Contemporary Wales

Volume 10

CALL FOR PAPERS

The editors are always pleased to receive papers on any topic relating to the economy and society of Wales for consideration for publication in *Contemporary Wales*. Contributions should, however, be written in a style which makes them readily accessible to non-specialists. Papers written in Welsh should be accompanied by an English abstract. The editors are very willing, if desired, to discuss proposals for papers with intending authors.

All articles are subject to a refereeing process. On acceptance by the editors for publication in this journal, copyright in the article is assigned to the University of Wales.

ACKNOWLEDGEMENTS

The Editors would like to thank all those who have acted as referees for this volume, and for the preceding volumes of **Contemporary Wales**. In future, they will be assisted in their work by an Editorial Board. We are also grateful for the invaluable assistance provided in the editing of this volume by Emeritus Professor John Black, who is an Honorary Departmental Fellow in the Department of Economics, University of Wales, Aberystwyth.

CONTEMPORARY WALES

An annual review of economic and social research

Volume 10

Editors

Graham Day

Dennis Thomas

Published on behalf of the Board of Celtic Studies
of the University of Wales

Cardiff
University of Wales Press
1997

First published 1998

British Library Cataloguing in Publication Data
A catalogue record for this book is available from the British Library.

ISBN 0-7083-1463-5

ISSN 0951-4937

Cover design by Strata
Typeset at the University of Wales Press
Printed in Wales by Dinefwr Press, Llandybïe

CONTENTS

CONTRIBUTORS

Graham Day, School of Sociology and Social Policy, University of Wales, Bangor.

Stephen Drinkwater, Department of Economics and Economic History, Manchester Metropolitan University.

Catherine Farrell, University of Glamorgan Business School.

Leslie J. Francis, Trinity College, Carmarthen, and University of Wales, Lampeter.

Nick Gallent, Department of Planning and Landscape, University of Manchester.

Peter Gripaios, South West Economy Research Centre, University of Plymouth Business School.

Heini Gruffudd, Department of Adult Continuing Education, University of Wales Swansea.

Gary Higgs, Department of City and Regional Planning, University of Wales, Cardiff.

Ian Humphreys, Department of Maritime Studies and International Transport, University of Wales, Cardiff.

Susan H. Jones, Centre for Theology and Education, Trinity College, Carmarthen.

Jennifer Law, University of Glamorgan Business School.

Max Munday, Cardiff Business School.

Michael J. Peel, Cardiff Business School.

Mark Tewdwr-Jones, Department of City and Regional Planning, University of Wales, Cardiff.

Alys Thomas, University of Glamorgan Business School.

Dennis Thomas, Department of Economics, University of Wales, Aberystwyth.

Sean White, Department of City and Regional Planning, University of Wales, Cardiff.

EDITORIAL

This is the tenth issue of *Contemporary Wales* and the first to appear in post-referendum, pro-devolution, Wales. For Wales, the opportunity to vote on devolved powers was the most direct and immediate effect of the election of a government of 'new' Labour. The major implications, initially at least, are constitutional, and relate to the governance of Wales, with the new Assembly destined to replace the activities and functions of the Welsh Office. Ultimately, however, there should be far-reaching social and economic consequences, as the Welsh population gradually come to terms with the result of what was a narrow majority vote, based on a low turn-out, and reflecting an apparently 'divided' Wales. The somewhat confused voting pattern within the various constituencies, and the marked variations in the vote across Wales, will provide rich material for the political analysts, and this presents an obvious topic for consideration in a future edition of this journal; but we also hope to continue to provide an outlet for the examination of the wider ramifications of this key political development.

Part of the argument for devolving powers to Wales lies in its capacity to represent itself successfully as a unified and separate 'region', both within the context of the UK, and more significantly perhaps now, in Europe. In various ways, a number of the contributions to this issue touch upon this theme. Alys Thomas uses the comparison between Wales and another 'Celtic' part of the UK, Cornwall, to highlight some of the problematic aspects of regional mobilization, and the various ways in which it can be conceptualized. Those in Cornwall who wish to assert their regional separateness find Wales offers a powerful model of how it should be done. Thomas examines several of the theoretical approaches which have been employed to make sense of the relationships between the Celtic peripheries and the English 'centre', and considers how helpful they are in illuminating the historical record. She notes the very complex way in which Wales has been constructed as a unique and distinctive region, and the difficulty faced by those who would like to do the same for Cornwall. Indeed, despite its distinctive and idiosyncratic features, there is an alternative view that Cornwall would fare better if united into a larger West of England region, which would include at least the County of Devon as well.

Somewhat similar questions arise from the illuminating comparison provided by Gripaios between the economic performance of Wales, and that of the regional economy of the South West, centred on Bristol. As Director of the South West Economy Research Centre at the University of Plymouth, Gripaios is well-placed to offer an informed, neighbourly view of recent developments. He casts a generally sceptical eye over the recent Welsh economic 'miracle' and notes that Wales is still lacking in a number of the attributes of an advanced modern economy, and that in terms of several key variables it remains very much towards the bottom end of the UK regional league table. He warns that too much attention may have been paid to 'headline' successes in attracting foreign inward investment, and that this may make Wales unduly vulnerable to recent and future cuts in UK and European regional funding. Pointing out that Wales seems to attract lower quality jobs, he refers especially to the slow growth of financial services and hence the relative dearth of the high-earning, higher-level functions associated with this under-represented sector. He suggests that growth and success on both sides of the River Severn might be better understood as aspects of an emergent economic 'super-region', in which Bristol and Cardiff may come to occupy distinctive roles. At the present time, it is the former which is acting increasingly as the centre for the developing economy of Severnside.

A more positive account of the role of foreign-owned companies within Wales is given by Munday and Peel. They examine the relative performance of foreign-owned manufacturing firms, compared to domestic rivals, during the recession of the early 1990s. Using a new and comprehensive data base, the authors are able to incorporate a large number of firm-specific variables into their analysis, reflecting a wide range of attributes of corporate performance. The results suggest that foreign enterprises experienced a smaller reduction in employment, and benefited from larger increases in labour productivity and sales growth during the recession. By contrast, domestic firms started the period with relatively high profit margins, but suffered a more serious erosion of profits. The findings offer some counter balance to various observations that have been made about the potentially 'footloose' nature of foreign direct investment, and the dangers of the 'branch factory' syndrome. The comparative stability shown by foreign employers would seem to provide some justification for continued expenditure on the marketing of Wales as a regional location. However, the authors caution that whilst the employment and output stability provided by foreign firms can contribute to prospects for regional growth and development, there are other grounds for doubts about the reliance placed upon a regional base of foreign capital.

Humphreys's contribution takes up a specific aspect of Cardiff's development, the part played by air travel and Cardiff airport. He details the airport's development from its humble origins under local authority ownership, through privatization to current ownership by the TBI property group. Although its role has been viewed by successive local authority owners, and by the Welsh Development Agency, as a catalyst for investment into south Wales, Humphreys suggests that it has not had a significant effect on foreign investment, its main benefit being the specific attraction of aerospace-related industry. The new title of Cardiff International Airport is part of the response to what are seen as the management challenges of becoming more customer-focused, raising more commercial income, and adopting a more aggressive marketing strategy: the description of an airport as 'a runway with a shopping mall beside it' is particularly telling. Humphreys concludes that a financially stable, market-orientated business able to invest in developing the airport and the surrounding land is as much in the interests of the region as it is those of the private owners. Given that private and commercial considerations of financial viability will dominate future decisions, it is no longer imaginable that the economic interests of the airport could be sacrificed for the good of the region as they were when the county council owners agreed to sell land to British Airways to enable the creation of a maintenance facility for its jumbo jets.

Two substantial contributions to this issue of *Contemporary Wales* revisit matters which have been of special, though not exclusive, significance for previous policy debates in rural Wales, access to housing, and deprivation. Both are aimed at helping to reorientate current policy emphases and to improve the targetting of rural problems.

The question of second-home ownership might appear to have gone off the boil somewhat in recent years, displaced from the centre of attention by newer concerns to do with permanent settlement via inward migration, and affordable rural housing. However, in their discussion of possible ways of regulating rural housing, Gallent, Tewdwr-Jones and Higgs bring all these matters together as different aspects of a situation in which persistent shortage of housing gives rise to a pressurized and unequal rural housing market in Wales, subjected to the impact of what they term 'residential tourism'. Both new and existing housing is exposed to competition between groups with highly unequal resources, invariably, it would appear, to the detriment of some local residents and their families. The authors review the range of planning controls that have been used to attempt to regulate this situation, and propose changes in perspective and in the operation of rules relating to alterations of housing use, which might enable local needs and interests to assume a higher priority in future. They point out however that all such controls tend to have unintended, and often negative, side-effects, and they emphasize the importance of the detailed local research and analysis required to inform and support the arguments advanced for such controls in relation to local housing needs, language erosion and so on.

With the recent shift in political climate, and power, in Wales and the rest of Britain, there is some evidence of a return to the policy agenda of issues of poverty and deprivation, for example as the new Welsh unitary authorities seek to develop their anti-poverty strategies. Higgs and White in their article examine the use Welsh authorities make of indicators of deprivation, as providing the necessary 'objective' underpinning for the various bids they have to make for assistance and funding. Such indices often take some geographical area or unit as their point of reference, and the authors show in relation to Wales how some of the key measures employed appear to be more successful and valid in picking up urban deprivation, in contexts where there are large aggregations of population and deprivation is spatially concentrated, than they are in pin-pointing rural poverty, which tends to be more dispersed and smaller scale. Research in progress is aimed at producing indicators that are more reliably attuned to rural circumstances, by drawing upon survey data produced at local community level, and by focusing on particular rural problems, such as access to services. Combined with knowledge from new geographical information systems (GIS) such data should enable a much better understanding of rural deprivation in Wales in future.

A vital aspect of the distinctiveness of Wales, upon which its claim to separate recognition and governance can be based, is the development and growth of a separate institutional framework for the administration of key social functions. *Contemporary Wales* has dealt with this previously, with regard, for example, to the political organization of the Welsh state (Jones, 1988), the regulation of agriculture (Murdoch, 1988), and the role of religion (Harris and Startup, 1995). In this volume Farrell and Law provide an overview of the development of educational institutions in Wales, describing the ways in which their path has intersected with and diverged from that of England. Despite a prolonged period of policy domination from Westminster, there have always been elements marking out Welsh education as different, both in content and organization, and as Farrell and Law show, the difference has increased in recent years, via the operation of processes of selective inclusion and exclusion of policy changes originating elsewhere. Thus Welsh education offered an early and enthusiastic home for the comprehensive principle, whereas in more recent years Welsh education authorities, headed by the Welsh Office, have resisted the implementation of such market-orientated innovations as nursery vouchers and opted-out schooling. With education now being brought under the supervision of the Welsh Assembly, its evolution is likely to continue to reflect the unique characteristics of Welsh society.

This issue includes two reports of findings from recent social surveys. In the second report based on questionnaire research into the attitudes of Welsh religious leaders, Jones and Francis describe the views of clergy working within the Church in Wales. Stimulated by worries that a high proportion of those ordained to work within the Church fail to take up or remain with the ministry, the survey does show a surprisingly critical evaluation among clergy of the state of the Church, especially in its organizational and administrative guise, and a marked sense that there are weaknesses in both the training and the level of personal support provided to clergy, whose work is confirmed to be demanding and stressful. In the views of quite a high proportion of its active clergy, the Anglican denomination within Wales compares rather unfavourably with its English neighbour, although there is approval for its distinctively Welsh character.

The article by Heini Gruffudd reports some of the findings from an in-depth study of language use among bilingual young people in south-west Wales. The survey data illustrate clearly the very marked differences in patterns of usage to be found between adjacent geographical areas, and shows how the encroachment of English as the dominant language is slowed by the propensity to use Welsh in the home, within the friendship networks of the young, and in the context of schooling. Key choices also have to be made by the young people with regard to their identity as Welsh or English speakers. There is evidence of quite positive attitudes towards Welsh among the sample, but the discussion concludes by emphasizing that, while it is important to sustain Welsh in home and school, there is also a need to move beyond these preoccupations into the domains where Welsh is weaker – such as leisure and popular culture. A number of research questions ensue, including the impact of the role of the mass media and of language use in the workplace in modifying the patterns of language acquisition and use laid down in the early years.

The customary survey of the Welsh economy concludes the volume. This is Stephen Drinkwater's second contribution to the series, and provides the usual commentaries on output, income and expenditure, employment and unemployment, earnings and house prices. This year's survey also includes an appendix containing information on the new unitary authorities. Drinkwater concludes by noting the challenges which lie ahead for Wales, both within the UK and Europe, in the years to come. Here, the influence of the elected Welsh Assembly will depend upon the powers it is given, and the role occupied by the new powerhouse that will be created by integrating the functions of the WDA, DBRW, and the Land Authority for Wales. Inevitably, the economic outcome of this power shift is uncertain. In his article Gripaios refers to the 'considerable envy' which Wales has attracted from across the Bristol Channel in recent years. The English regions have recognized the advantages Wales has gained from having a voice in the Cabinet, a Welsh Office to co-ordinate policy, and a strong and active Development Agency. This has helped stimulate the creation of the Western Development Agency which embraces the English counties of Avon, Gloucestershire, Somerset, Wiltshire and Dorset. With north Wales possibly looking to the north-west of England for a viable economic grouping, and the potential emergence of the Severnside 'super-region' in the south-west, inter-regional economic competition may take on a new dimension, and pose the new assembly some interesting strategic planning questions.

Graham Day
Dennis Thomas

REFERENCES

Harris, C. and Startup, R. (1995). 'The Church in Wales: a neglected Welsh institution', *Contemporary Wales* 7, 97–116.
Jones, B. (1988). 'The development of Welsh territorial institutions: modernization theory revisited', *Contemporary Wales* 2, 47–62.
Murdoch J. (1988). 'State institutions and rural policy in Wales', *Contemporary Wales* 2, 29–46.

1. REGION, CULTURE AND FUNCTION ON THE CELTIC PERIPHERY: WALES, CORNWALL AND THE EU

Alys Thomas

INTRODUCTION

> Wales is not a 'region' in the way that English regions are . . . Wales is defined by ancient political, cultural and nationhood factors and not by the latest bright idea to emerge from the Department of Trade and Industry. (Professor Garel Rees: 1992*)*

This quotation highlights the ambiguity and confusion in defining regions in Europe, particularly when issues of culture and identity are set against institutional and political factors. Kellas (1991) has argued that regions may be defined on economic, cultural and political bases but generally speaking regions will be a combination of these factors. The aim of this paper is to explore the impact of the regional dimension in Europe on two 'regions' of the United Kingdom which have traditionally defined themselves in terms of cultural distinctiveness based on a Celtic heritage. It will be seen that the politics of European Union regional policy has prompted a trend towards regional mobilization which has different implications for Wales and Cornwall.

In Cornwall, conflict exists between its identity as an historic region with territorial integrity, as recognized by the English Local Government Commission in its 1994 report (LGC: 1994), and the increasing trend towards its inclusion for functional purposes with Devon or in a still wider South West region (Thomas: 1994a). The creation of the West Country Development Corporation in 1993 and the establishment of the Government Office South West (GOSW) in Plymouth in 1994 point to the pressure on Cornwall to seek joint action with its neighbour for European participation and economic development. Furthermore, a body of academic thought such as that of Stanyer

(1996) and Hearl *et al.* (1991) argues that Devon and Cornwall form a natural unit and basis for a political and economic region.

Cornwall provides an interesting contrast to Wales because there is a notable tendency for those involved in the 'regional debate' within Cornwall to draw upon Wales as an example to emulate, whether it is in terms of the 'trappings' of a Secretary of State and an economic development agency or as an historic, Celtic territory. Wales is recognized as a nation of the United Kingdom and receives Government support for aspects of its culture, notably the language. Like Scotland and Northern Ireland it has representation in the Cabinet and a territorial office which it can be argued has served it well in projecting itself on a 'regional' basis in Europe. Nevertheless, in spite of Wales's claim to nationhood, in reality its economic and political autonomy is less than that of a German *Land* and critics argue that more robust Welsh-based institutions are required for Wales to sustain its role as a competitive regional player in Europe.

The term 'Celtic periphery' in the modern context will be considered in this chapter along with the concept of a 'Europe of the Regions'. Further consideration will be given to how institutions in the two territories have reacted to the emerging regional dimension in the EU. In conclusion, the experiences of Wales and Cornwall will be considered in the context of the United Kingdom as a whole and an assessment made as to how relevant cultural factors are in determining the future of individual regions as political actors within the European Union.

DEFINING THE CELTIC PERIPHERY

> In Continental Europe, nationalist thinking has become intertwined with Fascist and Nazi ideology. This was in complete contrast to Britain's wartime experience, where patriotism and the sense of nationhood had been the focus against Nazi totalitarianism. (Spicer: 1992)

This quotation, taken from a critique of the Maastricht Treaty by Michael Spicer MP, aspires to explain the difference between the United Kingdom experience and that of continental Europe which, he asserts, has made the latter disposed towards a 'United States of Europe' and accounts for the former's resistance to such a concept. Spicer defends nationalism and identifies supra-nationalism as the source of historical conflict, stating that 'nationalism represents the drive of a people united by language, religion, culture or tradition to form an independent, unitary and self-governing state'. In short, his critique of the integrationist thrust of the Maastricht Treaty is based on a defence of the 'British' nation which is assumed to be united on the basis of at least one of the criteria listed. This is an assumption which has been vigorously challenged and its employment in the context of the debate on European integration serves to highlight the ambiguous nature of 'British' identity (Spicer: 1992).

The political agenda of European integration has prompted the scrutiny of the functions of the nation state and posed the question at which level of government power is most effectively wielded. This has been felt very strongly within the United Kingdom where the Conservative government fought to secure a definition of subsidiarity which would bolster the role of the nation-state with regard to EU institutions. However, the growing importance of EU regional policy underpinned by the principle of partnership and the creation of the Committee of the Regions have led to new relationships being forged between local and regional levels of government and EU institutions, indicating a *de facto* recognition of a broader definition of subsidiarity which accepts that functions should be carried out 'at the lowest appropriate level'. Although they are essentially departments of central government, the existence of the Scottish, Welsh and Northern Ireland Offices indicates a recognition of territorial distinctiveness. The prospect of devolution for Wales, Scotland and the regions of England would seem to indicate that the concept of the unitary state in the United Kingdom is being seriously questioned. The administrative recognition of culturally distinct, Celtic parts of the United Kingdom, even under the unitary system, would seem to contradict the notion of homogeneous 'Britishness' identified by Spicer and it has been argued that the United Kingdom is more accurately described as a 'union state' (Rokkan and Urwin: 1982, Mitchell: 1996).

When looked at in the context of nation-building the history of the United Kingdom is *ad hoc* and haphazard. While it can be argued that England went through the process of nation-building at a relatively early stage so that at the time of the Norman Conquest it was more or less a coherent unit, the later evolution of the United Kingdom with the formal annexation of Wales in 1536, the Union with Scotland in 1707, and the repeated forays into Ireland culminating in Union in 1801 meant that the myth of the unity of the United Kingdom has always been imperfect. Moreover, it has been convincingly argued that the unity of England has been overstated. Payton (1992) has argued that Cornwall was never fully assimilated into England and has maintained a distinct identity with its passage through various stages of peripheralism.

A number of political scientists have attempted to provide a framework to define the nature of the United Kingdom and challenge assumptions about its homogeneity. In an overview of the literature, Neil Evans (1989) identified three central issues: the integration of the United Kingdom, regional identities and the pattern of core-periphery relationships and the problem of England within the United Kingdom. The integration of the United Kingdom underpins the centralized nature of the state which Evans argues should not be underestimated. With the coming of the Normans the territorial base of the aristocracy, and with it their close identity with particular regions, was destroyed. The struggle became one for a say in the government of the Kingdom, rather than for separate forms of government for the regions.

The significance of core-periphery relationships in relation to regional and cultural diversity has been explored through a variety of theoretical frameworks. With particular regard to Wales, Scotland and Ireland, Hechter (1975) attempted to apply the internal colonial model, transplanting it from Latin America to the United Kingdom with the assertion that England was the 'national' core region with the Celtic countries as peripheral 'regions' and that a colonial model existed whereby 'the English state attempted to rule the Celtic lands for instrumental ends'. On this basis the unequal relationship between core and periphery heightens existing cultural difference and acts against assimilationist forces. Hechter's thesis has been criticized on a number of grounds. The definition of England as a whole as a 'core area', for example, ignores differentiations both within England and within the Celtic countries. Equally, as Evans (1991) points out, it pays too little attention to divergent experiences within the Celtic territories, generalizing with regard to the cultural division of labour and ignoring the role of sub-national élites.

Other theorists have attempted to provide alternative core-periphery models for the United Kingdom which challenge the notion of England as a dominant core area. Bulpitt (1983) for example, identifies the core area as being based around the Westminster–Whitehall axis and Rokkan and Urwin (1982) identified London and the South East as the 'inner centre' and the rest of the United Kingdom being split into outer centre and inner and outer peripheries. Nairn (1979, 1988) contends that the 1688 constitutional settlement impacted on political culture in the United Kingdom in such a way as to remove any notion of popular sovereignty and thus the institutions of the nation-state have come to be synonymous with the state itself. This can be said to be significant in positioning British 'national' identity physically in the core area, where the symbols of the nation are located, and thus working against any evolution of a well developed regional perspective.

With regard to the nineteenth century it could be argued that the strength of the municipal ethos could have underpinned the emergence of regionally based politics and that the industrial revolution heightened regional difference and provincial pride in the short term (Butlin:1990). Cities such as Manchester and the Birmingham of the Chamberlains had a strong sense of civic identity and pride at the peak of their industrial strength. However, this coexisted with an equally, if not more, powerful imperial ethos. Harvie (1994: 8) has noted that 'book shops and library shelves make clear the literary and emotional investment in the war years which "freezes" British qualities – the Dunkirk spirit, living through the Blitz, and so on – less as living things, than as the memory of an uncertain people'. This observation ties in neatly with Spicer's view of the British experience of the Second World War. Crucially, this highlights the ambiguity with regard to Englishness and Britishness which is of significance in terms of the difference of perspective which exists on the Celtic periphery. Numerous commentators have pointed out that the territorial idea of England is very vague and in conceptual terms England is both larger and smaller than its physical reality (Nairn: 1988, Osmond:1988; Crick:1989).

Day and Rees (1991) highlighted the difficulty in defining both the terms 'Celtic' and 'periphery'. Arguing that the territories under scrutiny (Wales, Scotland and Ireland) exhibited 'a considerable diversity of economic, political and cultural characteristics' it was nevertheless concluded that 'what ultimately marks them off from elsewhere, is the *intensely problematic* nature of the interrelationships between four analytically distinguishable dimensions of contemporary social change: economic restructuring; political mobilization; the construction of social identities and the reorganization of state activities'.

Physical peripherality is difficult to dispute. Cornwall in particular lays claim to near island status. Still described as a 'land apart', Cornwall's character has been shaped by its geographical nature as a peninsula and the psychological significance of its border with Devon, the Tamar river. Currently it is viewed by others and to a certain extent by itself as on the periphery of the United Kingdom and Europe. The County Council worried that 'viewed from Brussels, London and even Bristol, the far south west peninsula may seem remote and peripheral' (Cornwall County Council: 1993). This 'mindset', however, has been criticized by Deacon *et al* (1988: 25–7) who claim that a sense of remoteness is a question of perspective and the fact that many of those formulating policy in local government come from outside Cornwall means that they do so on the basis that Cornwall is long way from wherever they came from. They therefore concluded that 'the first step towards a Cornish based policy is to stop thinking of Cornwall as far from other places but to think of it as the centre and other places as being remote from Cornwall'. Indeed, in the past, Cornwall lay at the centre of North Atlantic trade routes and was a focus for travel for the Celtic church and in later centuries it emerged as a hub of industrial and maritime activity.

It was the Saxon King Aethelstan who identified Cornwall as distinct from England in a settlement of 936 in which the Tamar was marked as the boundary beyond which lay the 'west Welsh', that is the Cornish. Payton has argued that the settlement established Cornwall as a geopolitical unit which was firmly annexed to England and yet was not part of it, either ethnically or in terms of territorial absorption (Payton: 1992). Building upon Cornwall's territorial separateness, a constitutional distinctiveness was to emerge in the medieval period through the Duchy of Cornwall and the Stannaries which grew out of a body of ancient rights and privileges enjoyed by tin miners. This distinctiveness has been evoked in a contemporary context in order to highlight Cornish 'difference'.

Much of the case concerning Cornwall's territorial and constitutional distinctiveness can be augmented by cultural factors such as the persistence of the Cornish language as an indigenous language until the eighteenth century. The issue of place-names is important as an indication of the historic, ethnic border between Devon and Cornwall but in contemporary terms the strength of a sort of 'folk memory' of Cornish, in the fact that it is known to have been spoken within the last 200–300 years, has a potent symbolism. Thus it is a popular assertion that the Cornish are 'different' because they have their own language, although the actual numbers of those involved in the modern language revival movement are quite modest. This provides an interesting contrast with Wales where tensions between the 20 per cent of Welsh speakers and the majority of non Welsh speakers have been discernible during the course of the century and where the language question can be said to be more 'politicised' (Thomas: 1994b).

It has been argued that a significant element of contemporary Cornish identity evolved from recent historic experience. Payton (1992), drawing on the work of Rokkan and Urwin, asserts that the industrial heights peaked by Cornwall in the nineteenth century and its relatively early decline left its mark upon Cornwall in terms a sense of difference born out of a peripheral status *vis-à-vis* the centre. This was true in spite of the phenomenal industrial success enjoyed by Cornwall in the eighteenth and nineteenth centuries as result of the copper and tin mines and the engineering expertise that developed concurrently. The problem was that Cornish industrialization was too specialized and when the mining industry experienced depression, and ultimately decline, this flaw became clear and strengthened Cornwall's peripherality as it became arguably the first 'post industrial' society. By the early twentieth century depressions in the mining industry had caused massive emigration from Cornwall to areas of the world where mining skills were in demand, notably South Africa and South Australia, which had a significant impact upon society and culture in Cornwall. Payton (1992: 49) concludes that the changing nature of peripherality has 'moulded the distinctive social, economic and political identity of modern Cornwall'.

Deacon has attempted to apply the internal colonial model, discussed above, to Cornwall's experience. Hechter himself judged Cornwall to have been successfully integrated into the English economy before 1600 when 'the English state began to seriously implement policies of cultural intolerance' and it was to be assumed that the diffusionist theory should apply, although he did concede that Cornwall was a 'partial exception' (Hechter:1975: 64). Deacon, however, contends that Cornish identity should have died out years ago if the diffusionist thesis is accurate. Measuring contemporary Cornwall against the four 'internal colony' criteria of territoriality, economic dualism, cultural discrimination and cultural division of labour, he finds that all apply to the Cornish experience, with the possible exception of cultural discrimination which is difficult to support beyond anecdotal evidence. Its territoriality is undisputed, economic dualism may be seen in the fact that unemployment figures have consistently been above average for the United Kingdom and there is a paucity of Cornish-based companies. The cultural division of labour can be found in the fact that the levels of Cornish people, as opposed to incomers, to be found on council estates is disproportionately high, just as it is low in professional occupations such as teaching and local government (Deacon:1983). However, the model does not appear to fit in terms of the minimal expression of political mobilization which exists and the fact that Cornwall is a focus for in-migration. The latter phenomenon, however, creates its own tensions and impacts further on Cornish identity. Deacon asserts that Cornwall is becoming a 'post-industrial leisure periphery', an experience which is serving to reinforce Cornish 'identity' in a modern context, and sums up Cornish history thus:

> Sometimes one gets the distinct impression that Cornwall has been chosen by history to act as a testing ground for major social changes. It was the first Celtic country to be incorporated into the English state; the first to lose albeit temporarily its native language; one of the first centres of European industrialisation – based on deep metal mining; and the first society in the British Isles to experience massive deindustrialization. (Deacon: 1988: 3)

If Cornwall was the first Celtic 'country' to be absorbed into the English state, Wales was the second. Wales as an entity existed in clear territorial terms, defined by the sea on three sides and Offa's Dyke on the other, from the ninth century onwards but proved elusive as a political entity. During the Middle Ages it was a constantly changing patchwork of princedoms and marcher and English royal lordships. There were successive attempts to unify the Welsh princedoms, notably under Llywelyn Fawr and Llywelyn the Last but these failed partly due to the Welsh tradition of gavelkind through which inherited lands were divided between brothers. After the death of Llywelyn in 1284 and his brother Dafydd in 1285 the Principality of Wales, centred on Gwynedd, passed to the throne of England and Edward I conferred the title on his eldest son, but unlike the Duchy of Cornwall the Princeship of Wales had no material or constitutional significance (Morris, 1995). A further attempt at political unification occurred with the rebellion of Owain Glyndŵr in 1401 which was successfully suppressed and by the time the Act of Union came about in 1536 the Tudor monarchy, with its Welsh roots, could present it as an exercise in rationalization, extending to its Welsh subjects the same privileges as to the English. There has been much academic debate in Wales about the intent of the Act of Union with regard to the language but certainly the Tudor period was crucial in maintaining the Celtic character of Wales. With the arrival of the Reformation and the translation of the Bible into Welsh the language was standardized, an important factor in explaining the survival of Welsh and its relative robustness in contrast with other Celtic languages. As Glanmor Williams has argued, the growth of nonconformity, literacy and industrialism in the eighteenth and nineteenth centuries were crucial in strengthening the language and making the Welsh conscious of their nationality (Williams: 1977).

Up until the earlier nineteenth century Wales was certainly peripheral in most senses of the word. To outside visitors it remained an inaccessible wilderness isolated by geography, language and culture. Lacking any town of significant size, London acted as a 'capital city' to Welsh literary and political figures such as Iolo Morganwg towards the end of the eighteenth century. However, at this time the Industrial Revolution was already underway with the beginnings of iron smelting in Merthyr. During the nineteenth century Wales was transformed as the coalfields opened up and as Gwyn A. Williams memorably wrote:

> the industrialising south-east sucked people in from the rest of Wales and from outside, until in the end nearly four fifths of the people of Wales were lodged in that continuously renovating and increasingly English speaking region. The centre of gravity of the Welsh population was wrenched bodily into the south-east. (Williams:1985: 174–5)

In applying the internal colonial model to Wales, Hechter argued that a specialized regional economy developed which provided England with primary products, namely coal, and remained highly vulnerable to shifts in demand from the 'core'. A case, therefore, was made for economic peripherality. However, historical scholarship has demonstrated that the industrialization of south Wales brought into being a vibrant and evolving society characterized by Smith as 'American Wales' (Smith: 1994). In linguistic terms Wales became split between the English-speaking industrial areas and Welsh-speaking rural areas but in terms of national consciousness the late nineteenth century and early twentieth century saw the crucial establishment of such institutions as the University of Wales and the National Library which were to provide an important institutional starting-point for later political institution-building (Jones: 1988).

So, how 'Celtic' and how peripheral is contemporary Wales? The transformation of the Welsh economy following the demise of heavy industry highlights the problem of oversimplifying notions of 'core' and 'periphery'. Parts of Wales remain geographically and economically peripheral but it can also be argued that areas of south Wales along the M4 corridor together with the city of Cardiff could be judged to be at least part of an 'inner periphery'. There has been recent concern that north and west Wales are losing out in terms of inward investment (Thomas: 1996). With regard to Wales as a 'Celtic' region, the Welsh language has a key role in defining Wales in this way. In contrast with Ireland, the linguistic issue has been a divisive factor in Wales since the late nineteenth century and has created a fragmented identity in Wales. In this sense it was the relative strength of Welsh which was important, the fact that in *y fro Gymraeg* Welsh was still the language of the majority of the community. In recent decades the language has become increasingly prominent with the Welsh Language Act of 1969, the creation of the Welsh-language television channel S4C in 1982, the inclusion of Welsh as a core subject on the national curriculum in Wales in 1988 and the creation of a statutory Language Board for Wales to oversee public bodies' adherence to agreed language plans under the terms of the 1993 Welsh Language Act. Superficially, therefore, Wales has become increasingly bilingual and the language appears to be a less divisive issue than it was a decade ago but some commentators on the language are concerned that too much effort is expended 'bilingualizing' non-Welsh-speaking areas rather than shoring up the language in those areas where it is still the natural community language (Aitchison and Carter: 1993).

The language has been a key factor in retaining Wales's difference since Union with England but it is now possible to talk of Wales as a political entity to the extent that it has a Welsh Office and numerous QUANGOs which operate on an all-Wales basis. It is the so called 'democratic deficit' with regard to the operation of these bodies which revived discussion of the need for a Welsh Assembly. The issue of identity in Wales remains controversial, not least because the decline of heavy industry has challenged the cohesive, working-class identity which was centred on coal and steel communities and challenged the self-confidence of that particular English-speaking Welsh identity. As Gwyn A. Williams argued, the Welsh have consistently reinvented themselves and it could be argued that Wales currently finds itself again at a crossroads (Williams: 1985).

'EUROPE OF THE REGIONS'

In 1975 Rhodes argued that much of the EC thinking behind the establishment of the ERDF (European Regional Development Fund) was an ill defined attachment to the concept of a 'Europe of the Regions' and he concluded that it was 'a nonstarter' because it had failed to distinguish between regional administration, regional economic planning, regional government and regional devolution and that the 'banner of regionalisation' had been adopted 'without assessing whether or not it is appropriate' (Rhodes:1975: 105). However, as the ERDF as grown to become the second largest item on the EC budget after CAP, the concept of a 'Europe of the Regions' has become very popular in some quarters. The reforms of the Structural Funds in 1988 and 1993 which brought the regions in as partners alongside the nation states and the Commission, and the creation of the Committee of the Regions have been highly significant in promoting discussion about a 'Europe of the Regions'.

In Wales and Cornwall the nationalist parties have both expressed enthusiasm for the concept. With reference to Plaid Cymru's self-government aims Dafydd Elis Thomas has noted that 'Our objective must no longer be defined purely within a British context. When we have considered this issue in the past, we have used the old post colonial model as if we were a colony which was winning self determination' (*Western Mail*, 27 October 1987). It is with this objective that Plaid Cymru went into the 1987 General Election calling for the establishment of a Welsh *Senedd* and fought the 1989 and 1994 European elections on a common platform with parties representing other minority ethnic groups within Europe. Elis Thomas has also argued that the charge of separatism could not be laid against Plaid Cymru after the establishment of a single market because the British state had become increasingly irrelevant.

Plaid has increasingly pointed to the experience of Ireland as a small but influential player in Europe and moreover one which is flourishing in economic terms. It is argued that 'Our constitutional relationship with Europe, via a

Westminster government which is skewed towards the priorities of south-east England has thwarted a full transformation of our economy' (Plaid Cymru: 1997). In particular it has stood between Welsh needs and the structural and regional funds and it is also claimed that British agriculture ministers fail adequately to represent the interests of Welsh agriculture.

Within Cornwall there exists a small but vocal and relatively high-profile nationalist element which will be considered in greater detail below with regard to attitudes to Europe. On a cultural level there are organizations such as the Cornish Gorsedd and the Cornish language movement. While membership of these groups tends to be limited, it is fair to say that they have succeeded in spearheading an active interest in Cornish culture through antiquarianism, literature, music and language revival. The broad movement has spawned two political parties, the Cornish Nationalist Party and Mebyon Kernow (the Sons of Cornwall), the latter being the stronger. Estimates of membership are small although MK did claim a membership of 4,000 in the early 1970s and a notable protest vote has been attracted in some local elections.

It can be argued that the idea of a 'Europe of the Regions' has allowed the nationalist parties to skirt around the tricky issue of viability and credibility which was often used by opponents as a stick with which to beat them in the past. Plaid Cymru asserts that 'Our vision is of a real partnership between the nations of Europe, among whom a self governing Wales will eventually take its place' (Plaid Cymru: 1997). However, asserting its support for the principle of subsidiarity it stressed that 'we start from the premise that all decisions should be taken locally whenever practicable and then at the regional, national and EU level as appropriate' (Plaid Cymru: 1997). This is perhaps indicative of a slightly more sceptical approach towards the 'Europe of the Regions'. Similarly, Mebyon Kernow views Europe as 'a rich tapestry of nations and regions' and sees its task as 'reasserting Cornwall's right to its place within a decentralised Europe of the Peoples' (Mebyon Kernow: 1994). The nationalist parties see Europe as an opportunity for minority ethnic groups to assert themselves and as a catalyst for institutional change. The arguments tend to take two forms: the Wales/ Cornwall in Europe argument of a highly idealistic nature based upon the sort of ideas put forward by Leopold Kohr and Yann Fouere and a more pragmatic and opportunistic stance which points out the advantages enjoyed by the smaller nation-states within the EU such as Luxembourg and Ireland. The MK are perhaps more typical of the former, Plaid Cymru of the latter.

However, if the nationalist parties can be said to represent the most idealistic aspirants towards a 'Europe of the Regions', other political actors have also latched on to the bandwagon. This has been particularly noticeable in Wales. In the 1996 document on its Welsh Assembly proposals, 'Preparing for New Wales', the Labour Party noted that 'If the most dynamic regions of Europe have a common denominator it is the fact that each has a proactive regional government' but stressed the need for direct links between a Welsh Assembly and the EU to run parallel to those of the Labour Government in Westminster (WLP: 1996).[1] The Liberal Democrats went into the 1994 European Elections reasserting their commitment to a Welsh *Senedd* and outlining its potential as an articulator of Welsh interests within the European Union (WLD: 1994).

Equally, local government interests represented, before reorganization, through such organizations as the AWC, adopted the language of a 'Europe of the Regions' especially through their dealings with such organizations as the CPMR (Conference of Peripheral and Maritime Regions) and Atlantic Arc and in the establishment of the Committee of the Regions. Welsh local government input into Europe has now shifted to the Welsh Local Government Association. In the ongoing debate concerning the establishment of a Welsh assembly, the changing context of Europe is cited as an important reason for establishing such a body (a significant change from 1979).

However, it must be asked as to how much of this is wishful thinking. Recent critiques have come from a number of directions. Borras-Alomar *et al.* (1994) have argued that it was the development of a 'Europe with the regions' rather than a 'Europe of the Regions' which was discernible. They argued that the role of regions is alongside that of the nation-state not in place of it and that the growing role of sectoral policy-making on a European level should not be ignored. Also, Hooghe and Keating (1994) have argued that the death of the nation-state has been exaggerated and that while regional mobilization can be identified, prompted by the competition for EU structural funds, the regions remain just one actor on the EU stage. However, in the context of the United Kingdom, Hooghe and Keating's identification of regional mobilization is noteworthy, not least if the Labour Party's plans for English regionalization are considered. Labour's consultation paper on English regions stated that 'the ability of England's regions to get the best deal from Europe is hampered by a lack of regional structure' and proposed that Regional Chambers, initially indirectly elected, should have a role in co-ordinating bids for European funding and in selecting representatives to the Committee of the Regions (Labour Party: 1995). This would seem to indicate that although the nation-state is not about to 'wither away' the impact of the EU is fostering an awareness of a regional dimension where previously little consideration was given to such notions.

WALES AND CORNWALL IN EUROPE

The European Affairs section of the Welsh Office was set up in 1975 to oversee administration of the ERDF in Wales. As pointed out by McAteer and Mitchell (1994), the primary interest of actors on the Wales-Europe stage is in 'attracting resources to Wales and in obtaining information about the development of EC legislation'. Local authorities (pre-1995 reorganization) are identified as key actors, notably the county councils through their European/Economic Development units and through the local authority associations, the Assembly of Welsh Counties (AWC) and to a lesser extent the Council of Welsh Districts (CWD). The twenty-two new unitary authorities and the Welsh Local Government Association have now taken over in certain areas. Prior to reorganization the AWC had co-ordinated Welsh membership of inter-regional bodies such as the CPMR and its sub-group the Atlantic Arc Commission and the Assembly of European Regions (AER). It also dealt with the co-ordination of ESF (European Social Fund) bids. Its role therefore could be described as something of a mixture of the practical and the visionary. On the one hand it interacted on European issues with individual counties, the CWD, the Welsh Office and the WDA. On the other hand, it used its links with ECTARC (European Centre for Traditional and Regional Cultures) and its Presidency of Commission VI of the AER to tackle a cultural and political agenda, notably advocacy of the role of regions within the European Union. These views were given coverage in a 1992 Policy Paper in which it advocated the establishment of a Welsh European Forum in which MPs, MEPs, the Welsh Office, WDA, local authority associations and groups such as the CBI and TUC could try to formulate common policy initiatives and actions with regard to Europe (AWC: 1992). The Policy Paper also advocated that a Welsh delegation in Brussels should be established which would be 'a point of reference for the Commission and an efficient means of contact with Welsh interests'.

Together with the WDA, the Districts, TECs and Universities, the AWC was one of the sponsors of the Wales European Centre (WEC) which was established in March 1992. Lewis (1995) has noted the 'turn key' role of the WDA in the creation of WEC and that the form WEC took in its mode of operation was 'determined by a combination of financial considerations, the interests of the main actors and the political climate'. In its memorandum to the House of Commons Welsh Affairs Committee in 1995 the AWC judged WEC to have played a significant role in 'firming up the profile of Wales' but also noted that because the Welsh Office's link with Brussels is via the Government UKREP, its relationship with and attitude towards WEC is an uneasy one. The Welsh Office is not a sponsor of WEC but it has an indirect association through the WDA. McAteer and Mitchell (1994) have argued that the Welsh Office and Whitehall retain the whip hand with regard to lobbying in Europe despite the growing role of local authorities. However, this does mean that there is a level of conflict between different European actors in Wales. When the debate was underway concerning who would represent Wales on the Committee of the Regions there was strong resistance from local government and Labour MEPs to the suggestion that the Secretary of State himself or Welsh Office officials should be appointed (Osmond: 1992), and the subsequent deal whereby representatives were appointed through political parties (Labour, Conservatives and Plaid Cymru) was criticized by the local authority associations because it meant that the second largest group in Welsh local government – the Independents – were effectively ineligible. With the appointment of John Redwood as Secretary of State in 1993, further tensions emerged when he suggested that the WDA should play down its 'Wales in Europe' campaign and stress its place in the United Kingdom. This represented a clear move to put a brake on growing momentum towards strengthening Wales's profile as a European region. A report by the House of Commons Select Committee on Welsh Affairs in 1995 welcomed a renewal of an active role by the new Secretary of State, William Hague, stressing the importance of personal contacts with regard to inter-regional networking (H of C: 1995). The report also recommended that Welsh Office Ministers should attend meetings of the Council of Ministers with more frequency.

The Committee expressed concern that WEC had been 'caught in politically motivated crossfire' between the Welsh Office and local government, referring to alleged Welsh Office and Foreign Office resistance to its establishment, recommended that the Welsh Office should actively encourage further sponsorship of the Office and urged that the WDA should maintain sponsorship until sufficient sponsors were found to secure WEC's future. These tensions indicate a dispute about the role of WEC. Mazey and Mitchell (1993) pointed out similar difficulties with regard to the establishment of the Scotland Europa office, that is whether the office should be there to act as a 'one stop' shop for interests within the territory or to act as a 'mini-embassy' for the territory. This clearly flags up the difference between a region projecting itself on a functional and cultural basis. The Welsh Office, through the WDA, takes a predominantly functional view, which is consistent with the way in which recent Secretaries of State have identified attracting inward investment as the key part of the job. The WDA's European section comes under its business services umbrella with the stated objective of helping Welsh companies to do business in Europe and establishing 'collaborative partnerships in key regions' (WDA: 1992). The Welsh Affairs Committee noted that 'Wales has undoubtedly benefited from having the WDA, an agency which has been able to deal with continental chambers of commerce on something like their own terms' (H of C: 1995).

In Wales, therefore, while central government and local authorities collaborate in European matters there is evidence of growing tensions arising from an increasingly political interpretation of the regional dimension in Europe. As Keating and Jones (1991) have argued, European integration has provided a stage for the articulation of Welsh and Scottish territorial interests which are frustrated in a United Kingdom context and the RECHAR controversy (Jenkins and Morgan: 1997) not only highlighted the effectiveness of regional actors but the tensions between central and local government in Wales. However, the impact of local government reorganization in Wales may alter the balance of power in that the disappearance of the Welsh County Councils has broken up some of the key units and departments which were involved with European affairs.

The investigations of the English Local Government Commission left the two-tier system in Cornwall intact so the county could remain committed to its objective, to 'establish Cornwall as a vibrant and prosperous European region which promotes a balance between a high quality environment and a thriving economic base, and where diversity of opportunity allows all citizens to develop and grow' (Cornwall County Council: 1994). This objective is certainly a bold assertion but ultimately vague as it is highly debatable whether Cornwall can in fact be considered to be a region in institutional terms. The Association of County Councils (ACC) declared that 'the day of the "lone ranger" in European Affairs is over' (1993) implying that local authorities in England should start grouping together on a regional basis in much the same way as local authorities had done in both Wales and Scotland. As will be seen, the impetus for Cornwall to co-operate with Devon exists with regard to a number of areas which make a joint European effort a natural progression. Support for a Cornwall-wide unitary authority emerged from the Campaign for Cornwall which it argued would 'facilitate the construction of clear strategic policies, both to deal with socio-economic problems within Cornwall and to project Cornish regional interests in Britain and Europe' (Campaign for Cornwall: 1994).

The privatization of public utilities in the United Kingdom has created increasingly complex administrative units and service delivery systems which have taken the place of central and local government for some functions. This has served to decrease the uniformity of territorial boundaries for different functions. On the one hand, the creation of Government Offices for the Regions

(GORs) in 1994 seemed to support a coherent regional structure in England, on the other hand some of the privatized monopolies such as British Gas have abolished their regional structure. For Cornwall, therefore, the assertion of its identity as a region is not just a question of cultural revival but of making a case for viability in a complex administrative context. On this basis, what has been described as Cornwall's *de facto* status within England must cause discussion of Cornwall's regional aspirations to be considered against the backdrop of the emerging regional debate in England.

As has been seen, in some respects Cornwall can lay claim to being a distinct region on the basis of its cultural separateness from its neighbour Devon and other English counties. Nevertheless, in purely administrative terms, Cornwall has been treated as an English county. Assistant Commissioner Flather summed up the situation succinctly in the 1988 European Parliamentary Constituency inquiry when he stated that 'this joinder (i.e. between England and Cornwall) has been carried on *de facto* for a very long period of time now' (Boundary Commission for England Report: 1988). The '*de facto*' inclusion of Cornwall with England raises difficulties for those advocates of territorial institutions which reflect Cornwall's cultural difference. There is an irony in the fact that the increasing differentiation in institutional terms since 1979 between Scotland and England and to a lesser extent Wales and England, as noted by Hogwood (1994) has served to highlight this difficulty for Cornwall. For example, with the creation of Historic Scotland, CADW and English Heritage Cornwall's inclusion in England is made manifest.

The impetus of the need to attract funding from the EU has led academics and policy makers to consider a regional context beyond the traditional territorial boundary. This has had significant implications for Cornwall in that there has been increased pressure for co-operation with Devon to create a regional unit more akin in terms of size to its United Kingdom and EU competitors. 'Devonwall' is a derisive term used to describe joint initiatives involving Devon and Cornwall on diverse administrative levels and between the local authorities. However, the pressures from the European context and from sectors such as the newly privatized monopolies have led to an increasing level of co-operation; for example, the creation of the Westcountry Development Corporation (WDC) in 1993 and the Devon and Cornwall TEC point to the use of Devon and Cornwall as a single unit for economic development purposes. One of the WDC's regional strategic activities for 1996/7 was 'Joint overseas marketing of Devon and Cornwall and increased coherence in the UK' (WDC: 1996).

There is some dispute about where the impetus for the 'Devonwall' approach originates. Opponents claim that pressures from the private sector through

, agencies such as the West Country Development Corporation reveal a 'hidden political agenda' which is pushed along by an 'élite' group of Councillors and Officers within Cornwall County Council, exacerbated by the *ad hoc* approach of many other local government politicians who tend to be strongly constrained by arguments for cost-cutting and rationalization. However, such arguments are disputed by officials and politicians in local government who contend that Cornwall is very much the senior partner in co-operative initiatives with Devon; thus, the transformation of the Cornwall European Bureau into a Devon and Cornwall operation in 1992 was not said to be a 'takeover' but an effective neutralization of a rival and an assurance of Cornwall keeping the upper hand.

Since the first direct elections to the European Parliament in 1979, the question of a Cornwall-only constituency has been an issue of controversy, resurfacing in 1988 and again in 1993/4. Prior to the 1994 European Elections the United Kingdom was awarded extra seats so the Boundary Commission once again reviewed European constituency boundaries and Cornish opinion was mobilized one more time to push for a Cornwall-only seat on the grounds of 'special geographical considerations', with the county council and all the district councils lodging objections. The two Liberal Democrat MPs, Paul Tyler and Matthew Taylor, together with their European candidate for the as yet undefined constituency, Robin Teverson, submitted an overtly nationalist submission. Adorned with crossed European and St Piran's flags, it stated that 'throughout this submission, the term England should be taken to refer to the counties east and north of the Tamar, and not to Cornwall' and asserted that 'Cornwall is a Celtic area and has more affinity with other Celtic regions than it does with Devon', noting that 'no seat in the other Celtic regions of Scotland or Wales is connected to any part of England within one seat'. Other factors cited were economic difference, Cornwall's status as a Duchy and the fact that the Highlands and Islands, with an electorate under 400,000, were afforded special geographical consideration (CLD: 1994).

With the creation of the GORs in 1993 the designated capital for the South West was named as Bristol, which elicited a strong reaction from different sectors within Cornwall and Devon. The *Western Morning News* (WMN) took a strong opposing line claiming that the new regional capital should be based towards the 'far south west where it is needed the most' (WMN 10.11.93). Local Liberal Democrat MPs concurred with this view and Conservatives sought reassurance that existing departmental offices in Cornwall would not be downgraded. Criticisms paid off as the Government created an Office in Plymouth which would work alongside that in Bristol, with its own Regional Director and a budget of £41m. The WMN welcomed the announcement because 'it recognises that Devon and Cornwall have distinct economic and social problems which cannot be tackled effectively from Bristol' and stated that the 'psychological effect of having a proper Government in Plymouth – not just a token fort manned by one man and a fax machine – cannot be underestimated' (WMN 12.5.94).

The establishment of the GORs pointed to an attempt by the Conservative government to mirror the regionally defined development functions of the Welsh Office in an English context. The WMN has consistently pointed to the benefits accrued by Wales by the existence of the Welsh Development Agency and the Welsh Office and views a 'Devonwall' region with similar agencies as the best way to compete (WMN, 1997). Nevertheless, interests within Cornwall argue that it is at a disadvantage from being considered with Devon. CoSERG (Cornish Social and Economic Research Group 1988) has argued that being locked into a partnership with Devon peripheralizes Cornwall further because research and higher education facilities and most of the headquarters of 'Devonwall' institutions are based in Devon (although a Cornish campus for the University of Exeter has been earmarked for Penzance). It has drawn comparisons with rural Wales and the Scottish Highlands and Islands by considering the establishment of the Highlands and Islands Development Board in the 1960s and the Development Board for Rural Wales in the 1970s and their objectives of halting outward migration and safeguarding cultural identity. Noting that the United Kingdom government 'will clearly not sponsor a Cornwall Development Board (despite the fact that Cornwall has more people and arguably greater potential than rural Scotland or Wales)' it also makes reference to the Irish Gaeltacht. The point made by CoSERG therefore, in opting for rural Wales and the Highlands and Islands as blueprints, is that physical peripherality and cultural features such as distinctive settlement patterns underpin Cornwall's case for separate treatment, hence particular attention should be paid to planning issues and the nature of economic development initiatives. The cultural element in CoSERG's case is implicit, as the issue of linguistic preservation is intrinsic to the existence of the DBRW, the Gaeltacht authorities and the Highlands and Islands Development Board.

Some advocates of a 'Cornwall alone' approach, therefore, believe that Cornwall, because it manifests 'difference' and a distinctive identity in the same way as Wales, should command similar recognition within the administrative make up of the United Kingdom as Wales or Scotland . This approach tends to ignore the nationalist tensions and political manœuvrings over the course of a century which have led to territorial recognition in Wales and Scotland. While Cornwall certainly manifests a distinct identity and Payton (1992) has identified ample evidence of anti-metropolitanism in Cornish politics, it is arguable whether this has manifested itself sufficiently strongly in political terms for a UK government to feel the need to 'accommodate' Cornwall to the extent of creating a Ministry or indeed a Development Agency.[2] In truth, the very fact that 'Devonwall' initiatives such as the location of GOSW in Plymouth and the creation of the WDC, are gaining ground would appear to indicate that current 'accommodation' of Cornwall reaches its limits at a recognition of aspects of its cultural heritage. In simple terms, Cornwall faces a problem if it wishes to make an impact upon the government and extract concessions in recognition of its territorial and cultural integrity in administrative terms in that when it comes down to pure mathematics even a united Cornish front would be hard pressed to operate as a political force within Parliament unless the government of the day were to find itself on a knife edge.

The problem facing Cornwall in seeking to define itself as a region (or indeed a 'country') is the lack of a regional context in the United Kingdom. Scotland maintained a measure of administrative devolution through the persistence of institutions such as its legal system and, as has been seen, Wales has achieved administrative devolution on a gradualist basis during the course of the twentieth century. Even mainstream politicians make much of Cornwall's Celtic heritage and argue that it should be taken into account when considering boundaries but 'Celticness' is not the issue, political and administrative factors are. To sum up, the ethos of the United Kingdom state remains very centralized. The lessons of the past show that central government only ever grants concessions as a last resort and it is doubtful whether Cornwall has the political muscle to carve out a regional status . Cornwall's 'pull' may well be tested in the event of the Labour government pressing ahead with its regional plans for England.

CONCLUSION

If a region can be said to be a combination of economic, cultural and political factors then it can be seen clearly that Wales and Cornwall have distinctive cultural identity based on a Celtic heritage. However, in the context of the United Kingdom Cornwall's political status is as an English county whereas Wales is recognized by administrative devolution of central government at a territorial level. The impact of European integration has strengthened interest in regional government in both territories but their respective administrative status has meant that this has differing implications. In Wales it may be be seen that tension between the Welsh Office and local authorities surrounds the issue of who represents Wales in Europe. This has also served to revive interest in a

Welsh assembly which is envisaged as having an important role in Europe. In Cornwall the tension lies in whether the functional case for a Cornwall and Devon regional unit should supersede the cultural claims of Cornwall itself.

However, the regional mobilization which Hooghe and Keating identify as taking place has important implications for Wales and Cornwall. On the one hand it may be argued that Wales possessed something of an advantage over regions in England in projecting itself in Europe and the world because of such institutions as the Welsh Office and the WDA. However, there is now evidence that English regions are beginning to mobilize, for example the North East (Elcock *et al*: 1990, Lanigan: 1996). This ties in with the trend towards 'bourgeois regionalism' identified by Harvie (1994), amongst others, which indicates that a 'Europe of the Regions' is not such a caring and sharing experience but rather a Darwinian 'survival of the fittest' exercise. Equally, it is arguable whether the EU is the friend of 'regionalism' some enthusiasts believe it to be in the sense of supporting regions based on minority cultures. Commission representatives have indicated that the growing body of regional representation in Brussels is diluting the effectiveness of many regional lobbies (Binns: 1992). On this basis the EU has been a factor in cementing Cornwall/Devon co-operation. When the European Offices merged in 1993 Commissioner Millan's adviser commented that 'The move towards inter-county collaboration is favourably regarded by the commission officials, and demonstrates a commendable local authority strategy, where local government boundaries are put aside in the spirit of a true Europe of the Regions' (Pyke: 1992).

Furthermore, the Commission is very anxious not to be seen to be stepping on nation-states' toes in according recognition to regions. A Commission publication stated:

> The terms 'region' and 'regional policy'constantly cause confusion. The EU countries are far too different in structure for there to be a clearly defined entity known as a 'region'. There are regions which have evolved naturally, some with their own regional languages, and they may or may not be supported by their country's regional structure. What the Union usually means by a region is a statistically defined area . . . (EC Commission:1994)

The establishment of the Committee of the Regions raised high hopes but even participants advise caution about how effective it will be and how it is supposed to operate as a regional forum. Charles Gray, leader of the United Kingdom delegation, stressed that its function was to provide a voice for the regional level of government, not to produce representation for specific regions (Brouwer *et al.*: 1994). Thus representation in England has been not been drawn along the lines of clear territorial delineation. Critics have pointed out that local authority representatives from the United Kingdom will be far weaker players in the context of the Committee than representatives from powerful regional administrations.

So, how does this affect Cornwall? Despite the County Council's avowal to promote Cornwall as a region, the impact of Europe has led to an increasingly integrated approach with Devon as evidenced by the establishment of the WDC in 1993 and the joint bid for Objective 1 status. In the light of regional mobilization elsewhere it would appear to be a sensible course of action. If the disparate groups in the ill defined North West (Burch and Halliday: 1993) can manufacture a regional identity then it should be easy enough for the counties of the 'far south west' to pool resources. The problem with this analysis of course is that it ignores the issue of cultural identity as it relates to Cornwall. Bearing in mind Garel Rhys's comments quoted at the beginning of this chapter, many in Cornwall would point out that Cornwall is not the bright idea of the DoE but should be recognized as a region on the basis of its distinct historic, economic, social and cultural heritage, and organizations such as CoSERG have argued that increased integration with Devon reinforces Cornwall's peripherality in the context of the United Kingdom and Europe. In this sense the trend towards regional mobilization could present a real threat to Cornwall as pressure mounts from political and economic actors within Devon and Cornwall, supplemented by encouragement from the European Commission, central government and local authority associations to forge a larger region. Further pressure may manifest itself as the regional dimension becomes more competitive. Are the natural parallels to Baden-Wurttemburg and Catalonia large city regions based around the likes of Birmingham and Manchester? If these conurbations find their regional voice, will Cornwall and, indeed, Wales find themselves pushed further into the periphery? Thus it may be argued that the aspirations of many in Cornwall and Wales concerning the positive impact of the EU on the articulation of regional/national identities and related institutional developments are oversanguine. In a functional context Cornwall is short on institutions to develop and has found itself innovating new ones in conjunction with Devon. Wales's apparent strength in terms of a regional profile came about due to the existence of institutions such as the Welsh Office and WDA but it is arguable whether it will be able to retain that 'head start' in an increasingly competitive context and if Labour's English 'Regional Chambers' come into being (Thomas: 1997).

NOTES

1. The White Paper on Proposals for a Welsh Assembly, '*A Voice for Wales*' (July:1997) outlines a role for the Assembly in scrutinizing EU documents and proposals and taking evidence, liaising with UKREP and the Secretary of State, and administering the Structural Funds in Wales. The continued role of the UK Government as the relevant and key player in EU affairs is reiterated.

2. In the General Election in May 1997 Cornwall became a 'Tory free' zone with four Liberal Democrats and one Labour MP. In the Queen's Speech the new Government put forward proposals for the creation of Regional Development Agencies. It is likely that the case for a separate Cornish Development Agency will be put forcibly by the four Cornish Liberal Democrat MPs. The new member for St Ives, Andrew George, is a member of CoSERG and co-author of the polemical work *Cornwall at the Crossroads* (1988).

REFERENCES

Aitchison, J. and Carter, H. (1993). 'The Welsh language in 1991: a broken heartland and new beginning?' *Planet*, February/March.

Association of County Councils (1993). *Local Government and Europe*, London.

Assembly of Welsh Counties Policy Paper (1992). *Wales and Europe*, Cardiff.

Binns, S. (1992). Commissioner Bruce Millan's Chef du Cabinet, Proceedings of AWC Conference, 'The Wales and European Union', Cardiff.

Borras-Alomar, S., Christiansen, T. and Rodriguez-Pose, A. (1994). 'Towards a "Europe of the Regions"? Visions and reality from a critical perspective', *Regional Politics and Policy*, 4, 2, Summer.

Boundary Commission for England Inquiry (1988). *Report*, HMSO.

Brouwer, F., Lintner, V. and Newman, M. (eds.), (1994). *Economic Policy Making and the European Union*, Federal Trust.

Bulpitt, J. (1983). *Territory and Power in the United Kingdom. An Interpretation*, Manchester University Press.

Burch, M. and Halliday, I. (1993). 'Institutional emergence: the case of the North West Region of England', *Regional Politics and Policy*, 3, 3.

Butlin, R. A. (1990). 'Regions in England and Wales *c.* 1600–1914', in R. A. Dodgshon and R. A. Butlin (eds.), *An Historical Geography of England and Wales*, 2nd edition, Academic Press.

Campaign for Cornwall (1994). *A Sense of Difference: A Submission to the Local Government Commission for England*, May.

Cornish Liberal Democrats (1994). Submission to European Parliamentary Boundary Commission.

Cornwall County Council (1993a). *Cornwall – A Land Apart: Issues for the New Structure Plan*, Truro.

Cornwall County Council (1993b). *Strategy for Europe 1992-1996*, Truro.

CoSERG (1992). *A Strategic Forum for Cornwall and Devon – Not a SWEL Idea*, July; Redruth.

Crick, B. (1989). 'An Englishman considers his passport', in N. Evans (ed.), *National Identity in the British Isles*, Coleg Harlech Occasional Papers in Welsh Studies No.3.

Day, G. and Rees, G. (1991). *Regions, Nations and European Integration: Remaking the Celtic Periphery*, University of Wales Press, Cardiff.

Deacon, B. (1983). 'Is Cornwall an internal colony?', in Cathal O'Luain (ed.), *For A Celtic Future*, Celtic League, Dublin. pp.259–72

Deacon, B. (1988). 'The smile on the face of the Cornish cat', *Planet 69*, Dec/Jan.

Deacon, B., George, A. and Perry, R. (1988). *Cornwall at the Crossroads?*, CoSERG, Redruth.

Elcock, H., Fenwick, J. and Harrop, K. (1990). 'Region, State and Europe: the case of North East England', paper presented to United Kingdom Politics Work Group Annual Conference, Oxford.

European Commission (1994). *Guidelines for Local Authorities in the EU*, Brussels.

Evans, N. (1989). 'Identity and integration in the British Isles', in Neil Evans (ed.), *National Identity in the British Isles*, Coleg Harlech Occasional Papers in Welsh Studies No.3, pp.6–22

Evans, N. (1991). 'Internal colonialism? Colonization, economic development and political mobilization in Wales, Scotland and Ireland', in Graham Day and Gareth Rees (eds.), *Regions, Nations and European Integration: Remaking the Celtic Periphery*, University of Wales Press, pp.235–64

Gray, C. (1994). Leader of United Kingdom Delegation to CoR, in F. Brouwer, V. Lintner and M. Newman (eds.), *Economic Policy Making and the European Union*, Federal Trust.

Harvie, C. (1994). *The Rise of Regional Europe*, Routledge, London.

Hearl, D. *et al.* (1991). 'Politics and government in the far south-west', in M. A. Havinden *et al.* (eds.), *Centre and Periphery: Cornwall and Devon and Brittany Compared*, University of Exeter Press, 1991.

Hechter, M. (1975). *Internal Colonialism: The Celtic Fringe in British National Development*, Routledge and Kegan Paul, London.

Hogwood, B. W. (1994). 'Whatever happened to regional government?: Developments in regional administration in Britain since 1979', *Strathclyde Papers in Government and Politics* No.97.

Hooghe, L. and Keating, M. (1994). 'The politics of European Union regional policy', *Journal of European Public Policy* 1, 3, 367–93.

House of Commons (1995). Welsh Affairs Committee, Fourth Report, Wales in Europe, Vol.1 Report, Vol.II, Minutes of Evidence, HMSO.

Jenkins, D. E. and Morgan, R. H. (1997). 'Rechar: too little, too late?', *Contemporary Wales 9*, 130–51.

Jones, J. B. (1988). 'The development of Welsh political institutions: modernization theory revisited', *Contemporary Wales* 2, 47–62.

Keating, M. and Jones, J. B. (1991). 'Scotland and Wales: peripheral assertion and European integration', *Parliamentary Affairs*, July.

Kellas, J. (1991). 'European integration and the regions', *Parliamentary Affairs* 44, 2, 226–39.

Labour Party (1995). *The Choice for England: A Consultation on Labour's Plans for English Regional Government*, London.

Lanigan, C. (1996). 'Business and regionalism in the north east of England', *Contemporary Political Studies Vol 1*, PSA.

Lewis, B. (1995). 'The Wales European Centre: its background, operation and significance', unpublished MA thesis, University of Wales.

Local Government Commission (1994). *Report on Cornwall*, November.

Mazey, S. and Mitchell, J. (1993). 'Europe of the regions: territorial interests and European integration: the Scottish experience', in Sonia Mazey and Jeremy Richardson (eds.), *Lobbying in the European Community*, Oxford University Press, pp.95–121

McAteer, M. and Mitchell, D. (1994). *Euro-Lobbying: A Comparative Analysis of the Strategies and Problems of Lobbying the EU by Scottish and Welsh Local Authorities*, PSA Paper, Swansea.

Mebyon Kernow (1994). Euro-election leaflet, Cornwall and West Plymouth Euro-constituency.

Mitchell, J. (1996). 'Conservatives and the changing meaning of Union', *Regional and Federal Studies*, Vol.6.

Morris, J. (1995). *The Princeship of Wales*, Gomer Press, Llandyssul.

Nairn, T. (1979). *The Break Up of Britain*, Verso, London.

Nairn, T. (1988). *The Enchanted Glass*, Paladin, London.

Osmond, J. (1988). *The Divided Kingdom*, Constable, London.

Osmond, J. (1992). 'A Europe of the Regions?', *Municipal Journal*, 21–7 February.

Payton, P. (1992). *The Making of Modern Cornwall*, Dyllansow Truran.

Plaid Cymru (1997). *The Best for Wales: Plaid Cymru's Programme for the New Millennium*, General Election Manifesto, Cardiff.

Pyke, B. (1992). Aide to Commissioner Millan, quoted in ACC County News, April 1992.

Rees, G. (1992). Speech, Proceedings of AWC Conference, 'The Wales and European Union', Cardiff.

Rhodes, R. (1975). 'Regional policy and a "Europe of the Regions": a critical assessment', *Regional Studies* 8: 105–14.

Rokkan, S. and Urwin, D. (1982). *The Politics of Territorial Identity: Studies in European Regionalism*, Sage.

Smith, D. (1994). *Aneurin Bevan and the World of South Wales*, University of Wales Press, Cardiff.

Spicer, M. (1992). *A Treaty Too Far: A New Policy for Europe*, Guardian Books.

Stanyer, J. (1996). 'The Janus faced periphery: Cornwall and Devon in the twentieth century', PSA 4 Seminar Paper: English Regions – Will they Happen?, Southampton Institute, 14 February.

Thomas, A. (1994a). 'European Region or "Westcountry" sub-region?: Cornwall's territorial crisis', *Cornish Studies 2* (Second Series), University of Exeter Press.

Thomas, A. (1994b). *Language Policy and Nationalism in Wales, Canada and Ireland*, unpublished Ph.D. thesis, University of Wales.

Thomas, A. (1997). 'Devolution in Wales: the English challenge', PSA Conference Paper, University of Ulster, Belfast.

Thomas, H. V. (1996). *The Place of North Wales*, Gregynog Papers No.1 Vol.1, Institute of Welsh Affairs, Cardiff.

Wales Labour Party (1995). *Shaping the Vision*, Cardiff.

Wales Labour Party (1996). *Preparing for a New Wales*, Cardiff.

Welsh Development Agency (1992). *Overview of Activities*, Cardiff.

Welsh Liberal Democrats (1994). *Unlocking Wales' Potential: European Election Manifesto*, Cardiff.

Westcountry Development Corporation (1996). *Regional Strategic Activities 1996/7*, Plymouth.

Western Mail (1987). 27 October.

Western Morning News (1993). 10 November.

Western Morning News (1994). Comment, 12 May.

Western Morning News (1997). 12 February.

Williams, G. (1977). *Religion, Language and Nationality*, University of Wales Press, Cardiff.

Williams, G. A. (1985). *When Was Wales?*, Penguin, Harmondsworth.

2. THE WELSH ECONOMY: AN OUTSIDE PERSPECTIVE

Peter Gripaios

INTRODUCTION

The South West Economy Centre of the University of Plymouth Business School has been researching the Greater Bristol area for well over a decade and it has become increasingly obvious just how close the links are between that part of the south-west of England and adjacent south-east Wales. Both are very much the economic dynamos in their respective regions and, while the links between them have long been firmly established, there is plenty of evidence that they have increased in recent years in response to a number of stimuli. One of course, is the impact of the first and now the second Severn crossing, another the gradual movement of economic activity westward from Greater London and Heathrow airport along the M4. Also of importance, as demonstrated by current work in the South West Economy Centre and the Welsh Economy Research Unit of Cardiff Business School, is an ongoing process of rationalization in what might be called Greater Severnside of financial and business services, the former public utilities, warehousing and distribution and indeed other industries too.

The extent of interlinkages and the pace of their intensification suggested that it might be appropriate to offer an opinion on the current state of the Welsh economy and its future prospects, from across the Bristol Channel. The article draws heavily on research on financial services and utilities, a summary of which appears in Gripaios (1997).

AN ECONOMIC MIRACLE?

Some commentators have argued that an economic miracle has occurred in Wales and cite as evidence the reduction in unemployment rate disparities compared with the UK in total, the better performance of Wales in employment growth from the early 1980s onwards relative to other UK Standard Regions, improved productivity growth and an industrial structure much less reliant than hitherto on heavy industries such as coal and steel.

There is certainly some validity in these claims. Employees in employment grew at nearly twice the rate of the UK from 1981–91, and fell by just 0.5 per cent in Wales during the 1991–3 recession compared with a 2.1 per cent drop in the UK.

TABLE **2.1**
Claimant unemployment rates

	Wales	**UK**	**Wales/UK %**
1981	10.4	8.1	128
1988	9.9	8.0	124
1989	7.4	6.2	119
1990	6.7	5.8	116
1991	9.0	8.0	113
1992	10.0	9.7	103
1993	10.3	10.3	100
1994	9.3	9.3	100
1995	8.5	8.2	104
1996	8.1	7.5	108

Note: Seasonally adjusted rates.
Source: Office for National Statistics (1996), *Regional Trends.*

That relative performance contributed to a narrowing of the unemployment rate differential between Wales and the UK as indicated in Table 2.1; indeed by 1993 it had closed completely.

As far as industrial structure is concerned, there has undoubtedly been a major transformation such that coal and steel now employ just 25,000, 2.7 per cent of the total, whereas there are currently some 16,000 workers employed in electronics, 100,000 in engineering and 90,000 in business and financial services (Thomas, 1996). There is also evidence of above average growth in output, particularly that of manufacturing and of productivity from the mid-1980s onwards (Thomas, 1996; Hill and Keegan, 1993) and this and other indices quoted above have encouraged bullish forecasts for the Welsh economy to the Millennium and beyond. Cambridge Econometrics (1997), for example, see the Welsh economy growing on average by 2.7 per cent per annum from 1998 to 2010 compared to 2.6 per cent for the UK in total. That sort of performance is consistent with the view that Wales has improved from an economy characteristic of the depressed UK periphery to one much more like the South East, East Anglia, the East Midlands and the South West. Certainly, there has been considerable envy from across the Bristol Channel of the relatively strong performance of Wales during the recession of the early 1990s, of the grants available to attract inward investment to the Principality and of the 'headline' foreign direct investment (FDI) successes, which continue to be announced. These in turn have focused attention in the English regions on the advantages of Wales in having a voice in the Cabinet, a Welsh Office to co-ordinate policy and a strong and active Welsh Development Agency. Indeed, the apparent success of Wales and the institutions referred to above was probably influential in the last Tory government deciding to allocate Cabinet and junior Ministers to look after the interests of English regions, sub-regions and individual cities. It was certainly also influential in encouraging the counties of Avon, Gloucestershire, Somerset, Wiltshire and Dorset to set up the Western Development Agency to try to compete with Wales for foreign inward investment. More directly, the improved performance of Wales suggested by the statistics referred to above led to a reduction in size of the Welsh assisted areas and of regional and WDA funding.

It is not at all clear to this commentator, however, that the current optimism on Welsh economic prospects is completely justified for, as Table 2.2 demonstrates, the Principality remains very much towards the bottom of the UK regional economic league table in terms of a number of key variables. Indeed Wales has the lowest level of average household income per head, the lowest level of average household expenditure per head, the lowest level of GDP per head, the lowest level of male weekly earnings, the lowest percentage of managerial and professional employees, the lowest male activity rate, the second lowest female activity rate and the seventh highest level of unemployment. That hardly seems reflective of an economic miracle, and neither does a second worst ranking overall with only the north of England doing worse. Moreover, the unemployment rate gap between Wales and the UK in total has seemingly begun to open up again (Table 2.1) and the growth of employees in employment from 1993 to 1996 in the Principality was less than half that of the UK (1.4 per cent compared with 2.9 per cent).

Quite simply, many observers within Wales, and outside it, may have paid rather too much attention to the 'headline' successes of the Principality in attracting inward investment and, as a result, Wales may suffer badly from the recent and any significant future cuts in UK and European regional funding. Though there have undoubtedly been many significant improvements in the Welsh economy, there are perhaps more clouds overhead now than many commentators have realized. This would suggest that a more balanced view of economic prospects should be entertained.

TABLE 2.2
Regional ranking by key economic variables

	SE	EA	SW	WM	EM	Y&H	NW	N	Scot	Wales
					Region					
Population growth 1991–5	=3	=3	1	7	2	=5	9	10	8	=5
Net migration 1994	10	3	1	8	2	6	9	7	4	5
Average household income per head 1994	1	3	4	7	5	8	6	9	2	10
Average weekly earnings (M) April 1996	1	6	3	5	7	=8	2	=8	4	10
Average weekly earnings (F) April 1996	1	=2	6	7	10	8	4	9	=2	5
Average household expenditure 1994-95	1	8	4	7	2	5	6	9	3	10
Consumer expenditure £ per head 1994	1	3	2	6	7	8	4	9	5	10
% of households with regular use of car 1993	3	1	2	6	5	7	8	=9	=9	4
% change in housing stock 1981-94	4	1	2	7	3	8	10	9	5	6
Average house price 4th quarter 1996	1	5	2	3	6	9	8	10	4	7
% change in labour force 1986-95	5	1	2	9	4	6	10	8	7	3
% change in employees in employment 1991–5	7	=3	1	6	2	=3	9	10	5	8
% managerial and professional employees 1994	1	3	2	5	4	8	7	10	9	6
Economic activity rate (M) Summer 1996	1	3	5	4	2	7	8	9	6	10
Economic activity rate (F) Summer 1996	1	3	4	5	2	7	8	9	6	10
Unemployment (at January 1997)	4	1	2	5	3	=6	=6	10	=6	=6
% long-term unemployed males (at January 1997)	9	1	=2	8	=6	=6	5	10	=2	4
% of workforce with HE qualification (inc. degree) Spring 1995	1	5	6	8	9	7	4	10	2	3
Stoppages of work (days lost per 1000 employees) 1995	4	1	2	7	3	6	10	8	9	5
GDP per head 1995	1	2	5	6	4	8	7	9	3	10
% growth of GDP 1985–95	4	5	=2	1	7	8	9	10	=2	6
Gross value added per employee in manufacturing 1993	1	6	7	9	10	8	4	2	5	3
Net business registrations 1991–5	1	5	9	4	3	6	7	8	2	10
R & D activity % of GDP 1994	1	2	5	6.	4	=8	3	=8	7	10
Total	67	76	81	146	112	166	163	210	115	166
Overall rank	1	2	3	6	4	=8	7	10	5	=8

Note: A rank of one indicates highest for all variables except unemployment, long-term unemployment and stoppages of work. In these cases, lowest ranks one.
Source: Gripaios (1997).

In the next section, we examine the role of FDI which has undoubtedly been a major factor in industrial restructuring within Wales and consider why its impact on the Principality has been less substantial than might have been both considered and hoped. The paper also examines some other likely key influences on future prospects for the Welsh economy, with a particular emphasis on developments in the Greater Bristol area.

THE IMPORTANCE OF FDI

There is no doubt that Wales has been extraordinarily successful in attracting 'assisted' inward investment. For the period 1979–94 the Principality had over 14 per cent of UK FDI notified to the Invest in Britain Bureau (IBB), and between 1988 and 1991 attracted over 20 per cent (ONS, 1996). In the period 1991–4, it recorded 188 'project successes' a figure only bettered by Scotland's 197. Over this period Northern Ireland had 51, the North East 113 and the other English regions combined just 724.

The result of FDI on such a scale was that by 1995 Wales had 353 plants of some 300 foreign-owned companies, employing over 73,000 employees or around 7.5 per cent of total employees in employment (Table 2.3). Around 40 per cent of employees in foreign firms were in North-American-owned businesses with 27 per cent in European-owned ones and 21 per cent in Japanese.

During the period 1979–94, there were 132 new manufacturing plant openings and during 1985–94 there were 101 (Welsh Office, 1995). The net change in total overseas-owned manufacturing plants over the latter interval was 94. It is interesting that during this period, the most important source of FDI was the European Union, which accounted for 56 of the net change in the stock of foreign-owned manufacturing plants and for 8,500 of the 21,700 new employed in such plants. However, Japanese-owned plants, the source of just 22 of the net change in stock, created 8,900 jobs (Welsh Office, 1995). New openings of American firms amounted to 32 over this time period. The net change was, however, just 17 in these firms creating 2,800 jobs.

Latest Welsh Office statistics show that the new businesses associated with FDI are concentrated in Chemicals, Electrical and Electronic Engineering, Rubber and Plastics, Motor Vehicles and Parts and Mechanical Engineering (Table 2.4) and include some of the leading international companies among them Sony, Matsushita and Bosch.

While FDI has been credited with greatly contributing to the improved competitiveness of British industry and of the UK economy in total (Eltis,

TABLE 2.3
Employment in overseas-owned manufacturing plants by country of ownership, 1995

	No. of plants	No. of companies	No. of employees (000s)	Employment in foreign plants as % of total
USA	135	112	30.7	41.8
Japan	36	26	15.4	21.0
EC	135	119	19.8	27.0
Germany	(42)	(37)	(6.2)	(8.4)
France	(22)	(20)	(4.5)	(6.1)
Italy	(7)	(6)	(2.2)	(3.0)
Denmark	(9)	(8)	(1.0)	(1.4)
Eire	(15)	(15)	(1.3)	(1.8)
Sweden	(15)	(10)	(1.8)	(2.5)
Switzerland	9	9	0.9	1.2
Other Europe	7	5	1.2	1.6
Australia	14	8	0.7	1.0
Canada	15	12	3.3	4.5
Other	13	9	1.6	2.2
Total	353	300	73.4	100.0

Source: Welsh Office (1996), *Digest of Welsh Statistics.*

TABLE 2.4
Employment in overseas-owned plants by industry, 1995

	No. of plants	Employment (000s)	Employment as percentage of total overseas
Chemicals	56	8.5	11.6
Electrical and Electronic Engineering	50	20.7	28.2
Rubber and Plastic	38	4.7	6.4
Motor Vehicles and Parts	30	9.9	13.5
Mechanical Engineering	30	3.0	4.1
Sub total	204	46.8	63.8
Other	162	26.6	36.2
Total	364	73.4	100.0

Source: Welsh Office (1996), *Digest of Welsh Statistics.*

1996), it would seem that it has, as already pointed out, done little to move Wales up the regional league table. Indeed GDP per head as a percentage of the UK was lower in 1995 than in 1984 while average gross weekly earnings were lower as a percentage of the UK in 1996 than 1984 (Tables 2.5 and 2.6). Finally, as argued above, unemployment differentials relative to other UK regions have begun to open up again while employment growth in Wales in the post-recessionary period has been disappointing. How then can the relatively poor performance of Wales be explained? It would seem to this commentator that a number of possibilities exist.

TABLE 2.5

Wales GDP per head and Personal Disposable Income per head: percentage of UK

	GDP per head	Personal Disposable Income per head
1984	85.6	89.3
1987	86.3	88.4
1988	87.0	87.4
1989	86.6	87.3
1990	85.9	88.0
1991	85.4	90.1
1992	83.7	89.3
1993	82.7	87.0
1994	83.7	89.4
1995[a]	83.2	na

Note: [a]Provisional figures.
Source: Office for National Statistics (1996), *Regional Trends.*

TABLE 2.6

Average gross weekly earnings of full-time employees

	Wales as % of GB
1984	93.7
1992	88.9
1993	88.7
1994	89.5
1995	89.8
1996	89.0

Source: Welsh Office (1995), *Welsh Economic Trends,* and Office for National Statistics (1997).

SOME POSSIBLE EXPLANATIONS

A poor starting position

Wales had been a poorly performing region since the First World War (Lee, 1971) so that it was already starting from a low position before de-industrialization in the 1970s added to the problem. It would, therefore, have needed a massive increase in economic activity simply to have stopped the situation from deteriorating further in the face of massive job losses in coal and steel.

The loss of well-paid jobs

The relatively well-paid jobs lost in coal and steel have been replaced with much lower-paying jobs in the new manufacturing industries associated with FDI and, as elsewhere in the UK, by jobs in the service sector. The latter employed 555,000 in 1984, 46 per cent of the total workforce, whereas by 1994 they employed 669,000, 52 per cent of the total. Moreover the growth of service sector jobs in Wales over this interval (20.5 per cent) was higher than that for GB (13.8 per cent) (Welsh Office, 1995). In 1971 coal mining had over 46,000 employees and metal manufacture nearly 90,000 persons, with these two sectors combined accounting for 14 per cent of employees in employment (SIC 1968). By 1981, the total figure employed in coal and steel (SIC 1980) had fallen to 73,000, around 7.8 per cent of the total. Today the total figure has fallen further to 25,000 employed in the two industries, just 2.7 per cent of total employees in employment. Even so, the proportion of the total workforce employed in services was still lower in 1994 in Wales than in Great Britain (56.9 per cent) despite a greater proportion of jobs in the public sector located in Wales.

While many of the new jobs associated with FDI may not pay as much (relative to the UK average) to male manual workers as the jobs in heavy industry used to, there is the added problem that many have gone to females who are traditionally lower paid. However, female employees in employment were a smaller percentage of total employees in Wales (37.3 per cent) in 1994 than in the UK (49.4 per cent) and the female activity rate, despite growing significantly in recent years, was just 65.9 per cent in Wales in 1994, the lowest figure in GB (Welsh Office, 1995). Moreover, earnings relative to the UK were higher for females than males in 1995 (Table 2.7). It is illustrative perhaps that Wales compares better in terms of manufacturing earnings compared with the national average than it does in all other categories except education, social work and health where (despite some recent changes) national bargaining still tends to pertain. It still compares badly, however.

TABLE 2.7
Average weekly earnings, Wales, April 1995 (UK = 100)

	Male	Female
All industries	88.7	91.8
Manufacturing	95.6	91.5
Distribution, Hotels etc.	84.8	85.4
Transport, Storage and Communication	87.6	–
Financial and Business Services	77.0	80.1
Public Administration and Defence	88.6	88.8
Education, Social Work and Health	96.4	96.0
Other	83.1	–

Source: Office for National Statistics (1996), *Regional Trends.*

In 1995, Wales ranked sixth in terms of males for manufacturing earnings and tenth for those in all industries. However, for females the corresponding figure for manufacturing was eighth, confirming, it would appear, the likely impact of the feminization of the manufacturing workforce referred to earlier.

A significant problem with manufacturing in Wales would seem to be that much of the foreign and domestic investment has primarily involved the setting up of relatively routine assembly-line production facilities with very little R and D, design and other higher order functions located there. Even in electronics, where jobs have been attracted in large numbers, there is no evidence of important R and D facilities such as that of Hewlett Packard across the Severn in Bristol (Gripaios *et al.*, 1997a). Unfortunately, as will be seen below, the same sort of division of labour may now apply to financial services where Wales compares particularly unfavourably in terms of earnings with the UK (Table 2.7).

A high level of leakages

A further problem involves large 'leakages' from the Welsh economy given the relatively poor backward linkages and limited integration between the foreign direct investors and local suppliers of goods and materials. There is no evidence that foreign manufacturing firms in Wales are any worse in terms of purchasing intentions than those in any other parts of the UK in this regard, but the small size of the Welsh economy, a possible relative dependence on foreign production plants and the proximity of industrial centres in England probably all conspire to reduce multiplier effects on the Principality.

This also seems to be true of the demand for higher order business services. Recent studies of the growth of financial services (e.g. Gripaios and Munday, 1997) certainly seem to suggest that much audit and banking provision for Wales-based foreign manufacturing firms goes to firms in Bristol and other parts of England. As can be seen from Table 2.8, of 83 Wales-based foreign manufacturers, 29 used English-based auditors. This is especially true of firms based in Gwent. Of 25 such firms, eight used Bristol auditors and two practices based in South East England (Gripaios and Munday, 1997).

TABLE **2.8**
Financial provision to Wales-based foreign manufacturers

	Location of auditor	Location of banker
South East	8	24
Bristol	11	1
Other England	10	8
Cardiff	46	21
Swansea	4	7
Other Wales	4	18
Total	83	79

Source: Gripaios and Munday (1997)

Interestingly, there was only one known instance of a South West foreign-owned firm (based in Gloucestershire) using a Welsh-based audit practice. Of course, this is explicable in terms of differences in the nature, as well as level, of financial provision in Wales compared with some English regions (considered below) in relation to the requirements of large multinational companies. Basically a good deal of what they require is only to be found outside Wales, possibly because of the small size of the Welsh market. Of course, there is the irony that much foreign investment has involved the take-over of indigenous companies, and reduced demand to local auditors, as multinationals have a tendency to use global auditing firms. Similar considerations may apply throughout the supply chain.

An issue of mis-reporting?
If leakages may have reduced the beneficial impact of FDI on Wales, there is
still the tantalizing possibility that it may be better than the published
figures on, for example, Welsh GDP might suggest. The problem is, of
course, 'transfer pricing' which foreign multinationals may use to minimize
global tax liability or for some other reason. As far as tax is concerned,
assigning corporate profits to areas of least liability may have the effect of
artificially inflating GDP there. Certainly Shirlow (1995) has argued that, as
a result of such considerations, GDP economic indicators for Ireland are
biased upwards. A similar situation may apply in Wales, given that the UK is
a relatively low corporate tax country by international standards. If
anything, therefore, figures for GDP in Wales may be overestimated. In any
event, Wales ranks badly on a lot more indicators than GDP. This would
indicate that, if there is an issue of mis-reporting, it could be that the share
of Wales in FDI attracted to the UK is overestimated. The reason is that so
much of Welsh FDI is grant-assisted, meaning that it is far more likely to be
picked up by the IBB, which monitors such investment, than a non-assisted
new opening in say Bracknell. Indeed, the IBB estimate that only a small
percentage of FDI is picked up in the figures of Tables 2.3 and 2.4.

A disadvantageous location?
Certainly, there is some evidence that despite the extensive attraction of
production plants of overseas-owned businesses, Wales seems to have lost
out to the Bristol area in terms of the attraction of the regional, and in some
cases national, service centres of major foreign IT providers such as IBM,
Digital and Canon (Gripaios *et al.,* 1997a). This may apply to a whole range
of industries and almost certainly applies to domestic suppliers too.
Companies tend to cite the advantages of locations close to the M4/M5
interchange from which they can service customers throughout south Wales,
most of the South West and indeed often the Midlands. One impact of the
opening of the first Severn Bridge was the rationalization of warehouse and
distribution centres generally to the English side of the Severn (Cleary and
Thomas, 1973), a process which seems to be continuing (Gripaios and
Munday, 1997).

Slow growth of financial services
A major growth industry of the last two decades has been financial services
and it would appear that, in this respect, Wales has lost out in relative terms
compared with the adjacent Greater Bristol area in particular. As is evident

from Table 2.9, the rate of growth of employees in employment in finance was less than half that of the South West from 1981 to 1991. Though Wales briefly did better during 1991–3, this may reflect a correction in the South West to the excesses of the last boom and also, possibly, some unreliability in the figures given the reclassification of industries in 1992. In any event, whilst employment in financial services was growing in the South West and Great Britain from 1993, it was falling in Wales.

TABLE **2.9**
Growth in financial services and % of employment in the sector, 1995

| | Growth in employment | | | % of total |
	1981–91	1991–3	1993–5	1995
Wales	28.7	0.5	–4.9	3.1
South West	60.5	–6.7	2.8	5.4
GB	33.5	–5.5	0.5	5.2

Source: Gripaios and Munday (1997)

Moreover, as with manufacturing and as already suggested, it may be more than an issue of jobs *per se*; the quality of jobs is also probably very significant. Relatively poor-quality financial services jobs in Wales are suggested by comparison of earnings in the sector and also by an examination of the major provision of financial services suppliers. It has already been pointed out that earnings in the financial services sector in Wales compare particularly unfavourably with the national average. Indeed, Wales ranks 10 out of 11 standard regions for both males and females. It compares very unfavourably with the South West. In financial and business services average weekly earnings in Wales were just 86.1 per cent of the South West figure for males and 89.7 per cent for females compared with 94.8 and 98.2 per cent for all industries (ONS, 1996).

Focusing on major financial services suppliers it would appear from Table 2.10 that these are heavily concentrated across the Severn, a great many of them in Bristol.

The population of the South West is roughly 1.7 times that of Wales so the existence of more major offices (for definition see table notes) in the South West would be expected. However, Wales has just 23 major offices compared with 81 in the South West, and it does particularly badly in terms of insurance. In recent years, there has been considerable rationalization in the financial sector and Wales has almost invariably lost out. Thus, for

TABLE **2.10**

Financial services representation: Wales and South West, 1996

	Accountants[a]	Banks[b]	Insurance cos.[c]	Finance cos.[d]	Total
Wales	7	2	8	6	23
(Cardiff)	(5)	(2)	(7)	(6)	(20)
South West	14	10	47	10	81
(Bristol)	(5)	(7)	(29)	(7)	(48)

Notes: [a]Big six.

[b]Regional and Head Offices of Clearing Banks plus Bank of England,
Chase Manhattan, Coutts, Bank of Scotland, Bank of Wales, excluding telesales.

[c]Area and Regional Offices.

[d]Top 12 Building Societies (plus Cheltenham and Gloucester), venture capitalists,
leasing agencies, credit insurers and commercial mortgage banks.

Source: Gripaios and Munday (1997)

example, two of the main clearing banks now operate Wales and the West super-regions from Bristol and another runs Wales from a regional office in the West Midlands. Cardiff has lost Chemical Bank (and 300 jobs) following the take-over by Chase Manhattan based in Bournemouth, and its office of the French specialist commercial lending bank UCB with operations transferred to Bristol. Wales has also lost large numbers of jobs following the merger of Lloyds and TSB. Some of the big six accountancy practices have never had an office in Wales while one that does, KPMG, is increasingly concentrating specialist provision in Bristol. Finally, Wales does not have headquarter representation of any of the top ten building societies (whereas the South West has three) and has only attracted two major insurers, Axa and Prudential. The former is the current national headquarters but may be affected by a proposed merger with the giant UAP, owners of Sun Life. The Prudential operation is a regional office.

What Wales has tended to pick up is direct line insurance brokers. One is Admiral, employing 800 in Cardiff and 200 in a satellite office in Swansea, and another is AA Insurance Services at Cardiff. It has also attracted the telesales operations of TSB to Newport, and Legal and General Insurance to Cardiff. In all these cases, it would appear that the 'soft' south Wales accent has been a major reason for locating (Turner, 1996; Wilkinson, 1996). Such jobs are not to be undervalued, but they are not the best paid in the sector and may reflect the same sort of division of labour between Wales and other UK regions as occurs in manufacturing. That division of labour may explain the high percentage of female jobs in Wales which are part-time

(49.6 per cent in 1994 (Welsh Office, 1995)). That is higher than in most UK regions and indeed the UK in total (ONS, 1996).

Just how important the attraction of higher-order business services may be is perhaps suggested by the GDP figure for South Glamorgan which is where, in Wales, such services are overwhelmingly concentrated. Cardiff has 20 of the 23 main suppliers of financial services in Wales (Table 2.10) and also all five of the top 100 UK (excluding London) law firms operating in Wales. It also has 12 out of 23 major consulting engineers. This feature may crucially explain the fact that, in 1993, South Glamorgan was the only Welsh county with an index figure for GDP per head above the UK average with 117.7 (UK = 100). All the rest were well below it, especially Mid Glamorgan (62.5).

Of course, the concentration of business services in Cardiff is far from the only contributory factor to this high degree of inequality within Wales. Also important is the location in the capital of large numbers of public sector jobs in the Welsh Office, Inland Revenue and major hospitals and Wales's largest university. We now consider the role of public expenditure in a wider context.

THE ROLE OF PUBLIC EXPENDITURE

Wales certainly benefits from some aspects of the allocation of public expenditure and tax but loses out in others. It certainly has had a very favourable allocation of Regional Selective Assistance (RSA) per head. The most recent data is for 1993–6 (specially provided by the DTI) and shows spending on RSA per head of working population in the Assisted Areas to have been £154.8 in Wales, a figure second only to Scotland (which had £189.9) in Great Britain. The GB average was £89.2 and the most expenditure in any English region was in the North East with £109.6. In the South West's assisted areas, the figure was just £68.9 a fact which has given rise to much antagonism in Devon and Cornwall where the Plymouth based *Western Morning News* has been campaigning hard for a 'fair' allocation of resources. Figures for Wales are frequently used to argue the case.

There is no question that Wales has also done very well in terms of the allocation of European Structural Funds and from government grants to local authorities. The latter is demonstrated by figures for average Council Tax paid in 1995 (ONS, 1996). The figure for Wales was just £330 compared to £560 in East Anglia, the lowest figure among the English regions. The figure for the South West was £599. At District level, figures of £770 for

Bristol and £620 for Plymouth compare with £299 for Cardiff. It is hard to believe that differences in 'need' justify such a disparity between the respective cities.

Overall, Wales does very well in terms of total identifiable 'General Government Expenditure' by region per head (Gripaios, 1995; HM Treasury, 1994) ranking only behind Northern Ireland and Scotland for 1991–2. However, such figures exclude some very important items of expenditure which vary significantly over space. Of particular importance is defence expenditure, and if figures for that are allocated to regions Wales falls to fifth in the spending league table while the South West climbs from ninth to third (Gripaios, 1995). The latter region has the highest per capita spending on defence of any UK region (Ministry of Defence (MOD), 1995) and there is no doubt that it operates as a hidden form of regional policy. The advantages to the South West look like being perpetuated for the foreseeable future. The latter region has recently benefited from the Trident refit programme, new orders to GKN-Westland for helicopters and, perhaps most importantly of all, from the concentration of MOD Procurement at Abbey Wood, Bristol. That is already pulling in MOD suppliers and may reinforce the pull in Wales from the east. Clearly, therefore, Wales benefits far less from government expenditure than a superficial examination of the figures would suggest. Equally such expenditure may continue to reinforce economic growth on the other side of the Bristol Channel.

FUTURE PROSPECTS

Though Wales continues to attract 'headline' foreign investments, such as that of South Korean microelectronics firm Lucky Goldstar to Newport, many of these are choosing locations just over the Welsh side of the Severn Bridge where they can get generous grant aid and yet be close to major markets and transport infrastructure. That probably means that businesses in the West of England and elsewhere are likely to benefit far more than they recognize or would ever admit.

Moreover the very success of Wales in attracting a major part of the grant-assisted FDI coming to the UK is causing great consternation in other parts of England such that the extent of Wales's preferential treatment may be further curtailed. Either way it faces stronger competition from across the Bristol Channel now that the five counties of Avon, Gloucestershire, Somerset, Wiltshire and Dorset have much more focused approaches to attracting such investment under the auspices of the Western Development

Agency. The new Labour Government proposals for a more coherent basis for regional strategy in England may have the same sort of impact. In any event, there must be concern about future levels of FDI particularly if, as looks likely, the UK is not an early entrant to a single European currency. That could have bigger implications for Wales than anywhere else not just because of what it may not get in the future, but also because of what it may lose.

Of final concern must be the ongoing rationalization in financial services and also other industries including the former public utilities (Gripaios *et al.*, 1997b). Most of this seems to be favouring locations further east and it may well intensify as the single market develops in Europe. An important competitor to Cardiff is certainly Bristol, which seems to be increasingly acting as a super-regional centre for a developing Severnside economic entity, just as Leeds seems to be doing for much of the North of England. Cardiff may as a consequence lose out and, as the capital city appears to be an economic oasis in an otherwise still depressed region, the implications should not be taken lightly. Bristol is more than ever aware of competition from the Welsh capital, and indeed other English cities, and is making great efforts to improve its image through a variety of ambitious plans including waterfront development. Cardiff, of course, was an early leader in this regard but it seems to this commentator that its image may have been tarnished by the well publicized problems over, and failed bid for, its proposed Opera House. That was to have been the jewel in the Cardiff Bay crown and its absence may deleteriously affect economic development from here on in.

It might, of course, be questioned whether competition between south Wales and the West of England is really the issue for, as argued above, there is some evidence of an emerging super-region encompassing both. The vitality of that super-region in total may be very important to the prospects of each component part even if Wales does lose out further in terms of the consequent division of labour. This raises interesting issues with regard to strategic planning and indeed effective regional government. Wales has concentrated on a 'Team Wales' approach considering its economy largely in isolation from that of its counterpart across the Severn. However, economic development on the ground ignores such niceties and there may now be a strong case for a joint approach to, for example, the provision of sites for different types of industry and key transport developments such as the location of a super-regional airport serving both sides of the Severn.

CONCLUDING REMARKS

There is no doubt that the Welsh economy has been transformed over the last two decades but, as Jones (1996) has recently argued, structural problems remain and Wales has done no more than hold its low position in the regional economic league table. The evidence for manufacturing and financial services reviewed here provides pointers as to why this may be so despite the fact that Wales has been a major beneficiary of FDI. Whether Wales can continue to attract as much FDI as it has done in the past is arguable. Indeed, if the UK does not enter the single currency Wales may be in danger of losing a good deal of what it has gained. Moreover, rationalization already occurring in a variety of industries raises concerns about the future strength of important sectors in which Wales is already poorly represented and particularly about the loss of higher-quality jobs of which Wales has always had too few. A major gainer in this regard certainly is the West of England. Wales on the other hand seems to attract lower-quality jobs whether in manufacturing or financial and business services, and all the relevant evidence suggests that the process is gaining momentum.

NOTE

I am grateful to Dennis Thomas, and to Max Munday of the Cardiff Business School for comments on an earlier draft of this article.

REFERENCES

Cambridge Econometrics (1997). *Regional Economic Prospects 1997*.

Cleary, E. and Thomas, R. (1973). *The Economic Consequences of the Severn Bridge and Associated Motorways*, Bath University Press.

Eltis, W. (1996). *How Much of the UK Competitiveness Gap Has Been Closed?*, Foundation for Manufacturing and Industry, London.

Gripaios, P. A. (1995). 'Government funding in the South West: an analysis', in Gripaios P. A. (ed.), *The South West Economy: Trends and Prospects*, seventh edition, University of Plymouth Business School.

Gripaios, P. A. (ed.) (1997). *The South West Economy: Trends and Prospects*, ninth edition, University of Plymouth Business School.

Gripaios, P. A. and Munday, M. (1997). *Uneven Development in UK Financial Services: The Case of the South West and Wales*, University of Plymouth Business School.

Gripaios, P. A., Gripaios, R. and Munday, M. (1997a). 'The impact of inward investment: the case of Bristol, Cardiff and Plymouth', *Urban Studies*, forthcoming.

Gripaios, P. A., Munday, M. and Thomas, M. (1997b). *The Impact of Utility Privatisation on Employment in the UK Regions: The Case of Wales and the South West*, University of Plymouth Business School.

HM Treasury (1994). *Public Expenditure Analysis*, HMSO, London.

Hill, S. and Keegan, J. (1993). *Made in Wales: An Analysis of Welsh Manufacturing Performance*, CBI Wales, Cardiff.

Jones, G. (1996). *Wales 2001: Three Years On*, Institute of Welsh Affairs, Cardiff.

Lee, C. H. (1971). *Regional Economic Growth in the United Kingdom since the 1880s*, Maidenhead: UK, McGraw Hill.

Ministry of Defence (1995). *UK Defence Statistics*.

ONS (Office for National Statistics) (1996). *Regional Trends*.

ONS (Office for National Statistics) (1997). *New Earnings Survey*.

Shirlow, P. (1995). 'Transnational corporations in the Republic of Ireland and the illusion of economic well being', *Regional Studies* 29, 687–91.

Thomas, D. (1996). 'Winner or loser in the new Europe? Regional funding, inward investment and prospects for the Welsh economy', *European Urban and Regional Studies* 3, 225–40.

Turner, R. (1996). 'Trustworthy accent helps bring in 250 more jobs', *Western Mail*, 22 May 1996.

Welsh Office (1995). *Welsh Economic Trends*.

Welsh Office (1996). *Digest of Welsh Statistics*.

Wilkinson, W. (1996). 'Legal and General picks capital site', *Western Mail*, 29 March 1996.

3. THE COMPARATIVE PERFORMANCE OF FOREIGN-OWNED AND DOMESTIC MANUFACTURING FIRMS DURING RECESSION: SOME DESCRIPTIVE EVIDENCE FROM WALES

Max Munday and Michael Peel

INTRODUCTION

The role of multinational corporations (MNCs) in the process of national and regional development is well established with a large number of studies highlighting the economic, social and cultural impact of foreign direct investment (FDI) in host economies. One potentially important contribution of the foreign sector to local economies is in the promotion of employment and output. However, research studies conducted during the 1970s and 1980s reported that MNC operations in host economies are both vulnerable to recession and the vagaries of changes in MNC corporate strategy (see e.g. Hood and Young, 1982). In particular, foreign-owned firms may be more prone to demand shocks in their home economies and key export markets. Furthermore, they may transfer host economy production to alternative locations and may prioritize domestic employment at the expense of host economy employment (see e.g. Davies and Lyons, 1991; McAleese and Counahan, 1979). In this context, studies which have examined the comparative stability of the foreign-owned and domestic sectors in the UK, Ireland, the US and Canada have reported that foreign sector employment is more stable than domestic-sector employment (see Killick, 1982; McAleese and Counahan, 1979; Li and Guisinger, 1991).

Based upon matched samples of foreign-owned and domestic manufacturing firms located in Wales, the main objective of this paper is to extend previous research by providing some comprehensive cross-sectional empirical evidence relating to the comparative performance of the foreign-owned sector through a recessionary period (1989–92). Across the periphery regions of the UK, there has been a continuing debate concerning the stability of employment and output within foreign plants. McAleese and

Counahan (1979) draw the distinction between 'stickers' and 'snatchers': that is foreign-owned subsidiaries who locate in host economies to reap the short-term benefit of regional production conditions and grants (snatchers), and those firms (stickers) with longer-term operational intentions in a region. From a policy perspective, the provision of grants and financial assistance to attract FDI presupposes that employment will be created over the longer term. Where foreign firms are able to relocate production facilities in response to economic shocks, or to close local operations to meet short-term global requirements, then public finance may effectively have been wasted. In addition, the relative stability of foreign plants during recession can indicate much about the underlying functions of local plants – with production-only operations relatively easy to contract during recession.

Whereas previous research has focused on comparative employment maintenance, this study provides evidence on a much wider range of variables encompassing corporate profitability, asset and labour productivity, employment, earnings, asset maintenance, stock efficiency, liquidity, gearing, credit risk and failure rates. The remainder of the paper is organized as follows. The first section reviews previous studies which have focused on the comparative performance and employment stability of foreign-owned sectors of regional and national economies. The second section examines the employment and output performance of the indigenous and foreign-owned manufacturing sectors of the Welsh economy at the macroeconomic level during the recent recession. The third section describes the data, method and variables used in the cross-sectional study. The next section uses data extracted from the FAME (Financial Analysis Made Easy) corporate panel database to provide a detailed empirical analysis of the relative performance of matched samples of foreign and domestic manufacturing firms located in Wales during the last recession. In addition, the relative failure rates and credit risk ratings of the population of Welsh foreign-owned and domestic manufacturing firms on the FAME database are analysed. The paper concludes with a discussion of the salient points to emerge from the empirical analysis.

OVERVIEW OF PREVIOUS RESEARCH

Initial theoretical developments explaining the activities of MNCs focus on their possession of ownership advantages, such as specific income-generating assets which more than compensate for the additional costs of MNCs locating operations in host economies. The possession of these superior tangible and intangible assets (whether in terms of patents, managerial expertise or superior technology) suggest that foreign-owned subsidiaries may be more efficient than their domestic competitors (see e.g. Dunning, 1993; Pitelis and Sugden, 1991; Shapiro, 1983).

In addition, it has been suggested that foreign firms may be more efficient than domestic firms, not just because of the possession of specific assets, but because of the way in which they internalize transactions in specific assets and intermediate products (including know-how) between productive units. For example, Buckley and Casson (1991) show that where uncertainty increases the transaction costs of a market exchange (e.g. via licensing production/technology to domestic firms), then markets are internalized within firms, decreasing uncertainty, and protecting proprietary knowledge and skills. Hence Buckley and Casson (1991) noted that MNCs may choose to locate their production facilities in host economies because the transactions costs associated with licensing or technology arrangements are relatively high and this may lead to a loss of key technical knowledge to domestic competitors.

However, it should be noted that any differences in the performance of the foreign sector may result from sectoral bias and/or location advantages (Luo and Chen, 1995). For example, Davies and Lyons (1991), who examined the productivity (gross value added per employee) of foreign-owned and domestic firms using 1986 UK Census of Production data, reported that, although the foreign-owned manufacturing firms exhibited a 40 per cent productivity advantage over domestic ones, only half was attributable to ownership differences. The remainder was due to structural effects, with foreign firms being disproportionately distributed in industrial sectors with relatively high productivity.

In an early study of 256 single-plant firms located in the UK mechanical engineering sector in 1974, Solomon and Ingham (1977) examined the significance of plant location as a determinant of relative performance of foreign and domestic firms. The authors reported that when location and industrial classification were controlled for, it was (contrary to expectations) indigenous firms which exhibited significantly higher labour productivity and superior export performance. However, despite this, the empirical results indicated that there was no significant differences between the profitability (return on capital employed) of domestic and foreign-owned firms.

Empirical research relating to the comparative employment and output stability[1] of the foreign sector, particularly during periods of recession, is more limited and has tended to focus on employment differentials. In this context, Dunning (1993) argues that concerns about the ability of MNCs to maintain employment in host economies is linked to the fact that foreign firms can relocate production units to meet global (parent) objectives, and can potentially cut back production in foreign affiliates during recessionary periods to concentrate on more lucrative markets. In a study focusing on the 1970s recession, McAleese and Counahan (1979) investigated the employment performance of multinational and indigenous firms located in Eire over the period 1973 to 1977 (a period which spanned the pre-recession peak and the post-recession recovery), in an attempt to ascertain whether employment levels in foreign firms were more unstable than domestic ones. The prime hypothesis tested in this study was that MNCs may contribute to local economic instability because of the relative ease with which they can transfer production (motivated by tax, government and legislation changes) during a major recession. The authors argued that the preservation of employment in parent-country plants may be given priority over employment in overseas plants, and that a recession may provide an excuse for MNCs to exit the host country.

McAleese and Counahan's samples comprised 191 foreign-owned firms established in Eire between 1952 and 1971, together with 151 domestic enterprises. No significant differences between the two sub-samples were found in respect of employment losses through the mid-seventies recession. However, the increase in employment in the foreign sample post-recession was significantly higher, with the study showing that by 1977 employment in the foreign-owned firms had returned to 1973 levels, whereas domestic firms continued to suffer job losses throughout the period. The authors also reported that larger MNC subsidiaries had weathered the recession relatively well, as had MNCs with a relatively high degree of marketing autonomy. It was suggested that this latter factor reflected the fact that some MNCs had the freedom to switch to other (non-recessionary) markets to mitigate the erosion of revenue in recession-hit local markets.

In the UK, Census of Production data indicates that over the period 1981 to 1986 total UK manufacturing employment fell by 17 per cent, from 5.78m to 4.77m; whereas the decline in the foreign manufacturing sector was substantially higher (28 per cent), falling from 858,000 to 620,000. Closures and rationalization in larger US manufacturing subsidiaries clearly contributed to this decline, with US manufacturing employment falling from 568,000 in 1981 to 394,000 in 1986. In contrast, according to the Census of Production, in the period 1986–92, employment in the UK-owned manufacturing sector fell by 9 per cent, whilst employment in the foreign sector grew by 26 per cent over the same period. However, to date there is only limited evidence charting the comparative regional performance of foreign-owned and domestic firms during recessionary periods.

THE MANUFACTURING SECTOR IN WALES (1985–1994)

The purpose of this section is to provide a brief overview of the performance of the Welsh manufacturing sector, over the period 1985 to 1994, to set the scene for the more detailed inter-temporal cross-sectional analysis that follows. The 1980s was a period in which foreign-owned manufacturing firms significantly increased their share of total Welsh manufacturing employment. Between 1985 and 1994 foreign manufacturing employment increased by 47 per cent (from 46,100 to 67,800), whereas domestic manufacturing employment decreased by 5.5 per cent, from 163,000 to just over 154,000 (*Welsh Economic Trends*, 1995). The growth of foreign manufacturing employment provides evidence of the region's success in attracting new inward investment, with the Welsh Development Agency (WDA) claiming a total of 679 new foreign projects and 48,000 new/ safeguarded jobs in the period 1982 to 1995.

Table 3.1 shows that between 1985 and 1994 the net increase in foreign manufacturing employment amounted to 21,700 jobs, with acquisitions of domestic plants representing a significant proportion of this growth – with the total increase in employment (17,700) in plants acquired from domestic firms accounting for 45 per cent of all new jobs (39,400) generated by foreign-owned plants during this period. It is also interesting to note that the bulk of the employment increase over the period is accounted for by plants controlled by Japanese (+8,900 jobs) and other European (+9,500 jobs) parent companies. In contrast, plants owned by US parents experienced a net increase of only 2,800 jobs. Table 3.1 also reveals that the 58 plant closures represented only a relatively small proportion (24 per cent) of the decrease in the stock of Welsh employment over the period analysed.

These changes have resulted in a diversified foreign manufacturing base in Wales which in 1994 comprised 353 plants, employing 67,800 employees – amounting to 31 per cent of all Welsh manufacturing employment (*Welsh Economic Trends*, 1995). Table 3.2 provides additional information relating to the foreign-owned manufacturing stock in Wales. It shows that in 1994 a high proportion of employment and plants were concentrated in a limited number of industrial sectors. For example, the electronics and office

TABLE 3.1

Changes in the stock of foreign-owned manufacturing in Wales 1985–1994

	Plants	Employment
Stock at 1985	259	46100
Stock Increases 1985–94		
New Openings	101	12300
Expansions	97	9400
Acquisitions	91	17700
Stock Decreases 1985–94		
Divestments	40	5800
Closures	58	4200
Contractions	62	7700
Stock at 1994	**353**	**67800**
Net Change 1985–94	**94**	**21700**

Note: Acquisitions include plants that have moved from UK to foreign ownership, and cases where overseas firms have taken over existing foreign enterprises in Wales. Divestments include foreign plants that have moved to UK ownership, and all plants which were overseas owned in 1985 and have been purchased by firms from other world regions. Expansions are additions to foreign-owned firm capacity that entailed 'significant' employment increases.
Source: Welsh Economic Trends, 1995.

equipment sector comprised 54 plants (15.3 per cent of all plants) and 18,400 employees, with the Japanese being particularly well represented in this sector (see Morris *et al.*, 1993). The motor vehicles and transportation sector employed the second largest number of employees (10,200). This sector has been specially targeted by the WDA for overseas marketing, and includes a number of large manufacturers, such as Bosch, Toyota, Calsonic and Valeo. North America is still the main origin of foreign manufacturing plants in Wales (145 plants in 1994, representing 41 per cent of all foreign-owned plants). However, as Table 3.2 reveals, North American plants generated only 12.9 per cent of the net increase in employment (21,700) accounted for by foreign-owned plants between 1985 and 1994 – with Japanese and European plants responsible for 85 per cent of the net increase in employment over this period.

A number of studies have also examined the impact of the growing foreign manufacturing sector in the Welsh economy from the perspective of its correspondence with regional economic needs and development objectives (see Hill and Munday (1994) for a review). For example, Munday

TABLE **3.2**
Foreign manufacturing in Wales by industry classification and source

Industry	Number of plants in 1994	Employment (000s) 1994	Employment change (1985–94)
Metal manufacture	16	2.9	−1.7
Mineral extraction	22	2.2	+1.1
Chemicals	55	8.2	+2.1
Other Metal Goods	29	3.8	+1.6
Mech. Engineering	28	2.8	+0.3
Electronics and Office Eqt	54	18.4	+8.9
Vehicles and Transport	31	10.2	+3.0
Instrument Engineering	11	2.4	+1.3
Food and Drink	20	3.8	+1.2
Paper and Related	27	4.6	+0.9
Rubber and Plastic	33	3.8	+1.2
Other Sectors	27	4.7	+1.8
Total	353	67.8	+21.7
Source:			
North America	145	33.9	+2.8
European	125	19.7	+9.5
Japan	32	12.4	+8.9
Other	51	1.8	+0.5
Total	353	67.8	+21.7

Source: Welsh Economic Trends, 1994

et al. (1995) demonstrated that Japanese transplants located in Wales had promoted long-term employment, diversification of the industrial base, and new methods of subcontracting and work organization. Using input-output analysis, Hill and Roberts (1993) attempted to estimate the direct and indirect economic impact of the local purchasing activities of foreign-owned firms. They concluded that, on average, foreign firms purchased only 12 per cent (by value) of their components in Wales. Consequently, the indirect multiplier effects on the local economy were limited. However, a further study of the Welsh manufacturing sector (Hill and Keegan, 1993) concluded that the foreign-owned sector played a significant role in reducing unit labour costs in the 1980s and early 1990s.

STUDY SAMPLE AND METHOD

To examine the relative performance of the foreign-owned and domestic firms located in Wales through the recent recession, a sample of firms was extracted from the FAME UK corporate database (produced by Jordans). This is an extensive database of UK public and private companies containing up to five years of financial and non-financial data for in excess of 100,000 UK firms. The database is available on CD-ROM, which is updated on a monthly basis. The data is derived (predominantly) from the audited annual accounts of each company. Corporate searches can be undertaken by reference to a range of attributes. These include location, corporate size, industrial sector and whether or not a company is foreign-owned (that is, where over 50 per cent of the share capital is owned by a non-UK parent company).

In selecting a sample of foreign-owned manufacturing firms, the database was first searched for firms with a registered office in Wales. Of these 2,035 firms, 551 (27.1 per cent) had a primary standard industrial classification (SIC) code in the manufacturing sector (SIC codes 2–4), of which 86 were foreign-owned subsidiaries (see Table 3.3). According to the Welsh Register of Manufacturing Employment (WRME) there were 273 foreign-owned manufacturing subsidiaries located in Wales in 1992, with 344 separate plants employing 66,100 employees. The sample of 86 foreign-owned companies used in this study therefore represents about 32 per cent of all foreign-owned firms located in Wales in 1992. The main reasons for the differences between the contents of the FAME database and the WRME are as follows:

- The FAME database is searched by reference to registered office, with some foreign firms having no registered office in Wales, although producing in the region.
- The search was based on firms with a primary SIC code in the manufacturing sector. Some foreign firms have primary operations in non-manufacturing classifications, whilst still undertaking some manufacturing activity (that is, they had secondary manufacturing SIC codes).
- A number of foreign-owned operations in Wales have turnovers below £1m, which are therefore under-represented in the FAME database.[2]

As Table 3.3 reveals, an attempt was made to match two domestic firms (from the available sample of 465) to each of the 86 foreign-owned ones by reference to the two-digit manufacturing SIC codes of each company in the latter sub-sample. However, the small number of domestic firms represented in some manufacturing sectors meant that it was not always possible to match two indigenous firms with a foreign-owned one. For example, the FAME database contained only 18 domestic firms in the electronic

TABLE 3.3
Industry classification of samples

Classification	All (n=216)	Domestic (n=130)	Foreign (n=86)
Metal Manufacturing	12	8	4
Chemicals	25	14	11
Other metal goods	12	8	4
Mech.Engineering	36	24	12
Elec/Electronic Eng.	45	21	24
Transport Eqmt.	26	15	11
Instrument Eng.	12	8	4
Rubber/Plastics	18	12	6
Other Manufacturing	30	20	10
Total	216	130	86

Note: Foreign-owned firms comprise 32 North American, 13 Japanese, 9 German, 9 French, 7 Scandinavian, 7 Swiss, 3 Eire, 2 Belgian, and one each from Australia, Italy, Netherlands and Liechtenstein.
Source: Derived from FAME (Jordans UK).

engineering (SIC 34) sector. Where more than two domestic firms were available, they were selected randomly.[3]

The data was collected during November 1994 and covered the annual accounting periods ending in 1989 and 1992. These years[4] were selected in an attempt to capture performance attributes (derived from company annual accounts and returns submitted to Companies House) in a 'boom year' (1989) and a 'recessionary year' (1992). The total number of observations for each variable reported in this study does not sum to 216 (86 foreign and 130 domestic companies) because some data items were missing from some company records. This is because small and medium-sized UK firms may choose under the Companies Acts to disclose less information in annual reports and accounts relative to larger companies. Furthermore, some firms had missing data[5] for one of the two years analysed. For example, only 76 foreign subsidiaries and 88 domestic firms reported employment data for both 1989 and 1992. As noted above, the company records held in the database include data extracted from annual balance sheets and profit and loss accounts. In addition to employment and remuneration data, a wide range of standard corporate performance indicators were generated from the database reflecting, *inter alia*, asset and stock efficiency, liquidity, gearing, productivity and profitability. A full list of the 57 variables used in this study together with their definitions is provided in Appendix 1 to this paper.[6] A list of the domestic and foreign-owned firms used in this study (including information on industrial classification and geographical location) is provided in Appendix 2.

The existing theory and evidence pertaining to MNCs outlined previously, would suggest, *a priori*, that foreign-owned manufacturing firms in Wales might be expected to outperform their indigenous counterparts with reference to a number of performance variables (see e.g. Dunning, 1993; Shapiro, 1983; Davies and Lyons 1991). More specifically, as noted above, the ownership of special intangible and tangible assets, combined with a reduction in transaction costs associated with the internalization of markets, should lead to a comparatively strong performance in respect of a number of the variables analysed, particularly those relating to profitability, efficiency and productivity. It should be noted, however, that in relation to some of the variables (which focus on gearing, liquidity and financial risk), there is no specific theory pertaining to how foreign firms might be expected to differ from their domestic counterparts. The issue is therefore essentially an empirical one. However, these variables (19–36 in Appendix 1) are standard ones used in corporate performance evaluation studies (see Van Horne, 1989), and by investment analysts to assess the financial performance of companies.[7] Hence, although there is no specific theory relating to these variables with reference to domestic and foreign-owned firms, they are analysed in an attempt to provide a comprehensive picture of comparative corporate performance.

In the analysis which follows, variable means, standard deviations (variance around the mean) and medians are reported for each sample for the years 1989 and 1992, together with changes in variable means and medians between these years. Following previous studies, Student's t-tests, using separate variance estimates (Norusis, 1988), were employed to test for significant differences between the mean values of continuous and ratio variables. Although there is no reason to suspect that the observations were not drawn from normally distributed populations (see Siegel and Castellan, 1988) there is a possibility that the matching procedure used for the domestic firms in this study may have infringed the t-test independence assumption. As noted by Norusis (1988) 'moderate violation of some (t-test) assumptions may not always be serious'. However, distribution-free nonparametric Mann-Whitney U tests were also conducted to test whether the variable distributions in the two samples differed significantly.[8] In all cases, two-tailed significance tests were conducted using the conventional 5 per cent (or better) statistical probability level.

EMPIRICAL RESULTS

Employment, remuneration and growth characteristics

Table 3.4 presents summary statistics relating to employment, remuneration and growth characteristics (variables 1–15 in Appendix 1) for the two sub-samples over the period 1989 to 1992. It reveals that in 1992 the average (281.4) number of employees (EMP92) employed in foreign-owned firms was significantly higher than in domestic firms (194.3). In addition, domestic firms shed more labour (mean = –15.4), between 1989 and 1992 than did foreign-owned firms (–1.54). However, the high standard deviations on the average change in employment (CEMP) for both sub-samples reported in Table 3.4, indicate that there is wide variation around the mean firm. This is also evident by reference to the more comprehensive frequency analysis of changes in employment reported in Table 3.5. It reveals that between 1989 and 1992, 53.9 per cent of firms in the foreign-owned sub-sample shed labour, compared with a much higher proportion of domestic firms (69.4 per cent) – with only 2.6 per cent of firms in the foreign sub-sample reducing employment by more than 200 employees, compared with 4.5 per cent of domestic firms. In contrast, Table 3.5 shows that 17 per cent of foreign-owned firms increased employment levels by more than 50, compared with just 8 per cent of domestic firms. In total, companies in the foreign-owned sample employed 21,508 employees in 1989 compared with 21,386 in 1992, a reduction of only 0.57 per cent (122 employees). Companies in the domestic sample employed a total of 18,455 in 1989 and 17,096 in 1992, a substantially higher reduction of 7.4 per cent (1,359 employees).

Overall the analysis of employment changes reported in Tables 3.4 and 3.5 demonstrates that, although both foreign and domestic firms maintained relatively stable employment levels through the recession, the wide variation around the average firm masks the volatility of employment changes, with 44.6 per cent of foreign-owned firms increasing employment between 1989 and 1992, compared with only 29.5 per cent of domestic firms. This may reflect (at least partially) the fact that a large proportion of 'surplus' employment in the Welsh manufacturing sector was shed during the early 1980s recession (see Hill and Keegan, 1993), and that in consequence the more recent recession has impacted less severely on manufacturing employment levels.

The 1992 Census of Production revealed that foreign-owned firms located in the UK paid their employees about 16 per cent more than their domestic

TABLE 3.4
Employment, remuneration and growth characteristics

Variables	Foreign-owned		Domestic	
	Mean (st.dev.)	Median (n=)	Mean (st.dev.)	Median (n=)
EMP92	281.4	165.0	194.3	99.5
	(323.9)††	(n=76)	(348.5)††	(n=88)
EMP89	283.0	178.0	209.9	109.0
	(320.1)†	(n=76)	(365.5)†	(n=88)
CEMP	−1.59	−4.00	−15.4	−9.5
	(106.5)	(n=76)	(116.5)	(n=88)
EREM92	15396.4**	15361.8	13758.1**	13939.7
	(4379.1)††	(n=74)	(4085.1)††	(n=87)
EREM89	10929.5	10628.4	10161.8	10080.0
	(2916.1)	(n=74)	(3612.7)	(n=87)
CEREM	4466.9*	4215.8	3596.2*	3696.6
	(3017.2)†	(n=74)	(2171.1)†	(n=87)
FASS92	6016.8	2846.0	3323.0	1070.6
	(11378.2)††	(n=79)	(9755.0)††	(n=97)
FASS89	4735.6	1861.0	2647.0	850.9
	(9260.3)††	(n=79)	(8284.6)††	(n=97)
CFASS	1281.2	370.0	675.7	42.3
	(4231.8)	(n=79)	(2718.1)	(n=97)
TASS92	15230.9*	8334.3	9018.2*	3621.4
	(19156.0)††	(n=79)	(24528.9)††	(n=97)
TASS89	13093.7	6865.4	8225.4	3187.0
	(17290.1)††	(n=79)	(24990.4)††	(n=97)
CTASS	2137.2	118.0	792.8	106.0
	(6648.5)††	(n=79)	(4877.3)††	(n=97)
TURN92	24962.1*	15556.0	13717.1*	5295.0
	(31883.8)††	(n=69)	(39768.4)††	(n=91)
TURN89	22050.5	11501.0	13987.6	4821.0
	(30471.3)††	(n=69)	(47926.3)††	(n=91)
CTURN	2911.6*	1869.2	−270.5*	11.9
	(9440.4)††	(n=69)	(11306.6)††	(n=91)

Notes: Means are unbracketed with associated standard deviations shown in parenthesis.
**,* Indicates means are significantly different at the 1% and 5% levels respectively (two-tailed Student's t-tests).
††,† Indicates sample distributions are significantly different at the 1% and 5% levels respectively (two-tailed Mann-Whitney U tests).

counterparts. North American firms were amongst the highest payers and Japanese firms the lowest (see Munday *et al.*, 1995). However, aggregated Census data should be interpreted with caution, since a relatively high proportion of foreign investment, particularly from the US, is located in sectors which tend to use more skilled labour, such as process engineering, chemicals, pharmaceuticals and the automotive sector. In this study we

TABLE **3.5**
Changes in employment 1989–1992 (frequencies)

Changes in employment	Foreign-owned (n=76)			Domestic (n=88)		
	Frequency (n=)	Percentage	Cumulative per cent	Frequency (n=)	Percentage	Cumulative per cent
–201 to –300	2	2.6	2.6	4	4.5	4.5
–101 to –200	8	10.5	13.1	8	9.1	13.6
–51 to –100	3	3.9	17.0	5	5.7	19.3
–11 to –50	18	23.7	40.7	26	29.6	48.9
–1 to –10	10	13.2	53.9	18	20.5	69.4
Zero	1	1.3	55.2	1	1.1	70.5
1 to 10	9	11.8	67.1	10	11.4	81.9
11 to 50	12	15.8	82.9	9	10.2	92.1
51 to 100	8	10.5	93.4	3	3.4	95.5
101 to 200	3	3.9	97.3	3	3.4	98.9
200+	2	2.6	100	1	1.1	100

attempt broadly to control (as noted above) for industry effects by matching foreign-owned and domestic firms. Table 3.4 reports mean and median remuneration levels (average employee pay) in the two sub-samples for 1989 and 1992 (EREM89/92), together with changes in average employee pay over the period (CEREM).

The results are particularly revealing, in that, although there is no significant difference in the average pay of employees in the foreign-owned and domestic sub-samples in 1989, the nominal pay increase of the average employee in the foreign-owned sector between 1989 and 1992 was significantly higher (40.9 per cent) than for the domestic sector (35.4 per cent), with real increases (RPI adjusted) of 20.7 per cent and 15.2 per cent respectively. This is reflected in the fact that in 1992 average employee remuneration was significantly higher in the foreign-owned sub-sample, with average pay in foreign-owned firms amounting to £15,396 in 1992 (median = £15,362), compared with £13,758 (£13,940) in domestic companies. As is discussed below, these changes may reflect the fact that foreign-owned firms were hiring (or training) more skilled employees with the aim of increasing productivity and output, with a concomitant increase in employee pay.

Table 3.4 also reports summary statistics relating to two asset (capital) variables. The first, fixed assets (FASS), which is the book value (at cost) of investments in land, buildings, vehicles, plant and machinery, is used to proxy for changes in the capital stock. A second variable employed is the value of the firm's total assets (TASS) which is the sum of fixed and current assets (that is,

TABLE 3.6
Changes in fixed assets 1989–1992 (frequencies)

Changes in fixed assets (£000s)	Foreign-owned (n=79)			Domestic (n=97)		
	Frequency (n=)	Percentage	Cumulative per cent	Frequency (n=)	Percentage	Cumulative per cent
−10968	0	0	0	1	1.0	1.0
−3001 to −5482	4	5.1	5.1	0	0.0	1.0
−1001 to −3000	6	7.6	12.7	4	4.1	5.1
−501 to −1000	3	3.8	16.5	3	3.1	8.2
−201 to −500	5	6.3	22.8	7	7.2	15.4
−101 to −200	3	3.8	26.6	9	9.3	24.7
−21 to −100	3	3.8	30.4	12	12.4	37.1
0 to −20	1	1.3	31.7	6	6.2	43.3
1 to 100	7	8.9	40.6	13	13.4	56.7
101 to 200	5	6.3	46.9	4	4.1	60.8
201 to 500	4	5.1	52.0	8	8.2	69.0
501 to 1000	12	15.1	67.1	10	10.3	79.3
1001 to 2000	10	12.7	79.8	8	8.3	87.6
2001 to 5000	10	12.7	92.4	8	8.3	95.9
5001 to 17000	5	6.3	98.7	4	4.1	100
22887	1	1.3	100	0	0.0	100

liquid assets comprising cash, debtors, and stock). Total assets is a standard corporate size variable (see e.g., Van Horne, 1989), and gives an indication of the scale (size) of a firm's operations. Table 3.4 reveals that, in both 1989 and 1992, the foreign-owned sub-sample is characterized by higher mean and median fixed assets, with mean FASS values of £6.02m and £4.74m in 1992 and 1989, compared with figures of £3.32m and £2.65m respectively for firms in the domestic sub-sample. However, the average increase in fixed assets (capital stock) between the two periods (CFASS) does not differ significantly between the two sub-samples, with a mean increase of 27.1 per cent for foreign-owned firms and 25.5 per cent for domestic ones. But Table 3.4 shows that there is again wide variation around the mean change in fixed assets. This is reflected in the fact that the median increase in fixed assets for foreign-owned firms (£0.37m) is substantially higher (a 19.9 per cent increase) than for domestic firms (£0.04m and 5 per cent).

This observation is reinforced by reference to the change in fixed assets frequency statistics presented in Table 3.6. It reveals that 68.3 per cent of foreign-owned firms increased their capital stock over the period 1989 to 1992, compared with 56.7 per cent of their domestic counterparts.

Furthermore, Table 3.6 also shows that a third of foreign firms increased the book value of their fixed assets by in excess of £1m between the two periods, compared with 20.7 per cent of domestic firms. Table 3.4 also shows that the pattern in respect of fixed assets is repeated for total assets. On average, foreign-owned firms were significantly larger in 1992 (TASS92) than their domestic counterparts, with the mean increase in total assets (CTASS) amounting to £2.14m (a 16.3 per cent increase) for foreign-owned firms, compared with £0.79m (a 9.6 per cent increase) for their domestic counterparts.

Finally, Table 3.4 reports summary statistics relating to turnover (sales revenue) in the two sub-samples. It shows that foreign-owned firms exhibit significantly higher mean turnover values in 1992, together with significantly higher mean growth in turnover between 1989 and 1992 (CTURN). Average turnover in the foreign-owned sub-sample increased in nominal terms by £2.9m (13.2 per cent), compared with a mean decline of £270,500 (-1.9 per cent) in the domestic sub-sample. After adjusting for inflation (RPI index), this represents a mean turnover reduction of 7 per cent and 22.1 per cent in the foreign and domestic sub-samples respectively.

Performance and efficiency characteristics

Tables 3.7 and 3.8 report a wide range of standard corporate performance variables (ratios) which are defined fully in Appendix 1 (variables 16–57). Table 3.7 reveals that average labour productivity (sales per employee) was significantly higher in the foreign-owned sub-sample in both 1989 and 1992. Furthermore, the mean increase in this measure of labour productivity is higher in the foreign-owned sub-sample (£12,602, a 16.7 per cent increase) than it is in the domestic sub-sample (£6,088 and 11.3 per cent). As noted above, this may be indicative of foreign-owned firms employing more skilled labour, and hence paying higher wages. Table 7 also shows that, despite foreign firms paying significantly higher average wages, the mean value of the wage bill expressed as a proportion of sales revenue (REMS) in the foreign sub-sample is significantly lower in 1992 (21.4 per cent) than in the domestic sub-sample (26.3 per cent). Furthermore, through a recessionary period, on average, the wage bill as a proportion of sales increased by a significantly higher (twice the) amount in the domestic sub-sample (4.8 per cent) than in the foreign-owned sub-sample (2.4 per cent).

In terms of the net profit before tax generated per employee (NPEM), Table 3.7 reveals that, although the mean values of this ratio do not differ significantly between the two sub-samples in 1989 and 1992, there is some

TABLE 3.7
Performance and efficiency characteristics

Variables	Foreign-owned		Domestic	
	Mean (st.dev.)	Median (n=)	Mean (st.dev.)	Median (n=)
SALEM92	88090.8**	72726.2	59884.2**	52571.4
	(66517.9)†	(n=68)	(30292.2)††	(n=85)
SALEM89	75488.6**	56919.8	53796.7**	42062.1
	(55261.2)††	(n=68)	(29145.8)††	(n=85)
CSALEM	12602.2	10048.6	6087.5	4892.3
	(28466.9)	(n=68)	(14697.6)	(n=85)
REMS92	21.38**	20.49	26.26**	25.21
	(8.62)††	(n=67)	(9.97)††	(n=87)
REMS89	18.99	18.07	21.50	21.44
	(8.96)†	(n=67)	(7.55)†	(n=87)
CREMS	2.39*	2.64	4.76*	4.09
	(4.82)†	(n=67)	(7.44)†	(n=87)
NPEM92	3735.1	1445.9	1738.8	1477.7
	(16485.6)	(n=75)	(5597.3)	(n=88)
NPEM89	3556.6	1359.6	3769.9	2407.8
	(11671.5)	(n=75)	(4504.2)	(n=88)
CNPEM	178.5	1003.4	−2031.1	−1200.5
	(11056.1)†	(n=75)	(5458.3)†	(n=88)
TUTA92	1.64	1.54	1.64	1.56
	(0.90)	(n=69)	(0.64)	(n=89)
TUTA89	1.56	1.49	1.71	1.54
	(0.89)	(n=69)	(0.80)	(n=89)
CTUTA	0.08	0.06	−0.07	−0.06
	(0.44)†	(n=69)	(0.82)†	(n=89)
TUFA92	11.45	5.39	10.85	4.86
	(33.71)	(n=69)	(33.56)	(n=89)
TUFA89	10.93	5.53	10.60	5.66
	(31.45)	(n=69)	(21.27)	(n=89)
CTUFA	0.53	0.17	0.25	−0.31
	(7.76)†	(n=69)	(16.52)†	(n=89)
NPMG92	2.17	2.10	2.23	2.47
	(12.82)	(n=69)	(11.01)	(n=91)
NPMG89	2.53*	2.49	7.14*	5.24
	(15.55)††	(n=69)	(8.02)††	(n=91)
CNPMG	−0.37*	−0.39	−4.92*	−3.65
	(12.87)†	(n=69)	(10.95)†	(n=91)
RCAP92	3.47	3.38	4.00	4.42
	(16.67)	(n=77)	(13.33)	(n=92)
RCAP89	4.65**	4.93	10.24**	9.54
	(14.16)††	(n=77)	(10.21)††	(n=92)
CRCAP	--1.18*	−0.61	−6.24*	−5.53
	(16.99)††	(n=77)	(15.94)††	(n=92)

Notes: Means are unbracketed with associated standard deviations shown in parenthesis.
**,* Indicates means are significantly different at the 1% and 5% levels respectively (two-tailed Student's t-test).
††,† Indicates sample distributions are significantly different at the 1% and 5% levels respectively (two-tailed Mann-Whitney U tests).

evidence that the mean change in this ratio (CNPEM) is higher in the foreign-owned sub-sample. Although foreign-owned firms exhibited lower levels of profitability per employee in 1989, relative to their domestic counterparts, they improved their performance over the recession. In this context, it is interesting to note that the median increases in net profit per employee between 1989 and 1992 in the foreign-owned sub-sample amounted to £1,003, compared with a decrease of £2,031 in the domestic sub-sample.

Table 3.7 also includes two standard asset efficiency measures, the ratio of sales to total assets (TUTA) and the ratio of sales to fixed assets (TUFA). As noted by Van Horne (1989), these variables focus on 'the relative efficiency with which the firm utilizes its resources in order to generate output' (with higher values of these ratios indicating higher asset efficiency). Table 3.7 reveals that there are no significant differences between the two sub-samples (in both 1989 and 1992) in respect of the means of the two asset efficiency ratios. However, there is some evidence that between 1989 and 1992 foreign-owned firms improved asset efficiency (CTUTA and CTUFA) relative to domestic firms.

In respect of corporate profitability, Table 3.7 focuses on two standard ratios: the net profit margin (NPMG), and the return on total capital employed (RCAP). It shows that, although foreign firms exhibit significantly lower mean net profit margins (2.5 per cent) than domestic firms (7.1 per cent) in 1989, they had significantly narrowed this differential (CNPMG) between 1989 and 1992 (a decrease of only 0.4 per cent), relative to the substantial decline experienced by domestic firms (4.9 per cent) – with both sub-samples exhibiting similar net profit margins in 1992 (around 2.2 per cent). This pattern is repeated with respect to the profit generated from capital employed. Table 3.7 reveals that, although domestic firms earned significantly higher mean returns on capital employed (RCAP) in 1989, this differential had been eroded by 1992 – with domestic firms experiencing a substantial (and significant) mean decline (6.2 per cent) in returns relative to foreign firms (1.2 per cent). Hence the results on relative profitability indicate that, although being significantly more profitable prior to the recession (1989), domestic firms suffered a significantly greater decline in returns during the recession – resulting in both sub-samples exhibiting similar profitability characteristics in 1992.

Stock, liquidity and gearing characteristics

Table 3.8 focuses on the stock, liquidity and gearing characteristics of the two sub-samples (variables 16–36 in Appendix 1). It reveals that there are no

TABLE 3.8
Stock efficiency, liquidity and gearing characteristics

Variables	Foreign-owned		Domestic	
	Mean (st.dev.)	Median (n=)	Mean (st.dev.)	Median (n=)
DAYST92	52.94	41.99	50.74	43.35
	(30.49)	(n=68)	(31.69)	(n=90)
DAYST89	62.23	57.86	62.44	52.68
	(34.96)	(n=68)	(43.77)	(n=90)
CDAYST	−9.29	−4.59	−11.71	−5.57
	(27.71)	(n=68)	(39.37)	(n=90)
DAYD92	55.66*	55.46	65.07*	67.28
	(28.79)†	(n=66)	(29.48)†	(n=89)
DAYD89	75.02	71.16	78.29	74.49
	(46.69)	(n=66)	(40.91)	(n=89)
CDAYD	−19.36	−10.39	−13.22	−8.29
	(39.14)	(n=66)	(51.28)	(n=89)
DAYC92	30.80**	28.59	44.86**	42.83
	(15.97)††	(n=68)	(22.70)††	(n=89)
DAYC89	57.45*	46.68	75.96*	59.88
	(40.67)††	(n=68)	(71.59)††	(n=89)
CDAYC	−26.65	−18.82	−31.09	−15.01
	(33.61)	(n=68)	(72.99)	(n=89)
CURA92	1.79**	1.53	1.39**	1.27
	(1.12)††	(n=79)	(0.62)††	(n=99)
CURA89	1.70	1.36	1.45	1.28
	(1.13)	(n=79)	(0.75)	(n=99)
CCURA	0.09	0.04	−0.06	−0.04
	(1.09)	(n=79)	(0.61)	(n=99)
QRAT92	1.23**	0.97	0.93**	0.85
	(0.96)†	(n=77)	(0.45)†	(n=97)
QRAT89	1.09	0.89	0.92	0.80
	(0.75)	(n=77)	(0.54)	(n=97)
CQRAT	0.14	0.09	0.01	0.02
	(0.69)	(n=77)	(0.43)	(n=97)
TLTA92	0.65	0.60	0.69	0.67
	(0.33)	(n=53)	(0.23)	(n=72)
TLTA89	0.61	0.62	0.64	0.63
	(0.28)	(n=53)	(0.19)	(n=72)
CTLTA	0.04	−0.01	0.05	0.03
	(0.26)	(n=53)	(0.18)	(n=72)
ICOV92	94.8	2.04	13.6	1.08
	(356.9)	(n=65)	(107.7)	(n=76)
ICOV89	49.9	2.96	55.9	3.18
	(186.1)	(n=65)	(203.2)	(n=76)
CICOV	45.0*	0.82	−42.4*	−1.69
	(240.1)†	(n=65)	(225.7)†	(n=76)

Notes: Means are unbracketed with associated standard deviations shown in parenthesis.
**,* Indicates means are significantly different at the 1% and 5% levels respectively (two-tailed Student's t-test).
††,† Indicates sample distributions are significantly different at the 1% and 5% levels respectively (two-tailed Mann-Whitney U tests).

significant differences between the sub-samples in respect of the days stock held (DAYST), with foreign-owned subsidiaries holding an average of 52.9 days stock in 1992, compared with 50.7 days for their domestic counterparts. However, it is interesting to note that (perhaps not surprisingly) both sets of firms reduced their mean stock-holding levels substantially during the course of the recession – with the average days stock falling by 11.7 days for domestic and 9.3 days for foreign firms between 1989 and 1992.

Cash flow management is clearly a key aspect of corporate performance (and indeed survival) during a recessionary period. Table 3.8 therefore includes two variables which focus on this facet of corporate performance. The first, days debtors (DAYD), represents the average number of days it takes to receive cash from debtors; whereas the second, days creditors (DAYC), represents the average number of days credit is received from suppliers. Table 3.8 shows that in 1992 domestic firms were characterized by significantly higher mean days debtor levels (65.1 days) than their foreign counterparts (55.7 days), indicating that, on average, domestic firms were less efficient (and/or experienced greater difficulty) in collecting cash from customers. However, it is interesting to note that, although not significantly different, foreign firms reduced the average level of outstanding debtors (19.4 days) by a greater degree than their domestic counterparts (13.2 days) during the course of the recession.

Furthermore, Table 3.8 reveals that foreign-owned firms had significantly lower mean days creditors outstanding (in both 1989 and 1992) than domestic firms. This may reflect the fact that domestic firms, relative to their foreign-owned counterparts, had to 'stretch' creditors to improve liquidity, since they collected cash from debtors less efficiently (above), and also exhibit lower liquidity measures (below). However, both domestic and foreign firms experienced a substantial reduction in the credit period granted by suppliers during the recession, with mean declines of 26.6 and 31.1 days respectively between 1989 and 1992.

Two standard variables were collected from the database to examine liquidity and solvency characteristics; that is, the relationship between a company's short-term (current) assets (usually convertible to cash within one year) and short-term (current) liabilities, generally due for payment within one year. The first variable is the 'current ratio' (current assets to current liabilities), with higher values of the ratio (CURA) indicating higher liquidity/solvency However, since current assets include the least liquid asset (stocks), a second variable, the 'quick ratio' (QRAT) is also employed, which is the ratio of current assets less stock to current liabilities. This ratio reflects a firm's ability to meet short-term claims from liquid assets (cash/debtors). Table 3.8 shows that in 1992 foreign-owned firms were, on average, significantly more liquid than domestic firms with reference to both solvency variables (a result consistent with the analysis of debtors and creditors above). It is also interesting to note that both liquidity variables remain relatively stable in both sub-samples between 1989 and 1992.

The final variables reported in Table 3.8 focus on corporate gearing (financial risk). The first (TLTA), is the ratio of total liabilities to total assets; whereas the second (ICOV) is the ratio of net profit before interest and tax to interest paid. Higher values of ICOV are associated with lower financial risk, with the converse applying to TLTA. Table 3.8 shows that there are no significant differences between the two sub-samples in respect of corporate gearing in 1989 and 1992. However, on average, foreign-owned firms significantly improved their interest cover (CICOV) relative to domestic firms between 1989 and 1992, with domestic firms suffering a substantial deterioration in interest cover during the recession.

Corporate failure and credit risk assessment

In 1995 (that is, subsequent to the time the data described in the preceding section was collected) the FAME database was extended to incorporate an additional 95,000 smaller firms. In addition, a further variable (credit score) was also included on the database. In this section we therefore provide some additional evidence relating to the failure rates and credit risk ratings of the population of all foreign-owned and domestic manufacturing firms located in Wales, which were included in the expanded database in April 1996. The purpose of their analysis is to supplement the matched sample performance analysis, by providing population failure rates and credit risk ratings.[9]

The FAME database contains a separate search procedure for firms originally included on the database, but which subsequently 'failed' (that is, corporate deaths resulting from liquidation/insolvency proceedings, together with those that had ceased trading). A search was made on the database to identify all manufacturing firms (that is, with a primary manufacturing SIC code) located in Wales which were 'live' (that is, excluding corporate deaths). In total, 866 firms with account year ends falling in 1994/95 met this criteria, of which 122 (14.1 per cent) were foreign-owned. A further search was then made on the database to identify all those Welsh firms with primary SIC codes in the manufacturing sector classified as corporate deaths (failures) between 1990 and 1995. This liberated 51 firms of which 5 (9.8 per cent) were foreign-owned.

TABLE 3.9
Corporate deaths: Welsh manufacturing firms (1990–1995)[a]

Year of death[b]	Foreign-owned subsidiaries (n=127)[c]	Domestic firms (n=790)[c]
1995	0.0 (n=0)	0.127 (n=1)
1994	1.575 (n=2)	1.266 (n=10)
1993	0.787 (n=1)	1.899 (n=15)
1992	0.787 (n=1)	1.266 (n=10)
1991	0.787 (n=1)	0.633 (n=5)
1990	0.0 (n=0)	0.633 (n=5)
All Years	3.937 (n=5)	5.822 (n=46)

Notes: [a] Analysis is based on all firms with a primary manufacturing SIC code located in Wales, accounts years ends falling in the period 1990 to 1995, on the FAME database.

[b] Deaths are defined as liquidations/ceased trading/insolvencies (including receivership and administration proceedings). Percentages refer to the proportion (per cent) of deaths in each year (relative to all firms in the sector).

[c] n= all firms on the database (including corporate deaths).

Based on this data, Table 3.9 shows corporate failure rates in Welsh manufacturing foreign-owned and domestic sectors respectively between 1990 and 1995. It shows that as a proportion of all foreign/domestic firms on the database, the proportion of failures between 1990 and 1995 in the foreign-owned sector (3.9 per cent) is lower than the failure rate (5.8 per cent) in the domestic sector, though the difference is not statistically significant on the basis of a chi-square test.[10] Table 3.9 also shows that, other than in 1991 and 1995, the proportion of failing firms is higher in the domestic sector. Overall, however, the failure rates do not differ significantly between the two groups; a result which is consistent with a previous UK study (Killick, 1982).

An analysis of the credit risk assessment of each firm (excluding failed ones) was also conducted. The results presented in Table 3.10 show the credit risk assessment categories ('high risk' to 'secure') of the two sub-samples. The five risk categories are based upon an analysis of each firm by a UK credit

TABLE 3.10
Credit risk assessment: Welsh manufacturing firms (1994–1995)

Risk assessment (credit score)	Proportion (per cent) in each risk assessment category	
	Foreign-owned (n=121)	Domestic (n=712)
High Risk (0–20)	9.92 (n=12)	10.39 (n=74)
Caution (21–40)	28.10 (n=34)	22.19 (n=158)
Normal (41–60)	23.14 (n=28)	32.72 (n=233)
Stable (61–80)	15.70 (n=19)	19.10 (n=136)
Secure (81–100)	23.14 (n=28)	15.59 (n=111)

Note: Analysis is based upon all firms with a primary manufacturing SIC code located in Wales on the FAME database in the period with financial year ends falling in the period 1994-95. Corporate deaths (Table 3.9) are excluded. One foreign-owned subsidiary and 32 domestic firms had missing values.

risk assessment company (Qui Credit Assessment Ltd), with a credit risk score allocated on a scale (score) varying between 0 (highest risk) and 100 (lowest risk). The risk categories reported in Table 3.10 refer to Qui's assessment[11] of the risk attached to extending credit (trade/loan creditors) to each firm in 1994/95. In relation to the high risk rating, the FAME manual states that companies in the high risk sector are unlikely to be able to continue trading unless significant remedial action is undertaken, there is support from parent firms, or other specific circumstances apply. Table 3.10 shows that a similar proportion of foreign-owned (9.2 per cent) and domestic firms (10.49 per cent) were classified as high risk, but that a significantly higher[12] proportion of foreign-owned firms (23.1 per cent) were rated as secure credit risks than were domestic firms (15.6 per cent); a result broadly consistent with the analysis relating to solvency (QRAT) and gearing (ICOV) characteristics, together with corporate deaths, discussed above.

SUMMARY AND CONCLUSIONS

Using a wide range of firm-specific variables, this paper has presented some new empirical evidence on the relative performance of matched samples of foreign-owned and domestic firms in the Welsh economy during the recent recession. The key results suggested that: (i) in total, firms in the domestic sample reduced employment levels by an average of 15.4 employees between 1989 and 1992, compared with a figure of only 1.5 employees in the foreign-owned sample, with 69.4 per cent and 53.9 per cent of domestic and foreign-owned companies, respectively, shedding labour through the recessionary period; (ii) average employee pay in 1992 was significantly higher in foreign-owned firms than it was in domestic firms. Perhaps more interestingly, mean earnings increased by a significantly larger amount in the foreign-owned sub-sample than in the domestic sub-sample between 1989 and 1992. Furthermore, over the same period, the wage bill to sales ratio increased by 4.8 percentage points in the domestic sub-sample, double that (2.4 per cent) in the foreign sub-sample; (iii) mean labour productivity levels were higher in foreign-owned firms in both 1989 and 1992, and also grew faster over this period. Furthermore, whereas mean sales revenue fell by around 2 per cent in the domestic sample between 1989 and 1992, it increased by 13 per cent in the foreign sample; (iv) firms in the domestic sample exhibited significantly higher profitability measures in 1989, but compared with the foreign firms, they suffered a significantly higher erosion of margins during the recession, resulting in domestic and foreign firms exhibiting similar profitability characteristics in 1992; (v) no significant differences were found in respect of the stock holdings of the two samples, but both foreign and domestic firms reduced stock levels substantially during the recession. In terms of liquidity and solvency, however, domestic firms (in both 1989 and 1992) exhibited higher debtor levels (that is, were owed more by customers) than foreign-owned firms. In contrast, on average, domestic firms had significantly higher days creditors outstanding (owed more to suppliers) than foreign-owned firms in both years; (vi) foreign and domestic firms exhibited similar gearing ratios, but financial risk (interest cover) was lower in foreign-owned firms in 1992, largely because of the significant improvement (relative to domestic firms) in interest cover between 1989 and 1992; (vii) an analysis of the population of Welsh manufacturing firms on the FAME database in 1995 revealed that, although domestic firms exhibited higher failure rates than foreign-owned firms between 1990 and 1995, the difference was not statistically significant. However, a significantly higher proportion of foreign-owned firms (23.2 per cent) were classified as being secure credit risks than were domestic firms (15.6 per cent).

This study suggests that foreign firms have maintained sales, assets and employment at a higher level in Wales compared with their domestic counterparts during the first part of the 1990s recession. The overall findings are comparable to those of McAleese and Counahan (1979) and support the view that foreign investment in Wales is relatively stable. This study, however, has some limitations. The findings refer to one region, and it would be valuable to compare the stability of the foreign sector in Wales with that in other UK regions which may have been more prone to recessionary forces. Furthermore, a future extension of the time period of analysis would allow the examination of the performance of domestic and foreign firms during the upturn in the UK economy. However, there is already some evidence that the Welsh economy came out of the 1990s recession relatively strongly. Wales was the fastest-growing UK region between 1993 and 1994, with the stability offered by the foreign manufacturing segment contributing to strong growth prospects (Cambridge Econometrics, 1995).

The regional policy resources available to market Wales abroad, and to provide financial assistance to inward investors, was reduced during the 1980s and early 1990s. However, the comparative stability offered by the foreign manufacturing sector in terms of employment and output does provide some justification for continued expenditure on regional location marketing. Whilst the stability offered by foreign capital can contribute to regional growth and development prospects, there are still a number of other questions concerning the region's foreign capital base. In particular, new foreign capital has tended to concentrate in the south-east and north-east of Wales, and has effectively served to highlight disparities in economic growth between the rural and western counties, and the counties of Gwent, South Glamorgan and (east) Clwyd.

The challenge for regional development organizations is perhaps to build upon the stability offered by foreign plants to spread their economic potential to western parts. Encouraging local purchasing within Wales might be one method of doing this, as is a finer distinction within Wales between areas where financial assistance for new foreign start-ups is targeted. In addition, there are still concerns about the limited production base of foreign manufacturing in Wales. Where foreign operations are relatively stable, there may be the opportunity for policy-makers to encourage the functional diversification of plants beyond production-only operations.

NOTES

1. In this paper, in common with previous research, 'stability' is defined in terms of the stability of employment and output in foreign and domestic firms through time.

2. At the time the data was collected (November 1994) the FAME database contained companies with turnover levels predominantly in excess of £1m. More recently (1995) FAME extended the database to include 95,000 smaller firms.

3. The matched sample design aims to control for corporate performance differentials which are related to industrial classification. In consequence, a limitation of the study (as with any study based on a matched sample design) is that the findings cannot be assumed to generalize to the population of Welsh manufacturing firms. However, there is no reason to suspect that geographical bias is present in the samples (e.g. based on any north/south Wales differences).

4. Clearly any empirical analysis of this nature may be sensitive to the time periods selected, with foreign and domestic manufacturing employment in the UK fluctuating significantly in the 1980s and early 1990s.

5. Again some firms which filed full accounts in 1992, filed reduced accounts in 1989 (that is, in 1989 they were able, under the Companies Acts, to file reduced accounts).

6. All the variables used in this study (including ratios) were generated from the information extracted (by FAME) from the statutory reports and accounts of each firm. The variables were selected with reference to the previous studies reviewed in this paper, together with a review of the standard financial ratios (i.e. relating to profitability, liquidity, gearing and asset and stock efficiency) which is used to evaluate corporate performance (see e.g. Van Horne, 1989).

7. For example, the FAME database (produced by Jordans, UK) was largely compiled for use by investment and corporate analysts (rather than academics). However, as noted by a referee to this paper, the standard variables (profitability, gearing, risk, efficiency and liquidity) collected for this study from FAME (i.e. those used by investment and corporate analysts), focus on different aspects of corporate performance and are thus 'performance' surrogates. For example, audited company annual accounts do not include data on the market value of capital stock, production output and labour hours worked. Hence, the productivity and capital stock variables used in this study may be viewed as surrogates for more conventional variables.

8. It should be noted that the Student's t-test tests for differences between sub-sample means; whereas the Mann-Whitney test tests for differences between sub-sample distributions. Although less powerful than the t-test, the Mann-Whitney test 'is one of the most powerful of the nonparametric tests' (Siegel and Castellan, 1988). It should also be noted that all the variables which were found to be significantly different (i.e. the means) at the 5 per cent level or better using a t-test, also differ significantly (i.e. the distributions) using the Mann-Whitney test. However, the t-test proved more conservative, in that seven variables (EMP89, FASS89, FASS92, TURN89 CNPEM, CTUTA and CTUFA) which differed significantly between the sub-samples using Mann-Whitney tests, did not differ significantly on the basis of t-tests. Hence, for the sake of comprehensiveness, although the tables in this paper highlight significant differences using both tests, interpretation of the results in the text focuses on significant mean differences using t-tests.

'9. As noted by a a referee to this paper, future research could expand the period of analysis for the matched company analysis (1989 to 1992) to incorporate more recent data on FAME. However, as noted in the paper, the expanded database contains a large number of additional smaller companies which are not available on earlier FAME discs. In addition, the credit rating variable is not available for years preceding 1995. The analysis in Tables 3.9 and 3.10 therefore relates to the population of Welsh manufacturing firms on the expanded FAME database and is not directly comparable with the matched sample analysis which precedes it.

10. For ease of interpretation, percentage frequency (as well as count) data are presented in Tables 3.9 and 3.10. However, standard chi-square tests were conducted on count data in all cases.

11. Each company case on the FAME database contains one of the five risk assessment categories shown in Table 3.10 (that is 'high risk' to 'caution').

12. The proportion of domestic and foreign-owned firms in the secure versus other combined bands differed significantly at the 5 per cent statistical level (chi-square = 9.49); whereas the proportion of foreign-owned and domestic firms differed significantly at the 10 per cent statistical level across the five risk assessment categories (chi-square = 8.80).

APPENDIX I Variable Definitions

Variables	*Definitions*
1. EMP92:	Number of employees in 1992
2. EMP89:	Number of employees in 1989
3. CEMP:	EMP92 – EMP89
4. EREM92:	Average employee remuneration (£) in 1992: wage bill/no.of employees.
5. EREM89:	Average employee remuneration in 1989
6. CEREM:	EREM92 – EREM89
7. FASS92:	Fixed assets (£000) in 1992
8. FASS89:	Fixed assets in 1989
9. CFASS:	FASS92 – FASS89
10. TASS92:	Total assets (£000) in 1992
11. TASS89:	Total assets in 1989
12. CTASS:	TASS92 – TASS89
13. TURN92:	Turnover (sales) in 1992 (£000)
14. TURN89:	Turnover (sales) in 1989
15. CTURN:	TURN92 – TURN89
16. DAYST92:	Days stock held in 1992: (stock/sales) *365
17. DAYST89:	Days stock held in 1989
18. CDAYST:	DAYST92 – DAYST89
19. DAYD92:	Collection period (days debtors) in 1992: (debtors/sales) *365
20. DAYD89:	Collection period in 1989
21. CDAYD:	DAYD92 – DAYD89
22. DAYC92:	Days credit period from suppliers (as a proportion of sales) in 1992: (creditors/sales) *365

23. DAYC89:   Days credit period from suppliers in 1989
24. CDAYC: DAYC92 – DAYC89
25. CURA92:   Current (liquidity) ratio in 1992: current assets/current liabilities
26. CURA89:   Current ratio in 1989
27. CCURA: CURA92 – CURA89
28. QRAT92:   Quick (solvency) ratio in 1992: (current assets-stock/current liabilities)
29. QRAT89:   Quick ratio in 1989
30. CQRAT: QRAT92 – QRAT89
31. TLTA92:   Gearing ratio in 1992: total liabilities/total assets
32. TLTA89:   Gearing ratio in 1989
33. CTLTA: TLTA1992 – TLTA89
34. ICOV92:   Interest cover in 1992: profit before interest and tax/interest paid
35. ICOV89:   Interest cover in 1989
36. CICOV: ICOV92 – ICOV89
37. SALEM92:   Sales (£) per employee in 1992
38. SALEM89:   Sales per employee in 1989
39. CSALEM: SALEM92 – SALEM89
40. REMS92:   Wage bill expense as a percentage of sales in 1992
41. REMS89:   Wage bill expense as a percentage of sales in 1989
42. CREMS: REMS92 – REMS89
43. NPEM92:   Net profit before tax (£) per employee in 1992
44. NPEM89:   Net profit per employee in 1989
45. CNPEM: NPEM92 – NPEM89
46. TUTA92:   Total assets turnover in 1992: sales/total assets
47. TUTA89:   Total assets turnover in 1989
48. CTUTA: TUTA92 – TUTA89
49. TUFA92:   Fixed asset turnover in 1992: sales/fixed assets
50. TUFA89:   Fixed asset turnover in 1989
51. CTUFA: TUFA92 – TUFA89
52. NPMG92:   Net profit margin (per cent) in 1992: net profit before tax/sales
53. NPMG89:   Net profit margin in 1989
54. CNPMG: NPMG92 – NPMG89
55. RCAP92:   Return (per cent) on total capital employed in 1992: net profit before tax/total capital employed
56. RCAP89:   Return on total capital employed in 1989
57. CRCAP: RECAP92 – RECAP89

APPENDIX 2 Surveyed Company Accounts*

*Location Key: (ISW) = Industrial South Wales i.e. old counties of Gwent, Mid, South and West Glamorgan including Llanelli; (NEW) = North East Wales i.e. Clwyd; (OA) = Other areas.

Metal Manufacturing:
Foreign: Pullmaflex (ISW); Alcoa Manufacturing (ISW); Aluminium Precision (ISW); Alcoa Extruded Products (ISW).
Domestic: David Matthews Limited (ISW); Rye Engineering (OA); ASW (ISW); European Electrical Steels (ISW); Stainless Services (ISW); Utterbest (ISW); Merton Wire (ISW); Evans and Reid (ISW).

Chemicals:
Foreign: Rockwool (ISW); Owens Corning (NEW); Peboc (OA); Agrisens (ISW); Cray Valley (ISW); A.Schulman (ISW); Conren (NEW); Viskase (ISW); PB Gelatins (ISW); Ondawel (ISW); Revlon (ISW).
Domestic: ARC (ISW); BDC Concrete (ISW); William Lewis (ISW); Merlin (ISW); Gower Chemicals (ISW); Clean Plastic (ISW); Boride Ceramics (ISW); Steltec (ISW); Chemical Corporation (ISW); Norgine (ISW); Sutures Ltd (NEW); Speywood Biopharm (NEW); Natural Beauty Products (ISW); Purolite International (ISW).

Other Metal Goods:
Foreign: Osprey Metals (ISW); Atlantic Services (ISW); Fiskars UK Ltd (ISW); Klockner Pentapack UK Holdings (ISW).
Domestic: Kaye Ltd (OA); Brockhouse Modernfold (ISW); Bridgend Timber Products (ISW); Ceka Works (OA); Technical Tooling (ISW); G Plan (ISW); Aman Metal Spinners (ISW); Price Fallows (OA).

Mechanical Engineering:
Foreign: Consort (OA); Goricon (ISW); Valentec International (ISW); Rizla (ISW); Facet Industrial (ISW); Hills Industries (ISW); Fram Europe (ISW); Eriez Magnetics (ISW); Saunders Valve (ISW); TRW Steering (ISW); Nacam (ISW); Sears Manufacturing (ISW).
Domestic: Walter Grenville (ISW); Fairfield Mabey (ISW); Caradon Catnic (ISW); Specialist Heavy Engineering (ISW);Unit Superheater (ISW); Steelfab (ISW); Rimer Alco (ISW); Ducant Limited (ISW); Assembly and Automation (ISW); Lacre PDE (ISW); Haven Automation (ISW); IMI Santon (ISW); CR Clarke (ISW); Coopers Filters (ISW); MacWhirter (ISW); Daniels Fans (ISW); Coinmaster Manufacturing (ISW); Alfred Cook (ISW); Rhos Precision (ISW); Harris Pye Marine (ISW) RHS Engineering (ISW); Teamseed (ISW); Formagrind (ISW); Wyndham Engineering (ISW).

Electrical Engineering:
Foreign: Brother Industries (NEW); Kyushu Matsushita (ISW); Aero Motive UK (ISW); Austin Taylor (OA); Industrial Capacitors (NEW); Yuasa Battery (ISW); Atlas Fire (ISW); Wall Colomnoy (ISW); Ascom Telecommunications (ISW); Mitel Telecom (ISW); Newbridge Networks (ISW); Lloret Electrical ((ISW); Molynx Holding PLC (ISW); Molynx Limited (ISW); DBK Technitherm (ISW); Gooding Sanken (ISW); Harman Motive (ISW); Hitachi Consumer Products (ISW); Matsushita Electrical (ISW); Bethesda 1994 Limited (OA); Race Electronics (ISW); Orion Electric (ISW); Sharp Precision (NEW); Advance Machine (ISW).

Domestic: Morganite (ISW); Pinacl Communications (NEW); Mills Associates (ISW); Datamatic (ISW); Afig Holdings (ISW); BIG Batteries (ISW); Elmatic (ISW); Denis Ferranti (OA); Control Techniques (OA); Electrotech (ISW); Control Techniques Drives (OA); Thermocouple Instruments (ISW); Pikington PE (NEW); Morganite Electrical Carbon (ISW); Control Techniques PLC (OA); A and A Electronics (ISW); Cornelius Electronics (ISW); Control Techniques Precision (OA); Quantum Electronics (ISW); Ultralight (ISW); Arnold Smart (ISW).

Transport Equipment:
Foreign: Trico (ISW); Pullmaflex UK Limited (ISW); Bosal Industries (ISW); Gillet Exhaust (ISW); Isringhausen GB (NEW); Calsonic Automotive (ISW); Valeo Wiper Systems (ISW); Valeo Climate Control (ISW); Portec UK (NEW); EMMS (ISW); Carters J and A (ISW).
Domestic: Thomas Hoskins (ISW); Laird (OA); J D Cleverly (ISW); K and J Withey (ISW); Ifor Williams Trailers (OA); J R Industries (ISW); Patron Enterprises (ISW); D W Williams Ltd (NEW); ROR Rockwell (NEW); Holyhead Marine (OA); Powell Duffryn (ISW); Annanvale (ISW); Thunder and Colt (OA); Aircraft Maintenance Supplies (ISW); Airborne Group PLC (OA).

Instrument Engineering:
Foreign: Lion Laboratories (ISW); MPD Limited (ISW); Biomet (ISW); Hoya Lens (NEW).
Domestic: Firsteel (ISW); Jones Chromatography (ISW); Minerva Limited (ISW); Nesbit Evans Healthcare (OA); Brevit products (OA); Nesbit Evans Limited (OA); Good-Life Medical (ISW); Laserscope (ISW).

Rubber and Plastics:
Foreign: Takiron UK (ISW); Klockner Pentapack Limited (ISW); Rexham Limited (ISW); Diaplastics (ISW); Solvay Automotive (ISW); Allevard Springs (ISW).
Domestic: Avon Inflatables (ISW); WA Thatcher (ISW); Brockington and Scott (OA); Just Rubber PLC (ISW); Development Plastics (ISW); Melanie Limited (ISW); Atlantic Plastics (ISW); Silvergate Plastics (NEW); Select Consumer Products (ISW); Microlink (ISW); Dipec (ISW); Nypo (NEW).

Other Manufacturing Groups:
Foreign: Champlain Protex (OA); Viscosuisse (ISW); New Venture Carpets (ISW); Spontex Limited (ISW); Kronospan (NEW); Record Industrial Brushes (OA); Chilham Limited (ISW); General Paper and Box (ISW); Staedtler UK (ISW); Fiskars Limited (ISW).
Domestic: Creamery Fare (NEW); OP Chocolates (ISW); Hicking Pentecost (ISW); Stewart Singlam (ISW); Western Fabrics (ISW); F Theak and Roskilly (ISW); W A Blyth (ISW); CAC Industrial (OA); Dendic (ISW); BCB International (ISW); Lifestyle Upholstery (ISW); S Dudley (ISW); Benders Holdings (NEW); Western Corrugated (ISW); Pontrilas Group (OA); Porth Decorative (ISW); Lefray Limited (ISW); Wendley Limited (ISW); EGA Limited (NEW); Powersport International (ISW).

REFERENCES

Buckley, P. and Casson, M. (1991). *The Future of the Multinational Enterprise*, London, MacMillan.

Business Monitor (1995). *UK Census of Production Summary Tables (1992)*, PA1002, HMSO, London.

Business Monitor (various years). *UK Census of Production Summary Tables*, PA 1002, HMSO, London.

Cambridge Econometrics (1995). *Regional Economic Prospects*, Cambridge, Cambridge Econometrics.

Davies, S. and Lyons, B. (1991). 'Characterising relative performance: the productivity advantage of foreign-owned firms in the UK', *Oxford Economic Papers* 43, 584–95.

Dunning, J. (1993). *Multinational Enterprises and the Global Economy*, Wokingham, Addison Wesley.

Hill, S. and Keegan, J. (1993). *Made in Wales*, Cardiff, CBI Wales.

Hill, S. and Munday, M. (1994). *The Regional Distribution of Inward Investment in the UK*, London, Macmillan.

Hill, S. and Roberts, A. (1993). *Inward Investment and Regional Economic Development*, Paper presented to the 17th Annual ANZRSA Conference, Armidale, New South Wales, Australia, December.

Hood, N. and Young, S. (1982). *Multinationals in Retreat: The Scottish Experience*, Edinburgh, Edinburgh University Press.

Killick, T. (1982). 'Employment in foreign-owned plants', *British Business*, November.

Li, J. and Guisinger, S. (1991). 'Comparative business failures of foreign controlled firms in the United States', *Journal of International Business Studies* 22, 209–24.

Luo, Y. and Chen, M. (1995). 'Financial performance comparison between international joint ventures and wholly foreign-owned enterprises in China', *International Executive* 3, 599–613.

McAleese, D. and Counahan, M. (1979). 'Stickers or snatchers? Employment in multinational corporations during the recession', *Oxford Bulletin of Economics and Statistics* 41, 345–58.

Morris, J., Munday, M. and Wilkinson, B. (1993). *Working for the Japanese*, London, Athlone.

Munday, M., Morris, J. and Wilkinson, B. (1995). 'Factories or warehouses: a Welsh perspective of Japanese transplant manufacturing', *Regional Studies* 29, 1–17.

Norusis, M. J. (1988). *SPSS-X Introductory Statistical Guide*, Chicago, SPSS Inc.

Pitelis, C. and Sugden, R. (1991). *The Nature of the Transnational Firm*, London, Routledge.

Shapiro, D. (1983). 'The comparative profitability of Canadian and foreign controlled firms', *Managerial and Decision Economics* 4, 97–106.

Siegel, S. and Castellan, N. (1988). *Nonparametric Statistics*, London, McGraw-Hill Inc.

Solomon, R. and Ingham, K. (1977). 'Discriminating between MNC subsidiaries and indigenous companies: a comparative analysis of the British mechanical engineering industry', *Oxford Bulletin of Economics and Statistics* 39, 127–38.

Van Horne, J. (1989). *Financial Management and Policy,* London, Prentice Hall International.
Welsh Office (1995). *Welsh Economic Trends*, Cardiff, Welsh Office.

4. DEVELOPMENT AND PRIVATIZATION OF CARDIFF AIRPORT

Ian Humphreys

INTRODUCTION

Cardiff is the only major airport in Wales, yet it is not the airport for Wales. It draws nearly all its traffic (81 per cent) from parts of south Wales (see Figure 4.1). The majority of passengers in north and mid Wales use Manchester and Birmingham airports respectively (CAA, 1992, 1993, 1995). The airport is currently the fifteenth busiest airport in the UK having served 1.04 million passengers in 1995/96, and returning pre-tax profits of £5.7 million. Located twelve miles west of Cardiff it currently offers over 120 scheduled departures each week to a selection of international and domestic destinations. The remaining 75 per cent of its business is shared amongst over 25 tour operators offering charter flights and package holidays to over 80 different holiday destinations ranging from the Mediterranean to the USA. On 16th March 1995, local-government-owned Cardiff-Wales Airport was sold to the Welsh property development group Thomas Bailey Incorporated (TBI) for £37.5 million, with its name changed to Cardiff International Airport.

This article examines the development of the airport at Cardiff including the conditions for its privatization. It also contains some reflections on the significance of the airport for the local economy. The paper begins with a commentary on air service development and the trends in passenger throughput. The role of the airport as a catalyst for inward investment into south Wales is then evaluated. Following an account of the airport's physical development under different owners, some implications of its recent privatization are discussed.

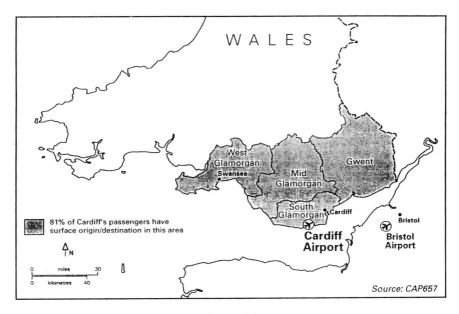

FIGURE 4.1
Cardiff Airport primary catchment area 1994/5

AIR SERVICE DEVELOPMENT

Air services provide two main benefits to the population of south Wales: access to business and leisure destinations; and revenue for the airport.[1] Passenger numbers provide a measure of airport development, with Figure 4.2 showing the growth in terminal passengers over the period 1955–1995. Initial development at Cardiff began in 1940 when the current airport site at Rhoose was requisitioned by the Air Ministry and a training base for RAF spitfire pilots was established. The first civil aviation developments at Rhoose came in 1952 when Aer Lingus received permission to operate a Dublin service because the city's existing airport at Pengam Moors, with its grass runway, was unsuitable for handling the aircraft used on this service. This marked the beginning of the end for the Pengam Moors airfield and by 1954 the airfield was closed and all civilian traffic transferred to Rhoose. The airport was renamed Cardiff (Rhoose) airport and began to develop in step with the expansion of services by the Cardiff-based Cambrian Airlines.

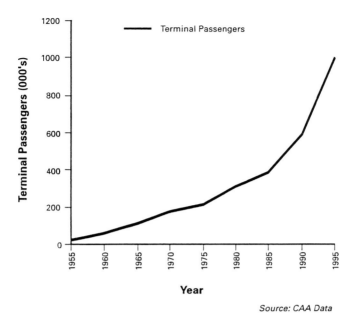

Source: CAA Data

FIGURE **4.2**
Terminal passengers at Cardiff Airport 1955–1995

Between 1955 and 1975 traffic at Cardiff grew by some 736 per cent, in line with national growth for this period. The links between airport growth and the activities of airlines are apparent throughout the development history of the airport. Cambrian Airways carried 25,000 passengers in 1955 and continued to develop new routes with new aircraft, so that by 1962 the airline was carrying some 100,000 passengers. Passenger throughput increased to 171,000 in 1970 as Cambrian continued to develop a network of services to points throughout Britain and the holiday resorts of Spain. Just as growth had been closely associated with the fortunes of airlines, so too was the decline in passenger figures. The oil crisis in the early seventies and the slump in the holiday market hit aviation throughout the UK; Cardiff was no exception as the services of a major package holiday airline, Court Line, were lost when the airline went bankrupt. A further blow for the airport came in 1974 when Cambrian services were phased out as a result of rationalization by its new owners, British Airways, because 'Cardiff services without exception were subsidised by the rest of British Airways' (Staddon

1979). The failure of several other airlines at Cardiff during the seventies constrained growth so that by 1975 traffic had only reached 209,000. Further growth then came from the charter holiday/inclusive tour business.

Charter holiday and inclusive tour traffic

From 1976 onwards the growth of passengers at Cardiff was driven almost entirely by the expansion of the charter holiday/inclusive tour market which accounted for over 80 per cent of traffic. Between 1976 and 1985 the introduction of jet services, low price package holidays and economic recovery from the oil crisis, led to an expansion of charter services to Spain. As a result, Cardiff's passenger numbers increased by 99 per cent compared with UK growth of 57 per cent. The eighties and early nineties saw the charter/inclusive tour business expand by 182 per cent between 1985/6 and 1995/6 compared to 66 per cent growth for the UK (see Figure 4.3). This was due to demand reaching levels that gave tour operators a critical mass for an expanded range of services. The number of destinations beyond the core Spanish market increased, with services to Greece, Cyprus, Bulgaria, Malta, Turkey and Yugoslavia.

Britannia, the airline of major inclusive tour operator Thomson holidays, has been a consistent source of passenger throughput throughout this period while a number of other airlines have come and gone. Most notable of these was the spring 1991 collapse of Air Europe, the second largest charter operator at the airport responsible for 200,000 passengers per annum. As a result of this and the negative impact of the Gulf War, passenger numbers declined to 492,429 in 1990/91 and continued to fall to 429,751 in 1991/92 (Greaves, 1991). As the demand for holidays improved again, passenger figures increased to 525,344 in 1992/93 and to 651,485 in 1993/4. Expansion by Britannia, from 200,000 holidays in 1992 to 350,000 in 1993, was a major reason for the growth of passenger throughput. Growth was boosted further when Airtours subsumed IEA and Aspro in a take-over that saw a second major tour operator with its own airline establish services from the airport during 1994. Further expansion of package holiday destinations by Airtours, Britannia and Monarch Airlines ensured that the 1994 and 1995 summer seasons were the most successful on record with a 33 per cent increase recorded in 1995/6 compared with 1993/4. Currently the people of south Wales have access to around 80 holiday destinations and 35 tour operators from their local airport.

Airspace, airport and surface congestion at airports in the south-east of England will make the option of offering flights direct from Cardiff increasingly attractive to charter holiday operators. The superior runway

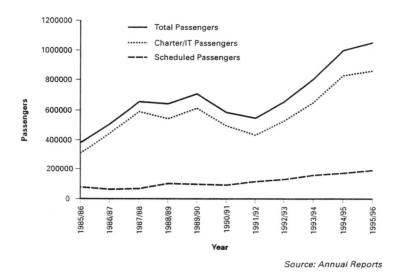

Source: Annual Reports

FIGURE **4.3**
Charter, scheduled and total terminal passengers at Cardiff Airport 1985/6 to 1995/6

length relative to its main competitor at Bristol will enable better economies of operation for tour operators who are able to operate larger aircraft such as the 757 (230 seats) and 767 (282 seats) aircraft at full payloads, from Cardiff but not from Bristol.

Scheduled services
Scheduled services provide access to business destinations either directly or through a link to a hub airport that allows connections with onward air services. Around 20 per cent of passengers using Cardiff travel on scheduled services.

Scheduled services from Cardiff have served a range of domestic and several short-haul European destinations (see Table 4.1). Although the number of destinations served (though not the mix) appears to have remained constant, the number of weekday departures has increased from 20 in 1986/7 to 120 in 1995/6 (see Figure 4.4).

TABLE **4.1**

Cardiff Airport scheduled service destinations 1985/6 and 1995/6

1985/6	
Domestic:	Belfast, Bournemouth, Gatwick, Guernsey, Jersey, Leeds-Bradford, Glasgow, Manchester, Newcastle
International:	Amsterdam, Dublin, Cork
1995/96	
Domestic:	Aberdeen, Belfast, Edinburgh, Glasgow, Isle of Man, Guernsey, Jersey, Manchester, Newcastle
International:	Amsterdam, Brussels, Dublin, Paris

Source: Cardiff Airport timetables

Up until 1990 services were frequently withdrawn. A key reason for this was that the frequencies and flight timings offered by airlines did not meet the demands of the market.[2] In 1990, surveys conducted by CBI Wales and the Institute of Welsh Affairs revealed that the business community required reliable, scheduled services with a twice daily frequency, timed to enable a full working day to be spent at the destination. In 1990 only the Amsterdam and Glasgow services fulfilled this criteria (Welsh Affairs Committee, 1991).

The vulnerability of services to financial pressures, the inability to make routes profitable and route rationalization, have combined to produce a scheduled service network that has been in a constant state of flux, with 26 services being withdrawn and 17 being started during the ten-year period 1981/2–1991/2. For example, by the end of March 1986, the withdrawal of services by Dan Air and Metropolitan Airways (route rationalization) and British Caledonian Commuter (end of an agreement with British Caledonian to feed passengers onto Gatwick services) left the airport with only four of the thirteen services that were operating in April 1985. The high number of scheduled services withdrawn from Cardiff caused services to be perceived as unreliable by the local business community. This led to locally based demand for air travel using the highly frequent and reliable services available from Heathrow instead of Cardiff: a 14 times per day service to Brussels and 21 times per day to Paris are available at Heathrow.

The turning point for scheduled service development came in 1991 when Manx Airlines invested £5 million setting up a network of eight scheduled services (*Western Mail*, 1991). This investment by an airline with the financial backing of the Airlines of Britain Group (40 per cent owned by Scandinavian Airlines) provided a new stability for the scheduled service

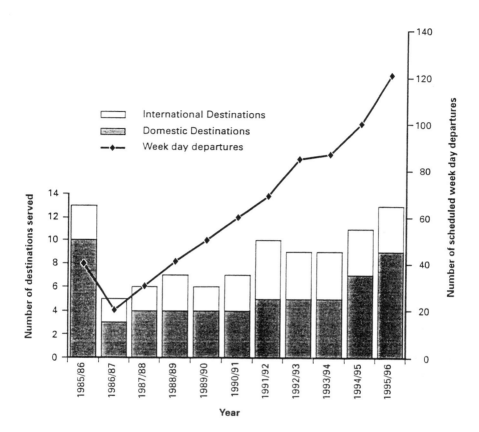

Source: Cardiff Airport Timetables, OAG

FIGURE **4.4**
Cardiff Airport scheduled service destinations and weekday departures

network and as a consequence only one service has been withdrawn since 1992. In 1990, there were 61 working-day scheduled service departures from Cardiff with Manx accounting for ten of these. By 1996 the number of working-day scheduled service departures per week had grown to 120 with 85 of these being flown by Manx. Day return trips to Belfast, Brussels, Edinburgh, Glasgow, Newcastle, Manchester and Paris were made possible by Manx's services. In 1990 passengers travelling to these destinations would have had to travel to Heathrow for a Brussels service, or would have had to stay two nights to gain a full working day in either Belfast or Paris. The airline tailored its operation to the needs of high-yield business travellers by operating sixteen-seat (Jetstream 31) aircraft that only require eight passengers per flight to break even. Manx has made its services pay where other airlines have failed. The concentration of a network of routes at Cardiff holds great potential for future expansion since, for Manx, the marginal costs of operating additional services from Cardiff are significantly lower than for operating new services from elsewhere.

In January 1995, Manx Airlines entered into a franchise agreement with British Airways (BA) that enabled its aircraft to operate with BA flight codes and wear BA livery. This move underpins Manx's position since it enables the airline to enjoy the benefits of the BA brand identity and the greater profile it gives them with passengers and travel agents. Inclusion under the brand of Europe's most profitable airline places Manx in a position to benefit from feeder traffic and new route opportunities as the liberalization of European air services continues to gather momentum.

Another important scheduled service development is the Cardiff–Amsterdam route operated by the Dutch National airline, KLM. Since 1988 the service has expanded from a 16-seat aircraft three times per day, to a five-times daily service using a mixture of 34- and 58-seat aircraft. The link is highly significant because it provides access to over 150 international destinations via connecting services at Amsterdam. In 1994/5 over half (53 per cent) of the 57,000 passengers using the route made connections to onward destinations (CAA, 1995).

Since 1991, the introduction of a stable, high profile network of services by Manx, the backing of the BA brand and the expansion of the KLM service have provided the south Wales business traveller with access to frequent, reliable, high quality, scheduled services.

Freight
The volume of freight traffic is a minor part of the airport's business with a

mere 2,487 metric tonnes handled in 1995/6, which represents just 0.001 per cent of the UK total (CIPFA, 1996). The volume of air freight from south Wales is such that it requires consolidation with freight from other parts of Britain at a major hub airport, such as Heathrow, to be an economically viable option. The majority of air freight travels in the holds of passenger aircraft. Heathrow, which offers air services to 220 scheduled destinations provides a natural focal point which Cardiff, with only 13 scheduled destinations, cannot effectively compete with.

While the economic benefits of handling freight are in the main lost to Heathrow, the most significant contribution of freight handling at Cardiff is the ability to accommodate *ad hoc* freight loads which maintain the supply chain for local industry, for example, Ford's air freight charters to supply car engines and other components to meet production demands at their Bridgend plant.

CATALYST FOR INVESTMENT

Cardiff's airport has been viewed as a catalyst for attracting investment into south Wales ever since Glamorgan County Council assumed control in 1965 (Glamorgan (Rhoose) Airport Joint Committee, CBI, Development Corporation for Wales and Wales TUC, 1975; and Welsh Affairs Committee,1991). The Welsh Development Agency (WDA) and the unitary authorities for the Vale of Glamorgan and Cardiff claim that the airport is a key selling point when trying to attract inward investment. This view, however, needs to be tempered somewhat.

Between 1 January 1983 and 1 January 1997 £3 billion of inward investment, just under half the Welsh total, has located in the vicinity of the M4 corridor in south Wales (WDA, 1997). An assessment for *Corporate Location* in 1995 found that firms were investing in Wales because of its competitive wage costs, high productivity in manufacturing industries, flexible labour force, greenfield site availability, WDA grants and WDA business support (Millward, 1996). The airport did not appear to play a significant role in the industrial location decision.

It can be argued that up until 1991 Cardiff had few, low-quality, and unreliable scheduled service links yet inward investment still poured into the south Wales M4 corridor. This would suggest that access to world markets via scheduled services from Cardiff Airport was not important as these links were not available. Moreover, access available to 220 direct international air services provided via Heathrow, the busiest international airport in the world, and only 2 hours 15 minutes away along the M4, is likely to have exerted more of an influence in attracting inward investment.

The one example where there is no doubt of the airport's role as a catalyst for investment was the establishment of the £70 million, 72-acre, BA jumbo jet maintenance facility at the airport in 1991.[3] It opened for business in 1993, and by January 1997 employed 870 people (Horner and Sherratt, 1997). Without the availability of a runway long enough to handle the Boeing 747, south Wales would not have been in the running to receive this investment. BA were attracted to the airport despite fierce competition from alternative sites because the then county council owners of the airport used it in a strategic way for the benefit of the region by selling the land to BA instead of leasing it. The sale of the land was not a decision the airport would have taken if it were a privatized entity, since the only economic benefit after the initial revenue from the sale is the landing fee for an empty jumbo jet every ten days. As such, the airport's immediate commercial interests were sacrificed for the economic and employment benefit of the region.

The strategic importance of BA's facility at the airport extends beyond the site itself. The county council owners recognized its role as a magnet for attracting related aerospace investment to the region. For example, BA located their £30 million main UK avionics workshop employing some 375 people at Llantrisant in 1994 and in 1996 80 people were employed when BA located a facility for aircraft interior work at Blackwood. A £4 million maintenance training facility and a German electrical firm have located on the airport business park, while an aircraft component repair plant at Blackwood, employing some 170 was announced in 1996. The RAF maintenance facility at St Athan employs some 3,000 servicemen and 1,500 civilians while the General Electric aircraft engine plant at Nantgarw employs around 1,000 people. In addition to these jobs, a further estimated 14,000 related jobs exist in south Wales (Henn, 1994). This concentration of the aerospace industry validates the region's credentials as a centre of excellence and makes further investment a strong possibility.

From this point of view, it would seem that the airport's principal benefit to the region has been its role as a catalyst for the location of aerospace-related industry in south Wales and the employment and other economic benefits this has brought.

AIRPORT OWNERSHIP AND DEVELOPMENT

Cardiff airport began its civil life owned by central government through the

Ministry of Aviation. The initial airport terminal development in 1952 took place on the south side of the airfield and was driven by the need to cater for the growing number of passengers being attracted by the airlines. After a number of loss-making years central government gave control of the airport to Glamorgan County Council in 1965. Run as a public utility the airport was far from being financially self-sufficient, making losses year on year. Investment in the development of the airport was not justified by the economic returns made by the airport but was justified by the county council owners in terms of the social and economic benefits that this infrastructure would bring to south Wales. This approach meant that the local taxpayer funded the two most investment-intensive developments at the airport during the late sixties/early seventies.

In the late sixties, airlines started to favour jet aircraft and the economic benefits these could bring, so the airport authority decided to upgrade facilities in order to cope with this trend. Failure to do this would have resulted in a loss of jet traffic to other airports The first part of the development strategy was to almost double the length of the runway, from 3,700 feet to 7,000 feet, to enable short- and medium-haul jet traffic to operate with full payloads; the extended runway was opened in March 1970. However, the terminal building struggled to cope with the rise in passenger numbers and in 1972 a £5 million investment was made in a new terminal building and tower. These developments took place on the current terminal site to the north of the runway and gave the airport a terminal building with a design capacity for handling one million passengers per annum. As passenger figures show the airport handled 285,000 in 1973 and it was not until 1995 that it handled over 1 million passengers for the first time. The new terminal building cost £12 million including interest by the time that the debt had finally been paid off (1983), and represented a costly over-provision of capacity. However, without the long-term, public utility view of the airport taken by the county council owners, the runway and terminal would not have been able to accommodate demand and airport development would have been severely constrained. Local government reorganization in 1974 saw further change in the airport's ownership with it being taken over by a consortium of the newly created Mid, South and West Glamorgan county councils. The name of the airport was changed to Cardiff–Wales airport in an attempt to emphasize the airport's national status.

In the financial year 1984/5 the airport owners were faced with a typical development dilemma. Should the runway be extended in the hope of attracting further traffic or should the airport wait until airlines showed an

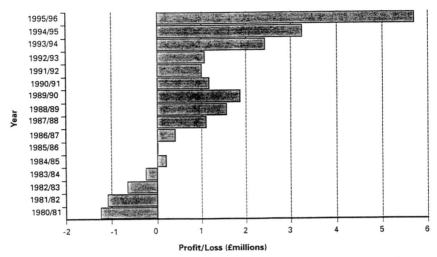

Source: *Annual Reports*

FIGURE 4.5
Cardiff Airport operating profit/loss 1980–1996

interest in operating services before an investment was made? Once again the owners took a proactive approach, and in 1986 they invested £1 million in a runway extension to increase the length to 7,723 feet, accommodating wide-bodied aircraft such as the Boeing 747, 767 and the DC10 which could reach the eastern seaboard of North America with a full passenger payload from Cardiff.

Under county council ownership the local taxpayers supported the airport through 32 years of losses. As traffic levels rose and utilization levels of the terminal improved, a profit was achieved for the first time in 1984/5 (Cardiff Airport, 1984/5). Improvements in capacity utilization ensured that the airport started to return pre-tax profits each year (see Figure 4.5). Profit figures fluctuated in line with passenger throughput and the level of utilization of the facilities. The 1989/90 boom in traffic produced pre-tax profits of £1.86 million, while the effects of the Gulf War and the loss of Air Europe constrained profit levels to around £1 million for each of the following years up to 1992/3 (Cardiff Airport, 1989/90, 1990/1, 1991/2,

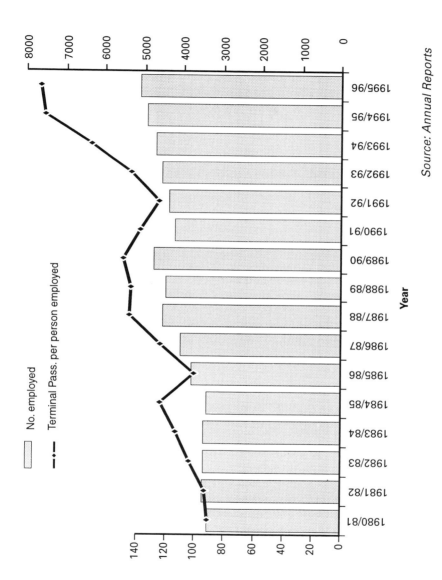

Source: Annual Reports

FIGURE 4.6 **Cardiff Airport workforce and productivity 1980–1996**

1992/3). From then onwards profits rose rapidly in 1993/4 to £2.4 million, and to £3.2 million in 1994/5 (Cardiff Airport, 1993/4, 1994/5). This success represented just reward for the long-term investment made by the county councils. The airport became financially self-sufficient, and profits benefited the local taxpayer in the form of dividends that were distributed to the county councils and spent on public services.

As the utilization of the facilities at the airport has improved, so has the productivity of the airport employees.[4] Employee productivity grew by 126 per cent between 1980/1 and 1995/6 from 3,382 passengers handled per employee to 7,637 passengers handled per employee (Cardiff Airport, 1980/1, 1995/6) (see Figure 4.6). In the five years prior to the airport being made a public limited company (plc) (1980/1–1985/6), productivity improved by 11 per cent. After 1986/7 a 36 per cent rise in productivity was recorded in the period up until 1990/1, followed by a 48 per cent growth up until 1994/95. The improvements in productivity provide further evidence of the successful role of the county councils in nurturing the airport's development.

The trend towards privatization began when the Conservative Government transformed UK regional airports into PLCs through the 1986 Airports Act. In Cardiff's case the shares were given to the original local authority owners which meant Mid, South and West Glamorgan maintained their ownership of the airport, but they could no longer subsidize its operation. In 1995 the county councils were effectively forced to sell their shares because the government restricted the amount of money that they could borrow to fund essential expansion plans to cater for the forecast doubling of traffic by 2010. Local government reorganization in Wales, scheduled for April 1996, accelerated the full privatization because if the airport was not sold by this date it would be given to a government residuary body and the proceeds would disappear into central government coffers. This meant that if the airport had not been sold the county councils would not have received a penny for their airport.

With reluctance, the county councils agreed to sell the airport and in doing so retained some economic benefits for the local taxpayers who had financially footed the bill for the airport's development. With pre-tax profits at £2.5 million in 1994/5 it was no surprise that ten bidders chased this prize asset with the Welsh property development company TBI emerging as the successful bidder, paying £37.5 million. The money was divided evenly between the three former county council owners, and allocated to amenities and services (see Appendix 1 for details). Ironically the airport was nearly bought by the Irish government, a reflection of the fact that not all governments are of like mind with regards to owning a profitable airport.

The county councils protected the interests of the region in two ways when they sold the airport. Firstly, they addressed concerns that the flat, stable and well-drained site would be bought for housing or retail development by protecting the site as an airport through a clause in the terms of sale. Secondly, the councils did not select the successful bidder on the basis of money alone. The airport was sold to TBI because of the company's Welsh roots and its extensive £20 million expansion plans which gave proof of its commitment to giving south Wales a first-class regional airport facility.

PRELIMINARY IMPLICATIONS OF PRIVATIZATION

It is too early to assess the impact of privatization as barely two years have passed since the airport entered into private control. However, initial changes and investment plans give a preliminary indication of the implications for south Wales.

An immediate and obvious change attributable to privatization was the change of name from Cardiff–Wales Airport to Cardiff International Airport which is intended to highlight the nature of the routes offered and provide a new identity to signify the change in ownership. TBI are a Welsh property development company that have consistently expanded their business, gaining a reputation for shrewd investment along the way. With airport passengers forecast to rise to 2.5 million per annum by 2004 (Cardiff International Airport, 1995) the acquisition of the airport may rank among its best deals yet.

The new airport management has stated its aims as: to be more customer-focused, raise more commercial income, and introduce an aggressive marketing strategy, viewing an airport as 'a runway with a shopping mall beside it' (Aitkenhead, 1996). This definition of the airport, as given by the first managing director following privatization, reflects the airport's new direction under private ownership. Central to achieving these aims is the £20 million plan for the airport which includes development of the airport terminal, the freight facility and the surrounding land. To date the first £5.5 million phase of this investment has been completed and includes the trebling in size of the international departure lounge to include 260,000 square feet of new retail floorspace, a new baggage reclaim area capable of processing three times as many passengers, eight new check-in desks and an overhaul of the current terminal facilities. The result has been an improved terminal environment with an increased choice of shops and food outlets, more terminal space and refurbished facilities. An investment plan of this scale and scope could not have been matched by the old county council owners because they did not have access to the private money markets like the private owners do. In 1992, surveys revealed that Cardiff was losing business because travel agents were promoting flights from other airports ahead of those from Cardiff (Humphreys, 1994a). The availability of financial resources has enabled TBI to address this by purchasing a chain of 22 travel agent shops in south Wales and the south-west of England in an attempt to promote flights from Cardiff at the point of sale.

During the first year of private ownership a £5.6 million pre-tax profit was announced (Cardiff Airport, 1995/6) and retained by the company. Although at face value this appears to be a 75 per cent increase, the accounts are not comparable because they were subject to different accounting practices. An interesting development was the transfer of £685,000, that had been put aside for resurfacing and maintaining the runway, into the airport's profit figures (Cardiff Airport, 1995/6. Note 4). Runways require major maintenance work likely to cost around £6–800,000 every seven to nine years. Any future maintenance or resurfacing expenses will have a direct impact on the airport's profit figure. How the financial markets view this remains to be seen.

Commercial income per passenger has continued to grow (see Figure 4.7). Once again improvements in capacity utilization have been the key to the upward trend. Under county council ownership a steady rate of growth in commercial income took place between 1981/2 and 1989/90 when an average 24p per passenger increase per year saw a rise from 76p to 292p per passenger. As passenger numbers fell and stagnated between 1990 and 1993 commercial income accelerated to a peak of 454p before declining to 358p in 1994/5 and rising to 410p during the first year of private ownership in 1995/6. Of the 62p increase in commercial income 44p is derived from increased retail spend by passengers. This is a stated aim of the private owners who have trebled the retail floorspace at the airport to provide fourteen shops in the international departure lounge and a revamped approach to retail with the introduction of new concessions such as Pizza Hut and Kentucky Fried Chicken.

Although the early signs suggest that TBI have made progress, with retail spending rising from 388p per passenger in 1993/4 to 432p in 1995/6, the commercial income per passenger has yet to regain its 1991/2 level. This can

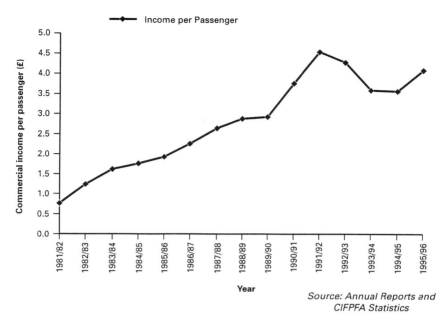

Source: Annual Reports and
CIFPFA Statistics

FIGURE **4.7**
Commercial income per passenger at Cardiff Airport

probably be accounted for by attractive initial deals to encourage retail outlets to locate at the airport and the fact that the new retail floorspace did not become operational until April 1996. In July 1995, the daily car park fee rose by 66 per cent (Roberts, 1995). Judging by the public outcry the drive for commercial income may have been taken too far on this occasion. The balance between commercial success and value for money service is likely to become an increasingly important issue for management and passengers.

It is too early to assess how the full privatization of the airport has affected employee productivity since only one set of figures is available. Early signs show a slight improvement from 7,540 passengers handled per employee in 1994/5 to 7,637 in 1995/6. It is difficult to attribute the slower growth of productivity during 1995/6 to the change of ownership. It is most likely that productivity grew at a slower rate because the airport passed the 1 million passengers per annum mark, a point at which available capacity utilization and staff productivity was close to a maximum given the current traffic pattern. It will be interesting to see if the airport's private owners can continue to improve employee productivity despite the currently high capacity utilization levels.

SUMMARY AND CONCLUSIONS

Cardiff's airport has had a positive impact on south Wales. It has provided direct access to a growing number of holiday destinations and a reliable, frequent network of scheduled services. It was used by its county council owners as a catalyst for the attraction of aerospace-related industry to south Wales, which in turn has brought employment and other related economic benefits. Airport expansion has been driven by the growth of charter holiday flights since the early 1970s. The county councils nurtured the development of the airport by using taxpayers' money to fund expansion and to support daily operations.

The current terminal operated at only one-third of its capacity during its initial years of operation in the 1970s. As traffic growth continued throughout the 1980s, the level of airport capacity utilization improved until a profit was returned for the first time in 1985. The continual rise in the level of terminal utilization accounted for the dramatic increases in employee productivity and profitability from 1986/7 onwards. Regular profits meant that the county councils reaped the rewards for supporting the airport through 32 loss-making years, in the form of a regular dividend that contributed to funding local amenities. Despite the airport's profitability, however, the lack of access to money for investment in the business and local government reorganization in Wales forced it to be sold to the private sector in 1995. The £37.5 million received for the sale was allocated to public services and infrastructure within the boundaries of the new unitary authorities.

Access to financial resources is now no longer a problem with TBI providing the backing of a major property developer and proposing £20 million worth of investment. The purchase of Cardiff does not appear to be a one-off, short-term venture. TBI has now become the second largest airport owner in the UK, with the acquisition of Belfast International in July 1996 and Coventry Airport in early 1997, and the company is reported to be seeking further airports to add to its portfolio.

The drive to increase retail spending and commercial income characterizes the direction of a management that must satisfy their shareholders with increased profitability. Achieving a balance between commercial maximization and passenger satisfaction in the context of ever demanding shareholders is the management challenge for the future. A financially stable, market-orientated business with the ability to invest in the development of the airport and the surrounding land, is as much in the interests of the people of south Wales as it is for its private owners. Expansion will enable the airport to maximize its share of the forecast rise in demand and will ensure more air services to business and leisure destinations. The position of the region will be enhanced in terms of its appeal to inward investors drawing further employment and financial benefits into the region.

The future of the airport looks to be assured as far as its contribution to the region's economy is concerned. However, it must be remembered that the economic interests of the airport will no longer be sacrificed for the good of the region, as it was for the BA project, because TBI will not entertain development unless they see a viable financial return.

APPENDIX 1

Utilization of airport sale receipts

The sale of the airport provided a one-off financial benefit of £37.5 million divided evenly between the three former county council owners (Mid, South and West Glamorgan), and allocated to amenities and services. Details of how South Glamorgan have already used the money and the proposed utilization by the new Cardiff County Council are given below.

The utilization of the proceeds from the airport sale by Cardiff County Council and its predecessor, South Glamorgan County Council, is typical of how the new unitary authorities that succeeded Mid and West Glamorgan have allocated their shares of the money.

In the case of Cardiff, most of the money (56 per cent) has been spent on transport-related infrastructure. The largest single allocation, £2.5 million, is put aside for a new rail freight terminal with £1 million allocated to a new airport access road, £1.5 million allocated to highway improvements, with environmental improvements to the city centre costing another £1 million. While these improvements can be viewed as providing general benefits in the region, the remaining money is directed at more specific needs such as the Pentwyn fire station (£263,000), Glan Ely High School (£500,000), and property renewal in various locations totalling some £1.4 million and several leisure-related developments.

TABLE A1

Capital expenditure met from the proceeds of Cardiff Airport, 1995/6

Proceeds	£000
Total useable resources	12.11
Less – Expense of sale and other expenditure	0.47
	11.64
Less – Rail Freight Terminal Allocation	2.50
Policy Committee 10/7/95 allocated the balance	6.50 (Cardiff area)
	2.53 (Vale area)

Expenditure	£000
Cardiff area expenditure	**(£000)**
Pentwyn Fire Station	263
Environmental improvements (city centre)	31
Asset renewal - property and highways	422
Glan Ely school (essential works)	15
Cardiff County Council proposed expenditure	
Glan Ely High School	485
Airport Access road	1000
Asset renewal - highways and property	2637
Safety works (various sites)	205
Proposed Welsh National Sports village (design)	115
Replacement Wales Empire Pool (studies)	85
Environmental improvements (city centre)	969
Leckwith all-weather pitch	310
TOTAL EXPENDITURE	£6,537

Source: Cardiff County Council 1997

ACKNOWLEDGEMENTS

Many thanks are owed to the airport's last two Managing Directors, Mr Graham Greaves and Mr William Aitkenhead, Councillor N. Salmon, the WDA and Cardiff City Council.

NOTES

1. In 1994 the published charges were £4.95 per arriving domestic passenger, £11.15 per arriving international passenger, and £14.10 per metric tonne landing fee. A 148- seat Boeing 737 operating on a charter service would bring in £2,000 (Cardiff Airport, 1994).
2. Scheduled service operators that have come and gone at Cardiff include Capital Airways, Ryanair, Dan Air, Air UK and Air France.
3. British Airways currently operate a fleet of around fifty 747s and carry out contract maintenance for a number of other world airlines, such as Gulf Air, Middle East Airlines and Pakistan International Airlines.

4. Although the numbers employed directly by the airport authority do not represent the total number employed by the airport, the responsibilities and duties these staff perform has remained constant. This provides a yardstick against which productivity can be measured.

REFERENCES

Aitkenhead, W. (1996). *Cardiff International Airport*, Managing Director's presentation at University of Wales, Cardiff, 7 February 1996.

CAA (1992). *CAP610 Passengers at the London Airports and Manchester in 1991*, CAA.

CAA (1993). *CAP618 Passengers at Central England Airports in 1992/3*, CAA.

CAA (1995). CAP657 *Passengers at Airports in Wales and in the South and South West of England in 1994/95*, CAA.

Cardiff Airport (1980-1997). *Timetables,* Cardiff Airport.

Cardiff Airport (1980/1). *Annual Report and Accounts*, Cardiff Airport.

Cardiff Airport (1982/3). *Annual Report and Accounts*, Cardiff Airport.

Cardiff Airport (1983/4). *Annual Report and Accounts*, Cardiff Airport.

Cardiff Airport (1984/5). *Annual Report and Accounts*, Cardiff Airport.

Cardiff Airport (1985/6). *Annual Report and Accounts*, Cardiff Airport.

Cardiff Airport (1986/7). *Annual Report and Accounts*, Cardiff Airport.

Cardiff Airport (1987/8). *Annual Report and Accounts*, Cardiff Airport.

Cardiff Airport (1988/9). *Annual Report and Accounts*, Cardiff Airport.

Cardiff Airport (1989/90). *Annual Report and Accounts*, Cardiff Airport.

Cardiff Airport (1990/1). *Annual Report and Accounts*, Cardiff Airport.

Cardiff Airport (1991/2). *Annual Report and Accounts*, Cardiff Airport.

Cardiff Airport (1992/3). *Annual Report and Accounts*, Cardiff Airport.

Cardiff Airport (1993/4). *Annual Report and Accounts*, Cardiff Airport.

Cardiff Airport (1994/5). *Annual Report and Accounts*, Cardiff Airport.

Cardiff Airport (1995/6). *Annual Report and Accounts*, Cardiff Airport.

Cardiff Airport (1994). S*chedule of Fees, Charges and Conditions*, Cardiff Airport.

Cardiff County Council (1997). *Utilisation of the Proceeds From the Disposal of Cardiff-Wales*, Cardiff County Council.

Cardiff International Airport (1995). *Cardiff International Airport Handbook*, Cardiff Airport.

CIPFA (1996). *The UK Airports Industry Airport Statistics 1994/95*, CRI, London.

Glamorgan (Rhoose) Airport Joint Committee, Confederation of British Industry, Development Corporation for Wales, Wales TUC (1975). *The Importance of Glamorgan (Rhoose) Airport in Relation to the Economy of Wales*, County of South Glamorgan.

Greaves, G. (1991). *Lecture on Regional Airports*, Managing Director's presentation at University of Wales, Cardiff, 15 March 1991.

Henn, C. (1994). 'An airport flying high', *Daily Telegraph*, 4 November 1994.

Horner, F. and Sherratt, P. (1997). *Interviews*, British Airways Maintenance Cardiff, Planning Group Management Team, Cardiff Airport, 13 February 1997.

Humphreys, I. (1994). 'Travel agents and regional air services', *Journal of Air Transport Management* 1, 151–60.

Humphreys, I. (1995). 'The privatisation of Cardiff–Wales Airport', *Planet* 111, 117–18.

Millward, T. (1996). 'From soot to Sony', *Corporate Location*, March/April, 47–54.

Roberts, S. (1995). 'Parking prices threaten airport', *South Wales Echo*, 9 August 1995.

Staddon, T. G. (1979). *History of Cambrian Airways, the Welsh Airline from 1935 to 1976*, Hounslow, Airline publications

Welsh Affairs Committee (1991). *The Welsh Affairs Committee First Report Cardiff Wales Airport*, HMSO.

Welsh Development Agency (1997). *Secured Project Analysis Data – 1/1/83–31/1/97*, Client Information Management System, WDA.

5. PLANNING FOR RESIDENTIAL TOURISM IN RURAL WALES

Nick Gallent, Mark Tewdwr-Jones and Gary Higgs

INTRODUCTION

Housing change is a fundamental component of more general social and economic changes occurring in rural areas and is worthy of closer examination. This paper focuses attention on residential tourism in rural Wales as particularly manifested in *built second homes*. Arguably, this phenomenon reached its political height in the late 1980s, spurred on by the property boom and the widening gap between house prices in affluent English regions and rural Wales. In 1987, it was estimated that 10 per cent of dwellings on Anglesey and around Caernarfon were second homes along with an unrivalled 25 per cent in the district of Dwyfor (Pilkington, 1990). In the popular press, it was claimed that as many as 60,000 Welsh families were being 'squeezed out' of their home communities each year by second-home purchasers and permanent inmigrants. Opposition and protest took many forms including a sustained arson campaign which claimed some 170 second homes between 1979 and 1990. For these reasons, residential tourism in Wales became a real and a literal 'burning issue' (Pilkington, 1990). At the beginning of the 1990s, second homes were at the forefront of housing issues and the more general debate concerning social change in the Welsh countryside. More recently however, economic recession and a less than buoyant housing market have put paid to many middle-class second-home aspirations and the issue has become increasingly hidden, as it was at the beginning of the 1970s (Jacobs, 1972). At the same time, it appears to have slipped from the political agenda whilst the issue of affordable housing supply has gained prominence (Barlow and Chambers, 1992; Barlow *et al.*, 1994; JRF, 1994).

This paper initially re-engages with the range of second-home issues before moving on to examine how specific problems arising in some local housing markets might be addressed in Wales's distinctive policy framework. Following brief descriptions of the Welsh 'housing problem' and the way in which rural markets might be conceptualized, the substantive part of the paper engages the main planning issues. Attention focuses on the use of occupancy controls, possible moves towards a situation where change of residential use might require planning permission and local presumptions against development grounded in clear evidence of potential disruptive impacts on the Welsh language and culture brought by second-home acquisitions or inmigration. Given a recognition of the problems introduced by residential tourism in some communities in Wales and the increasing level of lip-service that the planning system has paid local interests in recent years, the paper examines in detail how regulation of housing change might be achieved. In particular, the paper considers how land-use planning might be used to minimize the social costs associated with residential tourism whilst avoiding the undesirable situation where planning control alone dictates levels of housing supply and dwelling use.

KEY DEBATES IN RESIDENTIAL TOURISM

For the purpose of this discussion, 'residential tourism' (a term often applied to recreational housing developments across continental Europe; Barke, 1991) refers to the *built* second-home phenomenon in rural Wales and excludes static holiday caravans and commercial holiday developments. A range of general texts contain discussions on the definition of second-home types (Bielckus *et al.*, 1972; Downing and Dower, 1973; Coppock, 1977).

Much of the early 'second-home' literature (Coppock, 1977; Bollom, 1978) referred to the growth in residential tourism in the UK as being purely symptomatic of more fundamental changes affecting the economic bases of peripheral and growth regions in contrasting ways. Greater economic prosperity in some areas was generating higher disposable incomes, fewer working hours and a greater amount of available leisure time. But as some areas experienced growth, other areas were being relegated into a peripheral position as their economic bases (often founded on traditional heavy industry or agriculture) declined. In this context, leisure demand (and modern residential tourism) in prosperous 'exporting regions' became focused on marginalized rural 'importing regions' (Rogers, 1977) where property prices were lower, reflecting economic decline and the lower wages of rural households, and where the growing 'cult of nostalgia' for the countryside (Newby, 1980a; 1980b) could find physical form.

During the inter-war period, British residential tourism largely took the form of chalet development. When chalet development was brought under control by the Town and Country Planning Act 1947, demand for 'second homes' refocused on relatively inexpensive surplus rural housing. Until the greater economic prosperity of the 1960s, demand remained on a low ebb. From the mid-1960s onwards, however, residential tourist demand gradually rose until the market for surplus stock became saturated (DART, 1977; Shucksmith, 1983). The attraction of purchasing derelict rural housing with a view to bringing it into recreational use was also dampened by changes to improvement grant rules in 1974. New legislation effectively barred 'second home' owners from receiving grants and this move was at least partially responsible for the shift in demand to the mainstream housing stock which occurred when the market eventually recovered in 1977 (Shucksmith, 1983). Arguably, it was at this point that residential tourism began seriously to affect some rural housing markets, as a growing number of more prosperous groups competed for limited housing resources in the countryside.

Arguments for and against second homes are well-rehearsed. These range from the economic contribution derived from general expenditure (during the periods visitors spend in the importing region) and Council Tax, to the social disruption wrought by residential tourism when permanent residents are displaced by seasonal visitors as a result of uneven competition for housing in some sectors of the market. It is generally recognized that impacts are dependent on the degree of separation between the markets for first and second homes. Where demand is concentrated in the first-home market (i.e., in existing mainstream housing stock), any economic benefit may be negated by adverse social impact. In contrast, where demand is predominantly for surplus rural stock which had found no other effective use (a phenomenon recently observed in France; see Buller and Hoggart, 1994a; 1994b; Hoggart and Buller, 1995), the benefits of conversion may far outweigh any adverse impacts. In effect, the heaviest social and economic cost will be paid when residential tourist demand is focused in the market for existing housing and where local housing demand is significant.

The key argument levelled against residential tourism relates to house prices and the increases produced when markets become weighted in favour of more affluent buyers. Clearly, more competitive markets may bring house price inflation and a reduction in the housing choices of some lower income groups. However, house prices are also a function of restrictive planning control (the hall-mark of many rural areas; see Shucksmith 1981; 1990a) and the overall adequacy of local housing supply. Likewise, although second-home acquisitions may be blamed for decreasing the availability of rented accommodation in some rural areas, it must be noted that a lack of renting opportunities in the countryside may be largely attributed to the effects of successive Rent Act legislation since the 1920s, and more recently, to the huge impact that the 'right-to-buy' has had on housing choice (Shucksmith, 1990a). The arrival of second-home owners may be little more than a complicating factor in many areas, although it may be more important in specific communities where the displacement of local residents and the undermining of services, as a result of a changing social configuration and reduced year-round demand, combine to produce a real loss of community. For this reason, any policy must be grounded in an understanding of local circumstances. In Wales, this necessitates taking on board issues relating to language and culture.

In the long term, it is recognized that increased economic prosperity holds the key to reversing (where possible) the decline of many rural communities. When local incomes rise and a significant number of rural households become the competitive equals of middle-class town or city dwellers, the housing chances of local residents will increase whilst the housing and leisure choices of non-residents will adjust accordingly (as price differentials decrease). However, before this Utopian vision for the future is realized, intermediate steps may be required, perhaps to iron over the worst disparities of market allocation. In the past, suggested policy measures to deal with increases in residential tourism have focused either on the supply of rural housing (e.g., increasing housing choice and opportunity by providing more non-market options) or reducing external demand and housing consumption (either by increasing the price paid for second homes through taxation or differential Council Tax or licensing property acquisition and creating housing sub-markets in which local interests are prioritized). Measures to affect supply have largely fallen prey to decreasing public expenditure on housing in recent years. Recent emphasis on synthesizing the housing and planning functions of local authorities in order to procure affordable rural housing have, to date, proved unsuccessful on any significant scale (Barlow and Chambers, 1992; Barlow *et al*, 1994; Gallent, 1997). Unfortunately, the alternative of affecting demand and consumption runs contrary to Britain's dominant market ideology and may be grounded in a belief that policies implemented elsewhere in Europe, where devolved state structures enable local interests to be more effectively emphasized, may be readily deployed in Britain. Given the marked social and political differences between Britain and Europe, this is clearly not the case at the present time.

THE WELSH HOUSING PROBLEM AND SECOND HOMES

Rural Wales has a range of housing problems that may well be accentuated by residential tourism in some areas. In general, Wales has an ageing housing stock. Over a third (36.8 per cent) of the stock was built before 1919; in contrast, only a quarter (26.2 per cent) of the housing stock falls into this age category in Britain as a whole (Cole *et al*, 1995). The 1993 Welsh House Condition Survey revealed that 13.4 per cent of homes across Wales were 'unfit', often because of disrepair or inadequate ventilation, although more than 3 per cent of homes lacked at least one basic amenity. In an attempt to address these problems, thirteen renewal areas had been declared by the end of 1993, covering 13,300 properties (Cole *et al*, 1995). Such housing problems, combined with population growth and movement, had led to a shortfall in housing supply of almost 100,000 dwellings by 1989. Bramley (1991) estimated that there is a continuing need for 7,500 additional social housing units in Wales each year. Recent homelessness figures reveal that 12,382 cases were presented to local authorities across Wales in 1995; of these, 9,002 (or 72.7 per cent) were accepted (Welsh Office, 1995). In rural Wales, problems of poor stock condition (especially in the private rented and owner-occupied sectors) and a growing mis-match between housing demand and supply may be less visible, but these problems are certainly no less acute. Problems across rural Wales have common features, but they are certainly not homogenous. In 1992, those districts adjacent to the south Wales valleys (i.e., the old districts of Carmarthen, Dinefwr and Brecknock) recorded the highest homelessness rates (in excess of 6.1 cases per 1,000 households) whilst the northern districts such as Ynys Môn, Arfon and Aberconwy experienced the lowest rates (Welsh Office, 1993). The same three northern districts experienced the highest levels of population growth with the local authorities arguing that in-migration and residential tourism had produced greater competition for housing and led to elevated house prices.

In 1991, the UK Population Census estimated the number of 'secondary residences' in Wales to be in the region of 12,000 units (OPCS, 1993) compared with 92,550 units across both England and Wales. This contrasted with an earlier government estimation that there were 221,000 second homes in England and Wales in 1985 (Hansard, 1985), a figure that, given past growth trends and the property boom of the late 1980s, should have risen to at least a quarter of a million by the mid-1990s. On the assumption that the level of under-enumeration was roughly similar in England and Wales in

1991 (and that Wales has 13 per cent of all the second homes compared with just 6 per cent of all house spaces in England and Wales; OPCS, 1993), it might be estimated that there are presently about 32,500 second homes in Wales. Across the new rural districts (formed after local government reorganization in April 1996), the mix of housing problems (i.e., poor stock condition, homelessness or the lack of affordable housing for local people, accentuated by the level of residential tourism in some areas) are all present to a greater or lesser extent.

RURAL HOUSING MARKETS AND HOUSING CHANGE

With respect to the social construction of rural housing markets, Shucksmith (1990b) argues that housing class, in the Weberian sense, can be seen as a function of market power and therefore the rural property market has clear implications for the class structure of rural societies. However, the nature of the market and particular tenure divisions mean that there are no simple dichotomies between rich and poor or locals and newcomers. Saunders (1984), for example, argues that owner-occupiers form a middle 'domestic property class' who are advantaged by the cumulative potential of their tenure whilst those in rented accommodation have no comparable advantage. Clearly then, the effect that outside competition has on a rural market will depend on the level of indigenous owner-occupation and potential cumulative wealth (determined by local property values). Similar classifications have been developed by Ambrose (1974), Pahl (1966) and Dunn *et al* (1981). Domestic property classes are characterized by 'consumption cleavages' which define access chances and the ability of different households to compete in the housing market. Shucksmith (1990b) contends that access chances broadly differ between households with 'low income and low wealth' and 'more prosperous groups'. However, there are numerous sub-divisions within these broad categories. The first group will include young couples and single persons barred from entry to waiting lists (this group is often perceived as experiencing the greatest difficulties in gaining entry to the housing market; Cloke *et al*, 1994), other tenants of rented or tied accommodation, pensioners retired from local employment or former in-migrants now facing financial difficulties, and local authority tenants who are more fortunate and who may be eligible to buy their home with a discount. The second category might include indigenous owner-occupiers, retirement migrants with capital available from a previous home, second-home buyers and commuters.

This typology demonstrates that certain groups will face disadvantage in the rural housing market, not only in competition with newcomers but also with indigenous owner-occupiers who have the advantage of an established equity base. Shucksmith concedes that the above framework is empirically derived and will not have universal application; he notes, however, that all examinations of competing housing groups must recognize the importance of income and wealth, present tenure, life-cycle status and the motives for residing in the rural area in determining housing outcomes. Rural housing markets are more than just local interest versus second-home demands. However, it is clear that middle-class housing choices, built on a 'cult of nostalgia' for the countryside (Newby, 1980a) and a continuing desire to engage in residential tourism (Young, 1988), are causing significant changes in some rural markets and there is a need at least to understand the policy options available.

SECOND HOMES AND PLANNING CONTROL IN WALES

Past experience of the second-home phenomenon and the failure of local and national governments to deal effectively with the cumulative disadvantage felt by some social groups in the countryside mean that a need both to engage the various debates and to formulate an effective policy response is as strong as ever. Given the problems caused by residential tourism in some rural communities in Wales (and elsewhere across the UK), there is a need to review the government's options. In this section, we focus attention on how planning control may be used now to regulate the occupancy (and therefore use) of new housing and how planning control may, in the future, be used to restrict the number of existing dwellings becoming second homes.

The use of occupancy controls
In the 1970s, planning agreements (normally based upon Section 52 of the Town and Country Planning Act 1971) were used often by local authorities as a means of securing 'a contribution from developers towards the infrastructure costs' of new housing schemes (Barlow *et al*, 1994). By the middle of the decade, some authorities were using such agreements with developers to procure new housing units as well as other social infrastructure. Critically, Loughlin (1984) revealed that authorities were also using these agreements (and other conditions) to limit the occupancy of new dwellings in some rural areas to local residents. This phenomenon had

already been studied in detail by Shucksmith (1981) in the Lake District. Where planning agreements are used, the control of occupancy is closely linked to the actual development process (JRF, 1994; Barlow and Chambers, 1992; Barlow *et al*, 1994).

By 1985, more than 20 structure plans contained references to specific 'local needs policies'; that is, an explicit commitment to securing planning gains which emphasize the overriding importance of local housing needs (Bishop and Hooper, 1991). These policies invariably contained references to the control of occupancy. In 1981, Shucksmith argued that the housing problems faced by some rural communities could be alleviated in three ways; by discouraging or preventing houses from being used as retirement or holiday homes, by building more council houses and increasing rental stock, or through planning control with new dwellings going to local people. Through an examination of the Lake District Special Planning Board's [LDSPB] use of Section 52 agreements, Shucksmith found that controlling the occupancy of new units increased the competition for existing housing stock and caused further elevation of house prices. The experience of the LDSPB offered compelling evidence that it is impossible to restrict the occupancy of new dwellings whilst responding to local needs (Shucksmith, 1981). If prices for existing dwellings rise (because of the planning restrictions placed on the occupancy of new dwellings), then an increasing proportion of this stock will be unavailable to low-income, low-wealth rural households. The access chances of this group, therefore, will be increasingly dependent on the amount of new affordable housing being developed.

There is evidence to suggest that affordable housing provision is insufficient to meet growing need. The shortfall in housing provision nationally is usually estimated to be in the region of 100,000 units per annum in England (see Wilcox, 1990; Whitehead and Kleinman, 1991; AC, 1992) and 22,000 per annum in Wales and Scotland (Chartered Institute of Housing, 1992). In rural Wales, Bramley (1991) concluded that 'the deficiency [in provision] is dramatic where the need for social housing is 10 times the current building programme'. In 1994, there were just 2,797 public and voluntary sector completions across the whole of Wales (HM Government, 1996).

Occupancy controls (now achieved through planning obligations or the use of Section 106 agreements) may mean that affordable housing becomes increasingly associated with low-income groups and a social stigma may become attached to these developments, particularly where schemes are grouped together to form social housing 'ghettos'. A second problem is that these controls may inhibit the ability of associations to attract private finance on exception schemes, further reducing access opportunities for rural households (see RDC, 1995). Thirdly, and more significantly in this debate, they offer no route into the existing housing stock. Research has shown that the control of new property alone may accentuate more general problems in the wider housing market.

These difficulties may become more pronounced in the years ahead given the increasing support for occupancy controls as an element of affordable housing policies. Before 1989, it was widely accepted that the planning system could deal legitimately only with land-use issues and in the case of housing this excluded considerations of tenure, price and occupancy. It is difficult to judge how far the present system has moved away from this position over the last seven years although the debate surrounding the 'need' for social housing as a 'material planning consideration' has not yet been fully resolved. Department of the Environment Circular 13/96 (DoE, 1996) – which was not released simultaneously in Wales – seemed to confirm the overall legitimacy of affordable housing policies and it is clear that, in some circumstances, occupancy control is vital. In the case of rural exceptions policy, for instance, it is unlikely that the altruistic stance of landowners would be maintained if it was thought that dwellings built on land released at below development value would quickly be sold on at market value.

Occupancy controls are necessary in certain instances, but their social benefits may be outweighed by socio-economic costs if they are used too freely. In Ceredigion (a mid-Wales local authority), for example, moves to control the occupancy of all new dwellings along with conversions of existing dwellings is likely to have a serious impact on house prices in those communities where the housing market is affected by a significant number of outside buyers. However, the means to achieve more balanced control across the entire market are simply not available. If they were, more balanced communities might be attainable (with different consumption groups occupying a greater range of housing types and tenures) alongside the suppression of excessive demand and the relief of growing social tension.

Background to 'change of use' controls
Earlier in this paper, it was argued that the creation of housing sub-markets is unlikely to be a viable option in England and Wales where the national perspective prevails and the maintenance of a single and free property market is viewed as ideologically paramount. There is a way, however, to

maintain the integrity of market allocation and, at the same time, control the occupancy (or rather, the *use*) of existing dwellings. This could be achieved by drawing a planning distinction between property used for a 'primary' residential and 'secondary' residential function. All existing property would be classified in this way and, in effect, 'change of use' would subsequently be subject to planning permission (and controlled by local authorities); i.e., planning permission would be required for a dwelling used as a first home (for the last five or so years) to become a second home and vice versa. The demand for second homes would be suppressed and the value of properties might decline. All planning control may have an inflationary or deflationary effect on property prices and therefore, in this respect, opposition from existing owners would probably be limited. Despite the criticisms of occupancy controls in 1981, Shucksmith argued:

> Planning controls [focusing on use change] are potentially the most sensitive means of reducing the number of second homes, in that the policy would be operated by local authorities who could apply such restrictions in accordance with local circumstances. (Shucksmith, 1983, 189)

For instance, permissions might be granted where properties were surplus to general housing needs but refused where change of use from first to second homes was clearly resulting in house price inflation and social disruption.

The concept of bringing this type of use change under planning control has been canvassed by a number of interest groups for almost thirty years. In the early 1970s, it was recognized that the distribution of second homes in England and Wales was the product of dwelling use change and increasingly, the balance between change in surplus stock and mainstream stock use change was swinging in favour of mainstream housing with associated economic and social problems. In response, a number of observers commented that this change of use should be brought under planning control (Bielckus *et al*, 1972; Downing and Dower, 1973; Dower, 1977; Pyne, 1973; DART, 1977). By the 1980s, the idea had reached the political agenda with the introduction of a Private Member's Bill in 1981 by Dafydd Wigley, the Plaid Cymru MP for Arfon in north Wales. At that time, a number of criticisms were levelled at the possible creation of an additional use class. The government's argument hinged on the potential 'infringement to personal liberty' brought by such legislation. It could be argued, however, that given the way in which the government subsequently reduced the supply of rented accommodation (and thus infringed consumer choice) and its apparent approval of occupancy controls, any such criticism today might appear misplaced. In the early 1980s, however, it was clear that the type of material use change envisaged focused on the merits of the user and ran contrary to the spirit of planning law. The context today is much changed and there is perhaps little reason to believe that a system which allows the control of dwelling occupancy could not stretch to differentiating between types of residential use.

Despite government objections, which killed off the Bill during its first reading, the concept of change of use as a means of regulating second homes in the existing rural stock received a warm reception in Labour Party ranks. At the time, the Labour Party expressed support for the policy and said publicly that they would introduce such a measure, as part of a new planning package, on return to government. The political pledge made in 1981 regarding amending the planning system was clarified in 1990. At this time, the Labour Party argued that reductions in public subsidy for social housing revealed that the government was unable and unwilling to tackle rural housing problems. In contrast, Labour claimed to have a policy package which would create sufficient funding for the voluntary sector and reform housing finance in such a way as to bring home ownership within the grasp of a great many more households. One element of their wider rural strategy concerned second homes. Soley (1990) outlined the Labour position on second homes in the planning context:

> Our proposal is that local authorities involved would be able to restrict the growth of second homes in the affected areas by ensuring that an existing family home would need planning consent for 'change of use' before it could be sold as a second home in much the same way as change of use is required to change a home into an office, for example. The procedure would be subject to appeal. This is the practice in a number of European countries. There is no question of a ban on second homes. (Soley, 1990, 39)

In the Labour model, use change restrictions would not be applied retrospectively and would not affect those people requiring two homes for their work, those who are planning to retire to an area and those who live in tied accommodation. To some extent, the Labour Party has tried to win support for the policy by tapping peoples' nostalgic image of the countryside. In 1990, Soley argued that 'our villages are a very important part of our heritage and should not be allowed to die on their feet' (Soley, 1990, 39).

Change of use in current legislation

During the evolution of the use change debate, the planning system has been significantly overhauled and it is necessary to consider how such an amendment would fit into the current system. Clearly, some of the changes occurring may have increased the pressure for and viability of a future change to the Use Classes Order 1987 (in which development types are categorized). In particular, the increasing recognition in the British courts of affordable housing needs as a material planning consideration has moved the debate on at a positive pace over the last few years, assisting many rural authorities to develop local plan policies for the procurement of affordable housing where a clear need is demonstrated. Since the late 1980s, planners and academics have advocated reform of planning law and the introduction of a 'social' housing use class (ACRE, 1988). However, the failure to attract widespread support for this idea hinges on the fact that the Use Classes Order is not designed to be a mechanism for favouring particular types of occupants. Instead, it is 'intended to be an instrument for allowing changes of use which would constitute development were it not for the Order' (Barlow *et al*, 1994, 5). The insertion of 'primary' and 'secondary' residence functions would appear to be well within the scope of the Use Classes Order as this move would not necessarily mean control over new development. Change of use controls in Denmark, however, mean just that; planning permissions are granted to new development depending on proposed residential use type (Rossing, 1996). Therefore, local planning authorities wield control over both new second-home development and change of use. In Britain, this type of mechanism would fall at the same hurdle as the social housing use class with criticism that this type of development control is outside the legitimate purpose of the Use Classes Order. In order to overcome this problem, all new development would need the same 'residential classification'; the sub-classification would then be made only after the use became apparent (in Denmark, housing used as a primary residence for five years is subject to use change control) and therefore the Use Classes Order could not be abused by local planners.

However, the idea of a 'social' housing use class has been rejected on the grounds that 'it would lead to excessive general interest by planners in the personal circumstances of occupiers of housing' (Barlow *et al*, 1994, 5). Clearly, this criticism could apply equally to second-home use control despite the fact that planners would have no influence over the initial use made of a new dwelling. Where existing dwellings are concerned, 'change of use' control would amount to an invitation to control the occupancy of housing by reference to the circumstances of users. Another issue is the problem of distinguishing 'permanent' and 'temporary' residence. In Sweden for instance, a large proportion of 'second homes' are occupied for a large part of the year by the wives and children of businessmen who are employed in the cities and live in urban apartments which are 'officially' the family's first home (Bielckus, 1977; Rossing, 1996). The distinction, however, is blurred and it is almost as if the rural residence is the first home of half the family whilst the urban apartment is the first home of the working partner. The issue here is how easy and practical it would be to draw clear divisions between primary and secondary residences for planning purposes.

The recent Rural White Paper for Wales claimed that 'geographical location' is becoming 'irrelevant' in the new information age (Welsh Office, 1996a). This means that many more people, with access to computers and the internet, can work as easily from home as they can from a city office. In effect, people may have two work locations; one in or close to the city and another far removed, perhaps in remote countryside. If the cottage in the country is no longer used for 'mainly recreational purposes' and is more than an 'occasional residence' (the normal criteria for defining second homes), can it still be classified as a second home or does the household now have two residences with no distinction between primary and secondary? If the national legislators (and the local planning authorities) are unable to resolve this dilemma, then new legislation will either be generally ineffective or a large number of use change refusals will be overturned on appeal.

It is unlikely that new legislation will be water-tight. Many would-be second home owners may be deterred by the new legislation and it is likely that use control will have a significant impact on the demand for dwellings in the existing housing stock. However, national legislators, wary of giving local planners too much control over occupancy and the housing market, would probably impose tight restrictions on the use of any new legislation. It is likely, for example, that the use of new controls would have to be specified in the local development plan and only used where there was a proven need to ensure that housing did not change use. This 'need' might be based on an assessment of the consumer thresholds of local services, the need for housing for locals or proof that 'tourist accommodation' (development subject to holiday occupancy conditions) in the area was already at its optimum level. These assessments, however, are likely to be arbitrary with different authorities using different methods for measuring the indicators (this already happens with housing needs assessments). This process itself is likely to be controversial and disputes may frequently be played out in the courts. Many authorities will be keen to demonstrate the social disruption caused by second homes in the local housing market and may even overplay the social costs; other authorities, keen not to inherit the overspill of demand from their neighbours will be forced to play the same game and over time, with more authorities clamping down on use change, rural property prices may suffer a general decline. On the one hand, this might benefit local households who may find themselves in a far stronger competitive position in the housing market. On the other hand, the previous revenue from outside investment in rural property now stays in the exporting regions; marginally more money may be spent in rural guest-houses and hotels, but most will be invested in leisure pursuits either at home or abroad. The suppression of rural property prices (and a widening rural/urban differential) may generate new demand for permanent rural dwellings (particularly in the 'information age' when people can readily work from home) causing a total, and permanent, socio-cultural re-configuration of the countryside and further fuelling language decline in some communities in rural Wales.

The possible adverse effects of new legislation need to be examined urgently given the recognized inadequacy of occupancy controls over new development. Local authorities need to consider the overall effects that over-zealous implementation could have; they should recognize that the way in which they operate may affect both neighbouring authorities and the wider housing market. Any use change legislation would have to deal with establishing a workable distinction between 'secondary' and 'primary' residence. However, distinctions are likely to have limitations and many buyers will still be able to acquire what, to all intents and purposes, appear to be second homes.

Given the potentially charged political context and complex legal framework within which a use class classification would operate, it would be advisable for the government to design a fast-track planning appeals system in order to mediate in second-home cases. Such a system would be used by the government as a way of overturning local authority planning refusals where it is clearly demonstrated that the aspirations of second-home owners would have no land use impact – in the broadest sense – on the local community. Assessments of the costs and benefits of second homes are highly subjective and in this context, deciding whether or not to refuse a planning permission may prove extremely difficult and costly. Owners are always likely to forward some planning grounds for appeal unless the authority's case for refusal is water-tight. A local authority's case in this context would have to operate within the established planning parameters, according to the use class legislation, and be subject to conformity with central government guidance. In the latter case, this would necessitate not simply following Welsh Office planning policies regarding housing, but also policies relating to economic and historic development and environmental protection. Thus, a refusal for change of use that involved a derelict property would be a particularly sensitive point. Following the advice of Welsh Office planning guidance on derelict historic buildings (Welsh Office, 1996b), there would be little point refusing permissions on empty properties if a new use was advanced, even if the proposal was promoted by an individual living outside the locality. However, in the absence of specific exemption clauses (relating to properties that had been empty or on the market for a specified length of time), it may be anticipated that some authorities might attempt to refuse housing development simply as part of a wider political reaction against second homes which they hope will divert attention from their own failure to develop an effective economic strategy for the local area.

Change of use legislation might be effective in alleviating the problems of excessive second-home ownership in the existing housing stock in some communities so long as new powers were used sensitively. National legislators understandably would be wary of handing over such powers to local authorities which are already perceived by central government as operating 'on the fringe' of legitimate planning control. The ability to suspend use-change powers (on the part of the Secretaries of State for the Environment and for Wales) might be a prerequisite to any new legislation.

Planning policy in context
If formal amendment to the Use Classes Order is viewed as inappropriate or else excessively difficult to implement, could housing use be controlled through other planning mechanisms? In the mid to late 1980s, planners (encouraged by the Welsh Office) did take an interest in the occupants of new rural dwellings in their implementation of Welsh Office Circular 30/86 regarding housing for senior management (Welsh Office, 1986). This circular, which introduced another material planning consideration into the design of local plans, emphasized the government's desire for authorities to make land available for the development of housing suitable for senior management and executives. The planning justification for this requirement was economic and intended to facilitate inward investment by supplying housing of an appropriate standard and scale sought by senior executives. It is perhaps ironic that, at a time when the rural affordable housing question was causing considerable concern to local planners, the government was

making a planning commitment to facilitate high-priced housing for higher-income groups. The argument that planners should not take an excessive general interest in the personal circumstances of housing occupants was therefore undermined by central government policy.

Although Circular 30/86 is now cancelled and the senior management housing requirement has been deleted from Welsh Office policy, it does indicate that housing occupation can be a material consideration when it is justified on land use grounds. The same arguments apply to Welsh Office Circular 53/88 regarding the use of the Welsh language as a material consideration in development control (Welsh Office, 1988). This Circular requires that local authorities recognize the Welsh language as a planning issue, even though it is not strictly a 'land use' matter. Indeed, its role as a social issue within the planning system in Wales is still causing concern amongst local planning authorities eight years after its introduction, since little guidance has been provided to planners on how to implement the contents of the Circular. Secondary advice from central government, through Circulars and Planning Policy Guidance notes, could well be used to deal with second homes where areas are considered to be under pressure. What would be far more problematic, however, is stating how any future advice could be implemented within the existing statutory planning framework.

Circular 30/86 was used as a positive mechanism with which to provide for future housebuilding for particular social groups. Circular 53/88 positively makes the Welsh language a planning issue. Department of the Environment Circular 13/96 provides guidance on enabling affordable housing to be recognized within the planning system, again a positive move. However, the problem in covering the second-homes issue through the release of a central government Circular is that the underlying rationale for intervention appears to be, essentially, negative. As such, the prohibition or scaling down of the availability of housing for second-home purchasers would seem to run contrary to the positive stance of the British planning system. Welsh Office guidance states quite categorically that:

> It is not the function of the system to interfere with or inhibit competition between users of and investors in land or to regulate development for other than land use planning reasons. Applications for development should be allowed [...] (Welsh Office, 1996b, para.7)

The implications of this policy requirement are that it is virtually impossible to act negatively *per se* to prohibit future use. Under the present arrangements, a Circular could be introduced to promote further second homes in Wales, but not vice versa. If, however, the planning system operated negatively, i.e. there was a presumption against new development unless there were strong contrary reasons, it would be possible to introduce advice that restricted future development. This latter change, which would involve up-turning the entire land use process, would require the release of a central government policy document; there would be no need to introduce new legislation, since the current presumption in favour of development is merely a policy, as opposed to a legal requirement. Some elements within the opposition political parties have toyed with this idea over the years (on the basis that it would promote the environment as the primary consideration) but have since ruled out the change due to impracticalities.

How, then, could limiting second homes be acknowledged within the present planning system? It appears that the only way forward is to base the arguments against on strictly planning criteria, and then to present the problem as one existing at a local level. This would necessitate proving, beyond all reasonable doubt, that the existence and supply of local affordable housing was an interest of acknowledged importance that would be demonstrably harmed by the provision of further new housing priced outside the range of local buyers. A second and related interest of acknowledged importance could be the Welsh language, since provision already exists through the advice contained in Circular 53/88. If a local planning authority was considering using these issues to overturn the presumption in favour of development at the local level then a substantial amount of evidence would be required, firstly relating to language erosion (and related service disruption) and secondly, relating to the scale of the housing shortage in localities where a planning response might be warranted. The policy relating to the Welsh language, has not, as yet, undergone any testing in the British courts.

In terms of affordable housing, policies to generate future housing could be introduced. However, the control of second-home acquisitions from the existing stock could not be directly dealt with; control over existing stock could be subject to a locals-only restriction only if houses were owned by the local authorities or housing associations. Indeed, a future Government that proposed the reintroduction of council house-building (and additional grant support for the voluntary sector) could use the locals-only restriction and local covenants as an effective means of controlling the influx of second or multiple-home purchasers into settlements and also retain an appropriate stock of affordable housing for local people. Needless to say, such a policy change would require strong political backing and commitment at a national level and would, in any case, operate outside the planning system, requiring amendment to the 'right-to-buy' legislation. But the likelihood of such a move must be questioned. Given the growing pressure to sell voluntary sector units (using purchase grants scheduled to be introduced in April 1997) it seems unlikely that either non-market or market housing will, in the future, be retained for solely local needs.

The broader planning context
Given the inadequacy of simply protecting new housing from market forces and the problems created by residential tourism in the effective housing stock, new legislation at the national level and change of use control may, arguably, be long overdue. However, such a move would not be without its drawbacks and these must be carefully considered before new measures are implemented. An important principle to bear in mind is the fact that planning controls will form just one element of a wider policy approach required to manage residential tourism and rural housing problems more generally. They must be complemented with continuing support for the housing functions of the public and voluntary sectors and the recognition that peoples' leisure aspirations must be accommodated across both urban and rural landscapes. In order to gauge effectively the impacts of residential tourism, there is a need to consider how both the overall supply of rural housing and new demand pressures are juxtaposed in particular com-munities and come together to affect local housing opportunities. Only by deconstructing the housing market at the local level, will it be possible to judge the economic and social costs of second homes and formulate effective planning policies. If local plan policies are able to deal with local shortfalls in the supply of affordable housing, increases in new supply will doubtless soften the effects of external demand pressures. They will not, however, alleviate the problem of tenure polarization relating to the different housing options available to particular groups. Only change of use legislation or a significant improvement in the economic circumstance of rural areas may iron over this particular discrepancy in market allocation.

Measures which seek to both provide local affordable housing and satisfy the demand for second homes in a locality must ensure that the economic benefits of development are maximized while social costs are minimized. By adopting a strategy of control and development, the aspirations of second-home seekers and the needs of rural populations may be successfully balanced. However, there is a need for considerable more research in a number of areas.

First, it is not possible to develop policy recommendations for local areas without field research. Research must seek to separate local housing needs from second-home aspirations [i.e., wider market demand] and consideration should be given to the operation of the housing market, the needs of competing groups and the stock balance (including the current second-home situation through an examination of the types of dwellings used for this purpose). On the basis of such local research, policies could differentiate between settlement types and associated problems, providing a general framework which could be applied given a thorough understanding of the local housing market and local problems.

A second area of research might be the role second-home owners play in the market for surplus rural stock. After the rules governing improvement grants were amended in 1974 and second-home owners were effectively barred from receiving grants, demand shifted to the effective housing stock. This begs the question as to whether the saturation of the surplus rural market or the removal of grant rights was the root-cause of the cross-competition for mainstream housing which developed after the economic recession of the mid-1970s? More controversially, it may be questioned whether there is scope for giving second-home seekers grants to renovate some rural properties (unclaimed by the local population) where this will have a proven environmental benefit and decrease the competition for mainstream housing?

Thirdly, the potential impact of reform of the planning system needs to be carefully reviewed with particular reference to the additional power that might be given to local authorities. Policy and procedural changes to the planning system are on-going and our discussion has focused on the current system, although some reference has been made to alternative strategies. A future government may reform the planning system, associated with moves – particularly at the European Union level – to introduce greater certainty for local people and developers through the clarification of planning procedures. This might involve a move away from a discretionary political system and the introduction of administrative 'zoning' planning more commonly found in continental Europe. Although such a move may presently appear to be some years away, the recent interest in spatial planning taken by the Commission could well see 'local spatial planning matters' being placed on a (supra)national political agenda. Any change enforced at this level, either in the form of zoning or national physical planning, would require the traditional 'land-use only' definition of planning presently existing in England and Wales to be revised. Any amendments would require consideration being given to those policy areas where planning contributes to but is not directly responsible for; the most obvious area of local spatial planning that this could involve – within the context of this paper – concerns the supply of rural housing.

CONCLUSIONS AND POLICY IMPLICATIONS FOR RURAL WALES

Residential tourism is a component of social change which has received far less attention in recent years. Paradoxically, it is this apparent lack of concern which has brought second homes back onto the agenda at the local level. It was Bollom (1978) who argued that vociferous protest was often the hallmark of a healthy rural community, capable of mobilizing opposition against adverse social change. In contrast, where local interests had become submerged by outside influences, the dissenting voices had become silenced. Does the relative quiet in the British countryside today herald a new phase in social change where local interests have been overshadowed, or has residential tourism fallen prey to the wider economic recession? The truth probably lies somewhere in the middle ground. The slump in the housing market has undoubtedly affected second-home growth during the first half of the 1990s (Fisk, 1996) and communities have probably settled into an uneasy status quo. However, it would be wrong to assume that the issues identified in the 1970s are any less relevant today. After all, the same con-trasting social processes (between prosperous and less prosperous regions) are still apparent, with real incomes and leisure demand rising. Successive governments have been unwilling effectively to prioritize local interests in the countryside and this has led to the ingredients for the continuation of rural housing problems. Similarly, the solutions suggested are by no means new and it will be difficult to implement and sustain a strategy of balanced control and development.

With reference to the planning context, it is possible to highlight some very broad policy implications. Locally, these include the need to define the essence of second-home 'problems' in specific areas (given a thorough understanding of the housing market), comprehensive assessments of housing needs as a means of identifying 'pressure points', the continuation of local plan policies designed to synthesize local housing and planning functions and promote the provision of affordable housing and, in Wales, a focusing of attention on language and culture as material planning considerations. Nationally, there is a pressing need to reassess the Use Classes Order debate whilst being mindful that suppressing second-home demand in this way might reduce house prices, but also increase the inflow of permanent migrants. Likewise, occupancy controls continue to be controversial and their use requires careful monitoring. Presumption against development in certain areas may achieve some of the objectives established in WO Circular 53/88 and this is an option worth further consideration.

The argument traced in this paper is a circular one. Starting from the present position and the use of occupancy controls (affecting new development), the paper examined change of residential use (affecting existing dwellings) before considering the presumptions against development, particularly linked to opportunities offered by Circular 53/88 (returning again to new development). Arguably, this treatment of the issues represented a retreat from the more radical option and might be viewed as a 'fudging' of the central issue which involves local access to all housing, existing and new. However, the arguments forwarded in this paper are sensitive to the political and ideological constraints currently in place (and which are likely to remain given the Labour Party's much-changed political colouring and its own apparent 'fudging' of the devolution issue in Wales). A realistic set of policy options are outlined in this paper, whilst the possibility of pressing for more fundamental change in the planning system is certainly not neglected.

In the final analysis, the immediate way forward seems to lie with increasing housing supply rather than tinkering with the demand side of the equation. Attempts to control occupancy or curb development skirt around the edges of the real issue which is centred on the existing housing stock. Effective legislation to control occupancy in this sector may prove elusive and therefore only by increasing supply may tensions be eased. However, all new housebuilding must be subject to local circumstances, including the supply of empty properties, and pay particular attention to cultural and linguistic issues which are especially relevant in the case of rural Wales.

ACKNOWLEDGEMENTS

The research on which this paper has been based was funded by Gwynedd County Council (Gallent *et al*, 1996). The views expressed are those of the authors and may not necessarily represent those of the Council.

REFERENCES

Action for Communities in Rural England (ACRE) (1988). *Who Can Afford to Live in the Countryside? Access to Housing Land,* Cirencester, ACRE.

Ambrose, P. (1974). *The Quiet Revolution*, London, Chatto and Windus.

Audit Commission (AC) (1992*) Developing Local Authority Housing Strategies*, London, HMSO.

Barke, M. (1991). 'The growth and changing pattern of second homes in Spain in the 1970s', *Scottish Geographical Magazine*, 107, 1, 12–21.

Barlow, J. and Chambers, D. (1992). *Planning Agreements and Affordable Housing Provision*, University of Sussex, Centre for Urban and Regional Research.

Barlow, J., Cocks, R. and Parker, M. (1994). *Planning for Affordable Housing*, London, HMSO.

Bielckus, C. L. (1977). 'Second homes in Scandinavia', in Coppock, J. T. (ed.), *Second Homes: Curse or Blessing?*, Oxford, Pergamon Press.

Bielckus, C. L., Rogers, A.W. and Wibberley, G.P. (1972). 'Second homes in England and Wales: a study of the distribution and use of rural properties taken over as second residences', Wye College, School of Rural Economics and Related Studies.

Bishop, K. and Hooper, A. (1991). *Planning for Social Housing*, London, Association of District Councils.

Bollom, C. (1978). *Attitudes and Second Homes in Rural Wales*, Cardiff, University of Wales Press.

Bramley, G. (1991). 'Bridging the affordability gap in Wales: a report of research on housing access and affordability', Cardiff, House Builders' Federation and Council of Welsh Districts.

Buller, H. and Hoggart, K. (1994a). *International Counterurbanisation: British Migrants in Rural France*, Aldershot, Avebury.

Buller, H. and Hoggart, K. (1994b). 'The social integration of British home owners into French rural communities', in *Journal of Rural Studies*, 10, 2, 197–210.

Chartered Institute of Housing (CIH) (1992). *Housing: The First Priority*, Coventry.

Cole, A., Williams, P. and Ainger, B. (1995). *Housing in Wales: Attitudes and Issues*, London, Council of Mortgage Lenders.

Coppock, J. T. (ed.) (1977). *Second Homes: Curse or Blessing?*, Oxford, Pergamon Press.

Cloke, P., Milbourne, P. and Thomas, C. (1994). *Lifestyles in Rural England*, Salisbury, Rural Development Commission.

Dartington Amenity Research Trust (DART) (1977*). Second Homes in Scotland: A Report to The Countryside Commission for Scotland*, Scottish Tourist Board, Highlands and Island Development Board, Scottish Development Department, Publication No.22, Totnes, *DART.*

Department of the Environment (DoE) (1996). *Circular 13/96: Planning for Affordable Housing*, London, HMSO.

Dower, M. (1977). 'Planning aspects of second homes', in Coppock, J. T. (ed.), *Second Homes: Curse or Blessing?*, Oxford, Pergamon Press.

Downing, P. and Dower, M. (1973). *Second Homes in England and Wales*, London, Countryside Commission, HMSO.

Dunn, M., Rawson, M. and Rogers, A. (1981). *Rural Housing: Competition and Choice*, London, George Allen and Unwin Ltd.

Fisk, M. J. (1996). *Home Truths: Issues for Housing in Wales*, Llandysul, Gwasg Gomer.

Gallent, N. M., Tewdwr-Jones, M. and Higgs, G. (1996). 'Rural change in focus: rural housing supply and second homes in Britain and Europe', research commissioned by Gwynedd County Council; unpublished.

Gallent, N. M. (1997). 'Local housing agencies in rural Wales', *Housing Studies* (forthcoming).

Hansard (1985). *Housing Surplus in England and Wales,* Hansard Written Answer, Col. 16, London, HMSO.

HM Government (1996). *Housing and Construction Statistics No. 63 (September Quarter 1995),* London, HMSO.

Hoggart, K. and Buller, H. (1995). 'British home owners and housing change in rural France', *Housing Studies,* 10, 2, 179–98.

Jacobs, C. A. J. (1972). *Second Homes in Denbighshire; Tourism and Recreation Report No.3,* Ruthin, County of Denbigh Planning Department.

Joseph Rowntree Foundation (JRF) (1994). *Inquiry into Planning for Housing,* York.

Loughlin, M. (1984). 'Local needs policies and development control strategies. An examination of the role of occupancy restrictions in development control', Working Paper No.42, University of Bristol, School for Advanced Urban Studies.

Newby, H. (1980a). *Green and Pleasant Land?,* Harmondsworth, Penguin.

Newby, H. (1980b). 'A one-eyed look at the country', *New Society,* 14 August 1980.

Office of Population Censuses and Surveys (OPCS) (1993). *1991 Census: Housing and Availability of Cars,* London, HMSO.

Pahl, R. (1966). 'The social objectives of village planning', *Official Architecture and Planning,* 29, 1146–50.

Pilkington, E. (1990). 'Burning issue', *Roof,* 15, 2, 18–19.

Pyne, C.B. (1973). *Second Homes,* Caernarfon, Caernarvonshire County Planning Department.

Rogers, A.W. (1977). 'Second homes in England and Wales: a spatial view', in Coppock, J. T. (ed.), *Second Homes: Curse or Blessing?,* Oxford, Pergamon Press.

Rossing, Y. (1996). 'Legislation concerning the meaning of rural change', preliminary report to PACTE-funded Rural Change group, unpublished.

Rural Development Commission (RDC) (1995). Section 106 Agreements and Private Finance for Rural Housing Schemes, Salisbury, RDC.

Saunders, P. (1984). 'Beyond housing classes: the sociological significance of private property rights in the means of consumption', *International Journal of Urban and Regional Research,* 8, 202–27.

Shucksmith, M. (1981). *No Homes for Locals?,* Farnborough, Gower Publishing.

Shucksmith, M. (1983). 'Second homes: a framework for policy', *Town Planning Review,* 54, 2, 174–93.

Shucksmith, M. (1990a). *Housebuilding in Britain's Countryside,* London, Routledge.

Shucksmith, M. (1990b). 'A theoretical perspective on rural housing: housing classes in rural Britain', *Sociologia Ruralis,* 30, 2, 210–29.

Soley, C. (1990). 'Seconds out', *Roof,* 15, 2, 38–9.

Welsh Office (1986). *Circular 30/86: Housing for Senior Management,* Cardiff.

Welsh Office (1988). *Circular 53/88: The Welsh Language: Development Plans and Planning Control,* Cardiff.

Welsh Office (1993). *Welsh Housing Statistics No.13,* Cardiff.

Welsh Office (1995). *Welsh Office Quarterly Statistics,* October–December 1995, Cardiff.

Welsh Office (1996a). *A Working Countryside for Wales: Rural White Paper*, Cardiff.

Welsh Office (1996b). *Planning Policy Guidance Wales*, Cardiff, Welsh Office.

Whitehead, C. and Kleinman, M. (1991). *A Review of Housing Needs Assessment*, London, Housing Corporation.

Wilcox, S. (1990). *The Need for Social Rented Housing in England in the 1990s*, Coventry, Chartered Institute of Housing.

Young, K. (1988). 'Rural prospects', in Jowell, R., Witherspoon, S. and Brook, L. (eds), *British Social Attitudes 1988,* Aldershot, Gower.

6. A COMPARISON OF COMMUNITY LEVEL INDICES IN MEASURING DISADVANTAGE IN WALES

Gary Higgs and Sean White

INTRODUCTION

The aims of this paper are twofold: to review the current use of indicators of deprivation used by Unitary Authorities (UAs) in Wales; and to assess the spatial pattern of deprivation in Wales as revealed by the application of policy-relevant indicators at the community level. The study presents outputs from the first stage of a research project funded by the Economic and Social Research Council (ESRC) which is concerned with exploring the limitations of existing measures in accurately portraying deprivation in rural areas and with the development of indices which take into account factors such as declining levels of service provision in rural communities. This has involved the analysis of results from a survey of public service provision carried out in 1995/6 for all Welsh rural communities. Previous studies have identified 'declining levels of service provision' and 'reduced accessibility to these services' as important components of deprivation in rural areas, especially for certain target groups such as the elderly, single parents and the unemployed (e.g. Midwinter and Monaghan, 1990; Shucksmith *et al.,* 1996).

This study would seem particularly timely given recent debates into the kinds of indicators being used in resource allocation systems which are considered by some commentators to be largely urban biased and thus act to the detriment of rural areas (Hale and Associates, 1996). This project, although not explicitly concerned with the impacts of changes in the use of current indicators and the consequences in financial terms, has involved an investigation into the incorporation of more indicative measures of changes in rural areas. Previous studies have clearly highlighted the fact that deprivation is a multi-faceted concept which cannot be captured by a single indicator and that the heterogeneous nature of deprivation, especially in areas of dispersed population, suggests that census-based measures which use indicators biased towards urban areas have traditionally under-assessed levels of poverty and deprivation in rural areas (e.g. Midwinter *et al.,* 1988; Scott *et al.,* 1991; Walford and Hockey, 1991; Scottish Homes, 1993). It is not the purpose of this paper to provide a detailed review of this extensive literature. Rather, the main tenet of the paper is that area-based measures of deprivation still have relevance in the present policy environment and that, given that there are distinctive aspects to rural deprivation such as inaccessibility, social isolation and declining service provision, we need to explore the use of analytical techniques based on Geographical Information Systems (GIS), in order to examine spatial dimensions to rural deprivation.

The remainder of this paper is structured as follows. In the first section we outline the results of a survey of each UA in Wales in which we describe the use and derivation of existing indicators of deprivation. The survey has been concerned with exploring the relevance of area-based measures of spatial targeting in the current policy environment in Wales. We have also documented the perceived limitations of such measures and the need to develop indicators which are more representative of the socio-economic conditions prevailing in Wales. This provides the focus for the rest of the paper in which we describe the spatial pattern of deprivation as revealed by applying existing policy relevant measures at the community level. The analyses presented in the second section reveal a reasonable level of consistency in the communities identified as being in the most 50 deprived communities in Wales. Anomalies are explained largely in terms of the variables included in the individual measures. Urban communities in south and north east Wales with deep-seated problems of unemployment and housing deprivation appear in the worst 50 on each of the four measures employed in this study. However, the indexes appear far more limited in measuring facets of rural deprivation. In the next section we compare these trends to those identified in previous studies which have examined the use of policy measures at a range of spatial scales in England and Scotland. We outline the limitations of such measures as applied to 'rural' communities before proposing methods by which explicitly rural variables can be used to derive alternative measures of deprivation. Finally, we make some preliminary conclusions on the use of such indicators in rural contexts before providing some general comments on the use of spatial analytical techniques in general, and GIS in particular, in their derivation. This draws attention to the next stages of the project which will use case study regions in Wales in order to develop indicators in a variety of rural settings using such methodologies.

The main conclusions from this paper are twofold: firstly that area-based measures of spatial targeting are likely to continue to form an important component of UK government and European policies towards alleviating poverty and deprivation; and secondly that, given concerns expressed by those authorities with rural 'constituencies' regarding the appropriateness of applying such indicators in rural contexts, research into developing alternative, policy-relevant, indicators which reflect the changing socio-economic conditions prevailing in rural areas of Wales, would appear particularly timely.

EXISTING USE OF INDICATORS IN WALES

In August/September 1996 we conducted a postal questionnaire of all new UAs in Wales (Figure 6.1) in order to collate information on the levels of awareness within the authorities of the use and importance of indicators of deprivation. The aim was to establish if traditional approaches to tackling disadvantage using area-based measures of spatial targeting were still relevant in the current policy environment. The questionnaire was designed to assess the current use of indicators including their purpose and context across a number of departments in each authority. A secondary aim was to find out if a general purpose indicator was being used for all programmes or whether indicators were being tailored according to individual programme objectives. Comparisons could be made with, for example, the assertion made by Coombes *et al.* (1995), in a review of indicators used by central government departments involved in urban regeneration functions, that:

> the choice of indicators should not be driven by programme objectives – so it remains appropriate to develop a single 'general' index that each department can set alongside their own programme indicators (and later perhaps allow users to adjust it interactively to develop purpose-specific variants). (Coombes *et al.*, 1995, 13)

A secondary aim of the questionnaire was to gauge, where applicable, if particular authorities were attempting to develop indicators, or variables within indicators, that were a more accurate reflection of the unique facets of deprivation experienced in rural areas. A final response rate of 77 per cent was achieved for the survey (17 of the 22 UAs in Wales), the main findings of which are outlined below in relation to each of the four sections of the questionnaire.

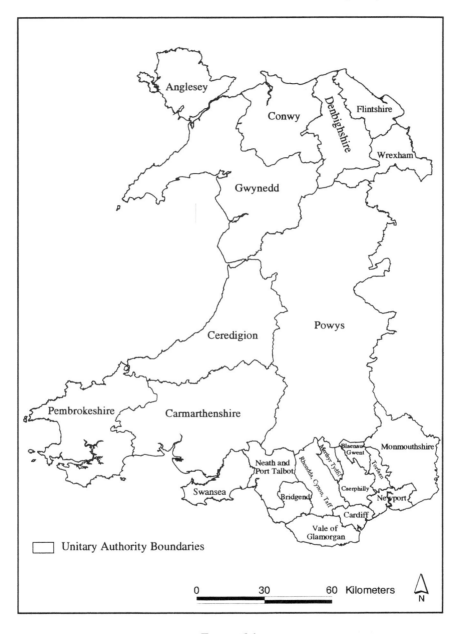

FIGURE 6.1
The new unitary authority structure in Wales

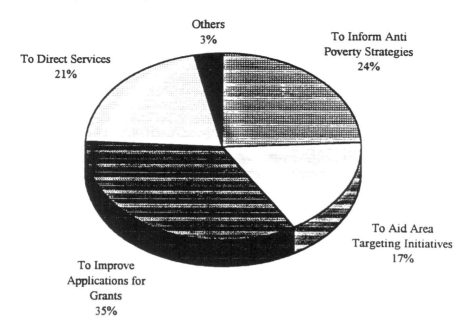

FIGURE 6.2
The use of deprivation indicators within Welsh Unitary Authorities

The first part of the questionnaire was concerned with describing the deprivation indicators currently in use within UAs, and the purposes for which they are employed. Figure 6.2 displays the response to emerge from a question related to the use of deprivation indicators to inform work or decisions undertaken in particular areas of the authorities' business. The majority of responding authorities employ deprivation indicators to inform and improve applications for funding, to prepare bids under a range of policy initiatives and to show the spatial pattern of socio-economic conditions in relation to their Anti-Poverty Strategies.

The majority of respondents were keen to stress the holistic, authority-wide approach taken towards the use of deprivation indicators and this is reflected in the large cross-section of UA departments currently using deprivation measures in their everyday activities. A number of authorities, however, have adopted a more focused approach to the measurement of deprivation with a specific targeting of particular issues or problem localities, perhaps in support of funding bids.

The second part of the questionnaire required respondents to evaluate critically the performance of deprivation indicators currently in use. Authorities were first asked if the currently used 'official' deprivation indicators provided an accurate picture of deprivation in the authority. The majority of respondents indicated that this was not the case. Prominent among the reasons given for concern over the pertinence of 'official' indicators is the problem of the robustness of the data used to construct the indicators. For instance, variables relating to unemployment are questioned due, in part, to the data now being out of date (1991 Census) and also to the fact that the variable does not give a true indication of under-employment or accurately highlight problem areas or localities at the intra-authority level. Concerns are also raised about the suitability of certain variables within current indicators; for example car ownership and population loss, and the methodologies used to combine such variables (for example, techniques for standardizing variables such as the Z score methodology). Many authorities call for a complete review of the official indicators currently in use within Wales with particular regard to; the variables used in the indices, possible alternative data sources to the UK Census (for example, benefits data or detailed employment statistics), and some measure of rural deprivation (for example, a measure of accessibility to services or life opportunities).

The third group of questions was concerned with: the nature of deprivation-based research being carried out within UAs in Wales, including work taking place to develop new indicators where current measures were deemed inappropriate; the data sources used to derive such indices; technical information related to the construction of indicators such as the weighting of variables; the spatial units used, and whether or not a GIS was used to derive new measures based on increased spatial analytical functionality within the UA. Response to this part of the questionnaire was poor, with only a fraction of the new authorities involved in such research. A number of the new authorities are currently at the stage of formulating an authority-wide response to the problem of deprivation through the instigation of Anti-Poverty Groups for instance, and have not, as yet, set about tackling the detailed measurement and definition of such problems. Research that has been undertaken is still largely census-based but some authorities are examining the possibility of using alternative data sources, for example free school meal data or Housing/Council Tax Benefits data. Opinion is split on the appropriate methodologies for combining such indices (Z Score values and signed Chi Square standardisation are the most commonly cited), but there is a consensus that GIS technology is most appropriate for research of this type.

The final part of the questionnaire concerned attempts to derive a rural dimension to deprivation. Authorities were asked to identify what, in their opinion, are the most important aspects of deprivation in rural areas, and whether or not these elements of rural disadvantage were being monitored or addressed within the authority. Probably the most common factor to emerge from the response to this question is the issue of poor accessibility to key services. Other important issues highlighted by respondents include poor housing conditions and a lack of suitable housing stock for first-time buyers which was seen to exacerbate the problem of rural out-migration among younger age groups. Linked to this last point is the problem of poor employment opportunities in rural areas, compounded by low wage rates and a prevalence of seasonal employment in some localities. Having identified the main features of deprivation in rural areas, respondents were asked to suggest variables that could be incorporated into an overall measure of rural deprivation. Authorities highlighted the need for some measure that would take account of the problem of poor accessibility to services in rural areas and stressed the need for a more accurate delimitation of rural employment problems. Clearly there is a call for an alternative to census-based measures in rural areas but, as yet, there is no clear methodology or consensus being adopted by the new UAs with a view to realizing such a measure.

The ESRC sponsored project underway aims to address many of the issues raised in the final part of the survey, relating to the rural deprivation problem. The aims of this project are to investigate the range of indicators of deprivation used by public service providers in rural areas and to critically evaluate their use in identifying areas of social disadvantage. Through the use of GIS spatial analytical techniques the project will provide practical ways in which accessibility to, and availability of, services, could be taken into account in an indicator of deprivation in rural areas. The rest of this paper is primarily concerned with the former task, namely with describing the geography of deprivation in Wales as revealed by applying the types of indicators identified in our survey of UAs at the community level. These indicators are derived from variables included in the 1991 Census of Population and in the next section we draw attention to the spatial patterns of deprivation prior to assessing the strengths and weaknesses of the indices in identifying deprivation in rural areas.

APPLICATION OF DEPRIVATION MEASURES AT THE COMMUNITY LEVEL IN WALES

A study of the use of a large number of indexes at the ward level in England and Wales and at the postcode sector level in Scotland (Lee *et al.*, 1995) revealed that, at these spatial scales, 'different indexes produce different results. Which index is chosen affects which areas are identified as the most deprived' (Lee *et al.*, 1995, viii). This study, the first of its kind in Great Britain, suggested that although such indexes are the 'most appropriate way of identifying areas with the greatest levels of multiple deprivation', a very different spatial pattern of deprivation is likely to result from applying these measures. The nature of the variables included in the indexes and the way in which they were constructed, influenced the overall patterns of deprivation and meant that interpretations of the overall patterns of deprivation were often contradictory.

A large literature exists on the construction of deprivation indexes and their use in problem identification and resource allocation (much of which was reviewed in Coombes *et al.,* 1995), and in a previous report we provide a detailed account of the spatial patterns of deprivation at the community scale in Wales (White and Higgs, 1997). In this section, we are concerned with comparing the performance of a sub-set of four policy relevant measures of deprivation, namely the Welsh Office Index of Socio-Economic Conditions (Welsh Office, 1994), the Department of Environment's Index of Local Conditions (DoE, 1994), the Townsend Index (Townsend *et al.*, 1988) and the Breadline Britain Index (Gordon and Forrest, 1995). These were chosen either because of their policy relevance in resource allocation mechanisms and their use as existing targeting measures in UK policy terms, or because, as in the case of the Townsend Index, they have been used as general measures of deprivation in a range of social applications. The latter, in particular, is widely used in the health sector to identify areas of relative need across a range of health and social services contexts. The Breadline Index was calculated in order to compare our research with a comprehensive study of deprivation at the small area level in Great Britain in which the authors found a very different pattern of deprivation when applying this particular indicator to that of a wider range of deprivation measures at the ward level (Lee *et al.*, 1995). The aim here is to examine the hypothesis that these indexes do not adequately assess deprivation in rural areas and that key aspects of rural deprivation such as declining service provision and spatial isolation are neglected.

Although some of these measures have been used by authorities in order to describe socio-economic conditions in their areas, this is (to our knowledge) the first attempt to provide a wider picture of deprivation at the community level in Wales. Each indicator is described in turn before a comparison is made of the relative rankings of communities on each. Unless otherwise stated, each indicator has involved the use of small area statistics from the 1991 Census of Population; the advantages and limitations of which have been documented elsewhere (e.g. Hirschfield, 1994; Lee *et al.*, 1995). The community (the Welsh equivalent of the English parish) was chosen as the spatial scale of analysis for a number of reasons. Firstly, as part of our analysis of changing service provision in rural Wales we have used the community as our survey unit, with each community clerk being asked to fill in a questionnaire relating to service provision levels (see Section 4). Secondly, denominator data from the 1991 Census is available at the community level through an aggregation of smaller spatial units offering a consistent spatial base. Thirdly, under the proposals included in the Rural White Papers for England (HMSO, 1995) and Wales (HMSO, 1996), communities in rural areas are likely to have an increased role in terms of funding opportunities partly through community appraisals. This, together with the move towards unitary authorities under local government reorganization (April 1996), will focus attention on communities as political units in their own right and thus an analysis of service provision in relation to socio-economic circumstances at the community level would appear to be particularly timely. The disadvantages of using the community are common to many of the area based approaches identified by Midwinter *et al.* (1988); namely the failure to take into account the nature of cross-boundary flows within communities, the disparity in the population bases of areal units, the dangers of assigning characteristics of areas to individuals or groups of individuals (the so-called 'ecological fallacy') and the impacts of the modifiable areal unit problem (Openshaw, 1984). A number of authors have suggested that such problems, when combined with the diverse and dispersed nature of deprivation in rural areas, precludes an area-based approach to deprivation and hence advocate client- or group-based approaches (e.g. Mason and Taylor, 1990; Scott *et al.*, 1991; Chapman and Shucksmith, 1996). Whilst agreeing with the general tenets of such an approach, involving the use of detailed community based-studies that have largely focused on rural areas of Scotland (Shucksmith *et al.*, 1996), results from the survey presented in Section 2 of this paper and the conclusions from similar research in other regions (e.g. Bruce *et al.*, 1995, for Cornwall) lead us to contend that area-based measures are likely to remain a component of government policy towards spatial targeting. This being the case there is a need to re-create measures of disadvantage for politically recognized units which are more representative of the underlying levels of disadvantage experienced by such groups. Firstly, we compare the use of existing policy relevant indicators at the community level in Wales.

The Townsend Index
Townsend (1987, 125) defines deprivation as:

> A state of observable and demonstrable disadvantage relative to the local community or the wider society or nation to which an individual, family or group belongs.

Townsend distinguished between two types of deprivation, namely social and material; the latter relating to the lack of resources available to individuals or households. The index of material deprivation developed by Townsend comprises four main census-derived variables (see Table 6.1), namely unemployment, housing tenure, overcrowding and the proportion of private households without access to a car, and uses a Z-score methodology to produce an overall index. This index has been used in a wide range of application areas, in particular in relation to health needs and in resource allocation (e.g. Townsend *et al.*, 1988; Phillimore *et al.*, 1994; Carstairs, 1995).

Figure 6.3 illustrates the spatial pattern of deprivation as revealed by the Townsend Index for Welsh communities. Appendix 1 contains a list of the 50 most deprived communities in Wales on this indicator. It is striking that of these, 22 (44 per cent) are located in the four main urban conurbations of Cardiff (10), Newport (6), Swansea (4) and Wrexham (2). Of the remainder, the majority are located in south Wales, with only four in north Wales other than the two communities in Wrexham, two of which, Bangor and Aberystwyth, have large student populations and score highly on the rented housing variable. There is a notable absence of traditionally 'rural' communities in the most deprived quartile. The influence of the 'no car' variable in this regard is significant. The necessity for a car in rural areas has meant that rural communities tend traditionally to have high levels of car ownership. This has led some commentators to suggest that high levels of car ownership in rural households should be regarded as an indicator of relative disadvantage rather than affluence in that such households may well

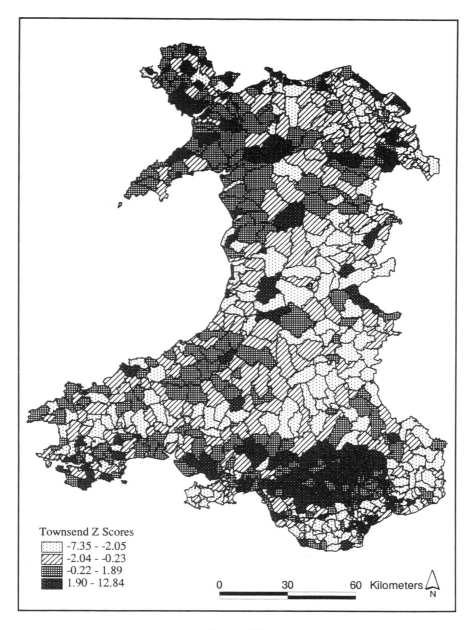

FIGURE 6.3
Townsend Deprivation Indicator at Welsh Community Council Scale

be 'deprived' of other basic household requirements considered to be necessary by modern-day living standards (e.g. Midwinter *et al.*, 1988). Patterns of deprivation in Figure 6.3 suggests that the incorporation of this variable in the Townsend Index, therefore, results in very few 'rural' communities falling in the top quintile on this measure. Similarly, the use of the housing tenure variable may be expected to discriminate against rural areas where rented housing forms a lower proportion of the housing stock. It should be recognized at this stage that, as with the other indices presented here, the Townsend index was not necessarily developed to assess rural deprivation. Nevertheless, the Townsend Index has been used as a measure of material deprivation in a number of studies especially in relation to health outcomes such as standard mortality ratios (e.g. Phillimore *et al.*, 1994). The spatial pattern of deprivation at the community level presented here would appear to suggest that the index is not necessarily suitable to analysing deprivation in rural contexts. Detailed analysis of spatial variations of individual community level constituent variables by some measure of rurality would be required to substantiate these assertions however.

The Welsh Office Index of Socio-Economic Conditions

This index has been used to assess applications for funding from local authorities in Wales under firstly, the Urban Programme scheme and latterly, the Strategic Development Scheme. Details regarding construction of the index are described elsewhere (Welsh Office, 1994). In summary a Z-score methodology is used to standardise eight 1991 Census of Population variables (Table 6.1) which are used as key indicators of economic and social conditions in Wales. The variables are given equal weighting in the summed index. Absolute and relative variables are used to calculate an overall index for each ward in Wales using a 25:75 split in favour of the relative value. The former is based on count variables, measuring the number of persons experiencing a given phenomenon in an area. For the latter index, these count variables were transformed to ratios of the population of individuals or households in a given ward.

As with the Department of the Environment's 1981 Deprivation score (DoE, 1983), the Z-score methodology which is used in the derivation of the Welsh Office indicator has been criticized for over-emphasizing the importance of areas with low population bases (ERI, 1993). This, in turn, has led to several attempts to use a chi-square or multi-variate approach based on factor and cluster analytical techniques when constructing such

TABLE 6.1
Variables in selected indicators

Variables	Townsend Index	Welsh Office Index	DoE Index of Local Conditions	Breadline Britain Index
Overcrowding	*	*	*	
No Car	*		*	*
Not Owner Occupied	*			*
Unemployment	*	*	*	*
Economically Active		*		
Single Parent Households				*
Low Socio-economic Group		*		*
Population Loss in the 20–59 years age group		*		
Permanently Sick		*		*
Lack of Basic Amenities		*	*	
Standard Mortality Ratio		*	*	
Children in Low-earning Households			*	
Children Living in Flats			*	
17 year olds No Longer in Full-time Education			*	
Income Support			*	
Low Educational Attainment			*	
Long Term Unemployed			*	
House Insurance			*	
Derelict Land			*	

measures (Folwell, 1995; Lee *et al.*, 1995). The Index of Socio-Economic Conditions does, however, have the advantage that it is relatively easy to construct, replicate and interpret and has been used by the Welsh Office when targeting funds.

Figure 6.4 shows the spatial pattern in deprivation at the community level as revealed by this indicator. Appendix 2 lists the 50 most deprived communities on the Welsh Office Indicator. Again, the urban conurbations are well represented with 19 out of the most deprived 50 communities in Cardiff (9), Swansea (6), Newport (3) and Wrexham (1). The two most deprived communities are Rhyl in the north and Barry in the south. Cardiff has 3 in the most deprived 10 communities (Trowbridge, Riverside and Ely). The presence of two Brecknock communities in the worst 50 is purely an artefact of the methodology, in that one of the variables (population change in the 20–59 years age group) is highly skewed for both communities as a result of the procedure of relating the 1981 enumeration district population-

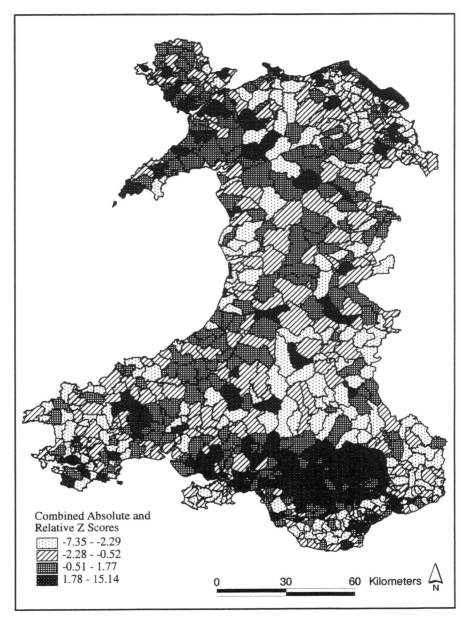

FIGURE 6.4
The Welsh Office Index of Socio-Economic Conditions at Welsh Community
Council Scale

weighted centroid to the 1991 community allocation. This results in what appears to be a dramatic increase in the population for this age group, resulting in an extremely large Z-score for this variable, which has a disproportionate effect on the final calculated index. Otherwise the patterns of deprivation illustrated are very similar to that presented by the analysis of the Townsend indicator. There are no explicitly rural variables in the index and so, methodological effects withstanding, rural communities do not figure strongly in the overall pattern of deprivation. Despite this a detailed breakdown of one of the relative variables (Standardized Mortality Ratio (SMR) for 1990-92 for the age group 0–74) shows that some rural communities have higher than average SMRs (SMR = 100) albeit that there are less than 20 deaths in the majority of these communities (Appendix 3). The rural district of Montgomeryshire, for example, has three communities with SMRs greater than 150 but in no instance does the number of deaths in this three year period exceed 11 so that much less statistical reliability can be placed on this particular variable. As with any other index, the choice of variables is open to criticism, and the use of a household amenity variable, in particular, has been questioned as a measure of 'long term and compounding deprivation' (Lee *et al.*, 1995, 30). Statistical analysis of the other variables incorporated in the index (not presented here) suggests that variations in these census-derived variables cannot be used to identify a specifically 'rural' dimension to socio-economic disadvantage (White and Higgs, 1997).

The Department of the Environment Index of Local Conditions

Criticisms of the Z-score methodology adopted for the DoE's urban deprivation index in the early 1980s (DoE, 1983), especially in relation to the perceived bias towards small areas and its inappropriateness particularly at the enumeration district (ED) level, led to a review of the use of indicators in targeting funds in England (Bradford *et al.*, 1995). This resulted in the development of a new index which differs in the way scores are standardized by adopting a signed chi-squared approach. The advantage of this approach is that greater weight is given to areas with a larger base population. Absolute and not percentage figures are used and the procedure involves summing the transformed variables for the relevant number of (unweighted) indicators (Table 6.1). The methodology also adopts a spatial hierarchical approach by using variables at a variety of spatial scales to create indices at enumeration district, ward and district levels which was felt to be advantageous given the importance of spatial scale on the resulting patterns of deprivation (Bradford *et al.*, 1995).

The Index of Local Conditions (ILC), which has been calculated for all 366 local authority areas in England, has been criticized both for the selection and the relative weighting of variables used in its calculation as well as the use of chi-square methodology in areas of unequal base populations (e.g. Folwell, 1995; Henderson, 1994; Simpson 1996). This weakness was recognized in the DoE report (1994, 5). The chi-squared method is also less appropriate for precisely measuring relatively low levels of deprivation.

Attempts to remove the skewness of data by use of the chi-square technique have also been criticized because of the need to retain the natural variation in the data (Martin *et al.*, 1994). In addition, the ILC, due in part to the nature of the housing variables, has been perceived to have a bias towards those regions containing large urban conurbations (Bruce *et al.*, 1995; Lee *et al.*, 1995). Applications of the index to rural areas of Cornwall reveal that, when compared with indicators such as wage levels and health status, the index underestimates the level of deprivation in rural areas and 'is inadequate in measuring the level of deprivation in West Cornwall because it fails to reflect the scale of the problems' (Bruce *et al.*, 1995, 20). The ILC has not, to date, been used in a Welsh context and has not been adopted by the Welsh Office in the targeting of funds. However, in order to gauge the performance of this indicator in Wales, we have calculated this indicator at the community level using enumeration district and ward level variables documented by the DoE (1994).

Figure 6.5 shows the spatial variation in the pattern of deprivation as revealed by applying the ILC for Welsh communities. Interestingly, no communities for Newport and only one for Wrexham (Caia Park) appear in the most 50 deprived communities in Wales (Appendix 4), although the two other main urban areas (Cardiff with 10 communities and Swansea with 5) are prominent in the list. The index, however, does highlight communities outside the 'core' urban areas identified in other indicators such as Neath, Aberdare and Caerphilly which have significant pockets of deprivation using the composite ILC variables highlighted in Table 6.1. The trends identified also tend to confirm the patterns in the Lee *et al.* (1995) study as being biased towards areas where flats form a significant component of the building stock. In this regard, areas of significant numbers of young and student populations are prevalent (e.g. communities in Bangor, Cardiff and Swansea) on this indicator. Towns in predominantly rural areas, such as Newtown and Carmarthen, also have communities appearing in the most deprived 50 communities for similar reasons. Overall, the spatial pattern

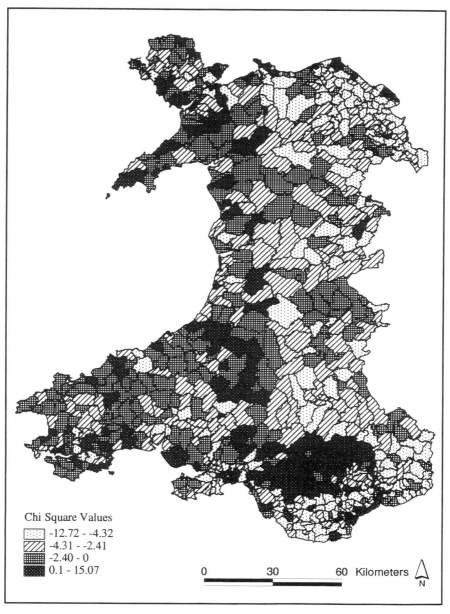

FIGURE 6.5
The DoE Index of Local Conditions at Welsh Community Council Scale

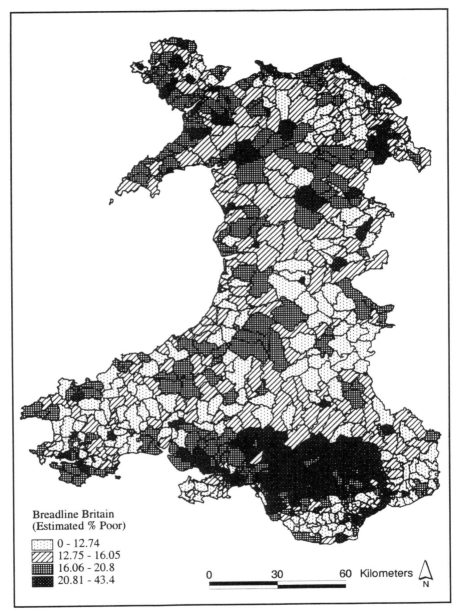

Breadline Britain
(Estimated % Poor)

- 0 - 12.74
- 12.75 - 16.05
- 16.06 - 20.8
- 20.81 - 43.4

0   30   60   Kilometers

FIGURE 6.6
Breadline Britain Deprivation Index at Welsh Community Council Scale

mirrors that found at the district level for Britain as a whole (Lee *et al.*, 1995) and confirms Bruce *et al.*'s (1995) suspicions of a bias towards areas dominated by certain types of building stock which precludes its use as an indicator of rural deprivation.

The Breadline Britain Index

The Breadline Britain Index uses census variables from the 1991 Census of Population, along with weightings derived from the Breadline Britain survey conducted in 1990 (Gordon and Pantazis, 1995) to estimate the percentage of poor households at the ward level (Table 6.1). The variables are weighted and validated against the poverty survey which, it is argued, gives the overall index an advantage over the use of Z- and chi-square methodologies. A statistical analysis of the relationships using the percentage of poor households revealed high correlations with both mean earnings and long-term illness at the ward level in England (Gordon, 1995). Lee *et al.* (1995, viii) suggested that this is 'the 'best' index for identifying the most deprived wards at a national level'. We have used a similar methodology to apply the index to Welsh communities using the same weighting scheme documented in the Lee *et al.* (1995) study.

Figure 6.6 shows the pattern of estimated percentage poor split into quintiles for Welsh communities. Overall, similar to the other indicators, the urban communities of south Wales figure highly amongst the most deprived in Wales (Appendix 5). The majority of the 50 most deprived communities are confined to the old counties of Mid, South and West Glamorgan along with some communities in Newport. The latter account for five communities, Swansea (4), Cardiff (7) and Wrexham (2). Only four communities north of Merthyr appear in the most deprived fifty – including Holyhead which appears in the most deprived list on all four indicators and Bangor which has a higher than average level of rented accommodation. In the rest of rural Wales, only towns such as Newtown, Llanidloes and Welshpool appear in the top quintile suggesting that the index is highlighting variables which are town- or urban-biased. Again, similar to the case with the Townsend Index, the presence of a variable on car ownership means that rural communities appear to have lower than average levels of deprivation on this index.

Comparison of the performance of deprivation measures at the community level

Clearly, the choice, weights and statistical manipulation of census variables and the spatial scale at which these measures are calculated are likely to have important implications for the patterns of deprivation observed. The importance of defining exactly what facet of deprivation is being measured at the outset of any project of this nature has been emphasised by Lee *et al.* (1995) in their national study. The focus of this paper has been to apply currently available policy indicators in order to try to assess the relative levels of deprivation of rural communities in Wales. Here, we compare the overall patterns as revealed by applying these indicators at the community level in Wales before advocating the use of a non-census-derived variable (based on the levels of service provision in rural communities) in developing indexes more in tune with levels of deprivation in rural areas. More comprehensive reviews of the applicability of census and non-census-based variables in deprivation indexes are presented by Coombes *et al.* (1995) and Lee *et al.* (1995).

Figure 6.7 and Appendices 1–5 show that there are some communities which are amongst the most 50 deprived on a number of indicators. These include urban communities in south and north-east Wales as well as that of Holyhead. The methods by which these indexes have been constructed clearly do have implications for the relative rankings of individual communities on particular measures but the overall picture is of a 'hardcore' of communities which are in the deprived category on each indicator. In a previous paper we have expanded on this analysis to include a wider range of deprivation measures and have statistically analysed the differences in the relative rankings of each community in Wales on such measures (White and Higgs, 1997). Results from this analysis, and the maps in Figure 6.7, suggest that certain communities in the four main urban conurbations in Wales are in the most deprived 50 across each of the main policy relevant indicators (e.g. Ely in Cardiff; Pillgwenlly in Newport; Townhill in Swansea and Caia Park in Wrexham). Clearly, there is a group of communities within south Wales, in particular, that can be classified as deprived on a whole host of census-derived measures. Indeed many of these urban communities have a long history of deprivation with deep-seated problems of low quality housing and poor employment opportunities which are at the heart of many of these indicators (Herbert, 1980; Morgan and Price, 1992).

Even accounting for factors such as the 'ecological fallacy' (where characteristics of areas are often erroneously attributed to individuals living within such areas) and the methods by which these indicators have been constructed, these urban areas are likely to contain larger numbers of deprived households, and people, than more rural communities. As with any area-based measure, however, there are pockets of deprivation which remain 'hidden' as statistical artefacts of the methods by which such indicators have been derived. Using finer zones of analysis, for example enumeration districts, may help to reveal such areas although very few studies present data on deprivation at this level and funds are usually targeted at higher spatial scales such as wards and districts. Previous research, such as that conducted in the Rural Lifestyles project, suggest for example, that there are households within communities in rural Wales that are disadvantaged in terms of factors such as poor housing and employment opportunities, low income levels and poor access to services (Cloke *et al.*, 1995a; 1995b). Using the types of area-based measures identified in this paper, however, we have not been able to identify consistently deprived communities in rural areas of Wales. The 'rural' communities that appear in the top quintiles in terms of deprivation tend to consist of small towns which, due to the biased urban nature of the composite variables in these measures, fare badly on the four deprivation measures presented in this paper.

It is important to stress at this point that the indexes analysed in this paper do not necessarily purport to measure deprivation in rural areas and that clearly it is important to establish at the outset of any project of this nature the concepts of deprivation that are being measured (Hirschfield, 1994; Lee *et al.*, 1995). However, our analysis has drawn attention to the limitations of current indicators of deprivation in identifying pockets of rural deprivation in Wales. Each of the four indicators included in this study can be criticized for not including variables which have explicitly 'rural' dimensions. Each index has been developed to measure different facets of deprivation and from different policy perspectives (largely dominated by the need to identify deprivation in urban frameworks). No one indicator has an explicitly rural focus. In part, this derives from the limitations of current census-derived measures and the non-availability of non-census-based data at fine enough spatial resolutions (see below). However, given that area-based measures are being used to allocate and target funds, and that there is the need to develop indicators that are more sensitive to the types of socio-economic changes that are taking place in rural areas of Wales, our research, which is focusing on one tenet of such change (i.e. changes in public service provision), would appear to be particularly timely. In the next section we describe the main features of our study, after firstly reiterating the main drawbacks of current area-based measures of socio-economic conditions in rural areas.

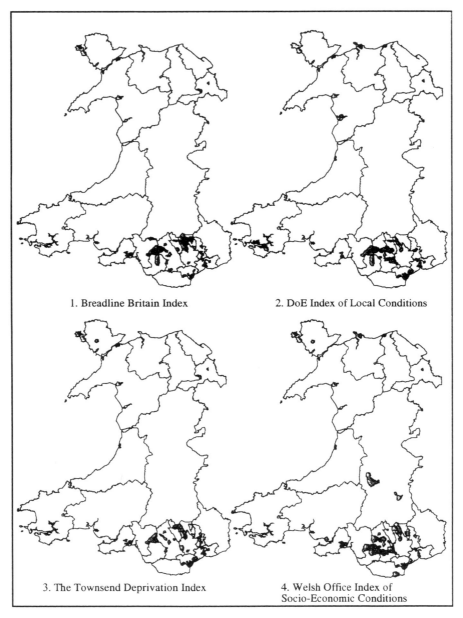

1. Breadline Britain Index

2. DoE Index of Local Conditions

3. The Townsend Deprivation Index

4. Welsh Office Index of
   Socio-Economic Conditions

FIGURE 6.7
**Most deprived 50 communities in Wales on four indicators of socio-economic
conditions**

MEASURING THE EXTENT OF RURAL DEPRIVATION

Weaknesses of current measures

Previous studies, based largely on questionnaire and ethnographic techniques, have shown that deprivation, due largely to its spatial and sectoral variation in rural areas, tends to be 'hidden' and 'undetected' in policy-relevant indicators (Scott *et al.*, 1991). The contrast between urban areas where there is often a spatial manifestation of social disadvantage has meant that area-based targeting policies are deemed to be less relevant to rural areas (Lowe *et al.*, 1986; Midwinter *et al.*, 1988; Scottish Homes, 1993; Shucksmith *et al.*, 1994a). As Shucksmith *et al.* (1994b, 33) stress 'an area-based approach is inappropriate to tackling rural disadvantage' and that 'instead, a diversity of policy responses is needed' at both national and local levels. However, despite the widely recognized view that inherent differences exist between multiply deprived households and multiply deprived areas and that area-based policies have largely failed to identify such disparities, it is also acknowledged that, from a policy perspective, area-based approaches are never going to be fully replaced and that targeting of this nature will always form a component of government policies towards rural areas. It has therefore been suggested as 'inevitable' that 'whatever the theoretical objections area-based indicators of need will be required by policy makers' (Bruce *et al.*, 1995, 17). Critics of such indicators as the DoE's Index of Local Conditions point out however that the use of such measures, largely based on urban-based variables, at a range of aggregate scales, is seriously flawed and that more effort needs to be made to incorporate measures more in-tune with the precise nature of social disadvantage. The Bruce *et al.* (1995) study of deprivation in West Cornwall, for example, drew attention to the limitations of variables such as car ownership, educational attainment and employment statistics (which are included in several of the indicators) in the context of rural deprivation studies. In the present study, the incorporation of variables such as car ownership, overcrowding and unemployment in the indexes has led to the majority of the communities falling in the most deprived quartile being located in urban areas of Wales.

Shucksmith *et al.* (1996, 26) identify the six principal factors associated with rural disadvantage as: old age (especially in association with low socio-economic groups), low wages, unemployment, low economic activity rates amongst married women, poor housing conditions and social isolation. As highlighted by the researchers, however, there is a dearth of information available with which to study these individual factors – particularly at fine spatial resolutions – such that developing an index based on these variables becomes problematic (ERI, 1996). This has meant that such research has often had to resort to the use of proxy measures of deprivation largely based on census-derived information (Cullingford and Openshaw, 1982). In one such study, Midwinter *et al.*, (1988) provide a comprehensive critique of the use of (largely) census-based indicators such as overcrowding, car ownership and a number of household amenity variables in rural Scotland – problems with which are compounded in studies of multiple deprivation, they suggest, through double counting. In addition, the dispersed nature of deprived households has meant that the use of such coarse statistics at the area level is deemed unsuitable by many local authorities and rural agencies (Hodge *et al.*, 1996). This has led researchers both to investigate the use of alternative measures of deprivation in rural contexts such as income support and benefit data (Midwinter and Monaghan, 1990) and to advocate client-based approaches to studying deprivation which recognize that deprivation is experienced by people and not areas and that, in order to gain a fuller understanding of the experiences of potentially vulnerable groups, we need to study the root causes of deprivation and to recognize the social dimension to deprivation (Townsend, 1987; Midwinter *et al.*, 1988; Shucksmith, 1990; Chapman and Shucksmith, 1996).

Despite these methodological problems, attempts have been made to apply such indicators in rural contexts. Bruce *et al.* (1995) compared the DoE's Index of Local Conditions (see Bradford *et al.*, 1995) with a variety of other indicators of disadvantage in three districts in West Cornwall. This indicator, calculated for all 366 local authority areas in England, has been criticized both for the selection and the relative weighting of variables used in its calculation (Henderson, 1994; Simpson, 1996). In their paper, Bruce *et al.* were solely concerned with the application of the index in identifying rural deprivation. This revealed that when compared with indicators such as wage levels and health status, the index (being urban-based) underestimates the level of deprivation in rural areas. The three districts studied were seen to fare differently on variables not used in the calculation of the index which were thought to be more appropriate in rural environments and on the individual composite variables leading the authors to conclude that:

> It is clear that any really robust rural deprivation index would require either different variables or the weighting of particular measures, e.g. car ownership. In practice, given the current dearth of information on rural deprivation this is an almost impossibly difficult task. (Bruce *et al.*, 1995, 20)

There are severe methodological problems in any study of this nature, many of which are not unique to rural deprivation studies (Hirschfield, 1994). A recently published review of previous studies relating to disadvantage and deprivation in the British Isles, highlighted five key data problems facing researchers in this area namely; data availability, spatial resolution, timeliness, validity and reliability (Scottish Homes, 1993). Firstly, one of the key shortcomings of data available to British researchers is the lack of data at disaggregate levels. Confidentiality constraints, for example, prevent data relating to income for such spatial units being made available to British researchers. In-depth studies of rural disadvantage could, for example, include analysis of house insurance premium data (as a proxy for crime risk; Coombes *et al.*, 1995), house transactions prices or access to leisure facilities (Sports Council for Wales, 1991). Further work would be required to assess the suitability of these variables as being appropriate quantifiable indexes of rural deprivation but, to date, there has been little empirical research in this area either due to the commercial sensitivity of the data or because it is beyond the resource capabilities of authorities to routinely collect and update such information. Secondly, there is a relative dearth of information available to researchers faced with identifying specific aspects of rural deprivation. There are no spatially consistent data series relating to wage levels in rural areas, for example, nor data on within-household variations in access to cars highlighted by many researchers as a significant factor in social isolation. Both these measures have been suggested as more appropriate indicators in rural areas (Midwinter *et al.*, 1988; Bruce *et al.*, 1995; Shucksmith *et al.*, 1994b) but the lack of nationally available statistics precludes the study of these fundamental aspects of rural deprivation. There are no indicators of public service provision in the standard deprivation measures, nor measures of (in)accessibility of facilities. The majority of such studies take no account of the accessibility dimension which previous studies have suggested represents a significant factor in the socio-economic processes that are taking place in rural areas (e.g. Clark and Woollett, 1990; Cloke *et al.*, 1994). This is particularly problematic for as Midwinter *et al.* (1988) suggest from a comparison of urban and rural approaches to deprivation studies: 'the difference is that whilst the spatial factor is a central part of rural deprivation, it merely characterises the distribution of urban deprivation but is not a central dimension of it' (Midwinter *et al.*, 1988, 46).

Studies of rural deprivation in Scotland have led researchers to suggest that a combination of such area-based targeting with client-based approaches may offer more insights into the nature of rural disadvantage (Midwinter *et al.*, 1988; Shucksmith *et al.*, 1994b, Pacione, 1995). In such cases, incorporating levels of service accessibility and variations in service provision in rural communities within existing government-derived indicators may provide a much more profitable insight into the true nature of deprivation as well as providing policy makers with improved targeting measures for existing funding mechanisms.

In addition, the recently published Government White Papers on Rural England (HMSO, 1995) and Wales (HMSO, 1996) have again drawn attention to the need for measures to reverse the decline in service provision in rural areas, with the latter, for example, reiterating the government's commitment 'to improving the services to the people who live and work in rural Wales' (Foreword by the Secretary of State for Wales, HMSO, 1996, 1). This, in turn, has focused attention on the methods by which current levels of provision can be adequately monitored including the need to create a nationally consistent baseline survey of facilities in rural areas with which to gauge change.

In this paper we draw attention to one such survey which is being collated for all rural communities in rural Wales. The survey methodology and the advantages of a national approach to the study are highlighted in the next sub-section. The use of current spatial analytical techniques, and in particular GIS, have provided the project team with a powerful array of techniques with which to assess the extent of service provision in rural Wales and to monitor change in subsequent years. Furthermore, the availability of such a database at the small area level permits an extension to existing methodologies which have focused on the use of census-based information, the use of which has largely been discredited in rural studies as neglecting explicitly rural dimensions to deprivation.

Extensions to existing indicators in rural areas

Above, we drew attention to studies which suggest that current, largely census-derived and urban-based, policy based indicators of deprivation are insensitive to the heterogeneous nature of deprivation in rural areas. A recent study by Cheshire County Council (1994), for example, noted disparities between standard indicators of disadvantage from the 1991 Census of Population and service provision as gauged from the Rural Development Commission (RDC) survey in the county, in that deprived enumeration districts were actually well served in terms of services. Clark and Woollett (1990) draw attention to previous studies which have investigated changes in service provision in rural areas and conclude that there is, as yet, no spatially or temporally consistent data source with which to gauge national trends in provision. Others have attempted a more comprehensive survey of facilities using sample-based approaches, for example, Moseley and Packman's (1985) survey of 6,000 branches of Women's Institutes in order to examine the distribution of nine so-called 'fixed' services, including post office, general foodshop, school, playgroup, butcher, GP, breadshop, library and bank, and eight mobile services. A still more comprehensive survey has been carried out by the RDC (in 1991, 1994 and 1997). This involved detailed questionnaires sent to clerks in rural parishes in England (equivalent to communities in Wales) with a population of less than 10,000. Information was collected on thirteen service categories including shops and retail, education and social services, recreation, and information and public transport, and a response rate of 80 per cent was achieved with some information from clerks being supplemented by information provided directly by the rural community councils or county councils. Analysis in the RDC reports has been confined to pre-defined population bands and is purely descriptive with tables produced expressing provision rates for service sub-groups across the population bands. Six 'essential' services were identified and variations in provision ratios analysed; namely schools, post offices, permanent shops, pubs, village halls and bus services and these were also identified in the 'Lifestyles in Rural England' project as important services in rural areas especially for less mobile members of the community (Cloke *et al.*, 1994). The 1994 survey was a follow up to the 1991 Survey of Rural Services and, as such, a large part of the report is concerned with comparative analysis of changing rates of provision over the three-year period. The RDC Report (1995) does not identify any major changes in provision rates in most service categories over the three-year period and comments are limited to comparisons of service provision rates between different counties. The question of access to services in rural areas is not explicitly considered except in as much as the levels of public transport provision by population bands is quantified.

Research in the Grampian Region of Scotland has taken this approach further through a GIS-based survey of facilities (Bochel and Chapman, 1995). The need for alternative measures of deprivation in rural areas was highlighted using a combination of census-based indicators of deprivation, such as number of single-parent households, unemployment and dependency, with access to facilities such as shops, primary schools, petrol stations, GPs and post offices. Census-based measures were judged to be inadequate in identifying deprivation in areas outside urban settlements which led the researchers to explore the use of GIS techniques to develop indicators based on the provision of services. The levels and range of services available were considered important components in maintaining the vitality of these communities. Thus, the nature of the settlements lacking these services and the changes over time in service provision in relation to settlement size permit an analysis to be made of gaps in provision across the county which can then be compared to standard Scottish Office indicators of disadvantage which have, like the policy indicators analysed in the present study, largely been developed to try to combat deprivation in urban areas, for example, through Urban Programme funding (Shucksmith *et al.*, 1994b). In addition, the disaggregate nature of the data held within the GIS permit changes in accessibility to be measured, e.g. changes in proximity to post offices. There are other important, less quantifiable, components to such studies; for example, the need for data on the quality of provision, the limitations of using straight line distances and the need to consider the ability of residents to pay for such services rather than just the geographical availability of services. Nevertheless, using the Grampian Region as a case study, the authors were able to point the way to the types of GIS-based analyses that could benefit studies of rural disadvantage. Until recently, however, there has been a dearth of appropriate data sources in Wales with which to develop alternative rural-based indicators based on factors such as the provision of services and facilities. This has been redressed with the creation of a database of public service provision at the community level which is described in more detail below.

The 1995/6 Survey of Public Service Provision in Rural Wales
Background to the survey
The RDC report (1994, 5), *Rural Services: Challenges and Opportunities*, suggests that 'the state of rural services has major implications for rural people and countryside policy' and that one of the policy goals of the RDC is that 'rural communities have reasonable and affordable access to services'. The lack of any nationally consistent baseline survey of such facilities has inevitably hindered researchers faced with investigating the implications of declining service provision. Although some of these problems have been addressed in recent RDC surveys of services in England (admittedly with sample level data), no comprehensive, spatially and temporally consistent, survey exists at the national level.

Rural deprivation studies in both England (Howes *et al.*, 1993) and Scotland (Mackay Consultants, 1989) have drawn attention to the need to develop measures of service provision, or access to facilities, in order to assess the implications of declining provision levels in rural areas. Such studies have inevitably brought into focus the types of survey methodologies most relevant to researchers concerned with analysing rural deprivation. A Welsh Consumer Council survey carried out in the late 1970s, for example, used data at the most disaggregate of levels; namely that of the individual facility. An alternative approach is to aggregate numbers of facilities to an areal unit such as the parish or community. Several recent studies have involved a combination of these techniques. This is the approach adopted in the present study. A recent research project, carried out by the authors and sponsored by the Higher Education Funding Council for Wales (HEFCW), has been concerned with assembling information on a wide range of service sectors in Wales, including health, education, emergency services, housing and transport. Large amounts of data relating to the various sectors has been collected at the individual facility level and a public services GIS has been constructed for Wales to store, analyse and display the data. The project has adopted a hierarchical data model within a GIS to allow effective, spatially referenced, organization of the information and to enable the processing of data using the range of spatial analytical functions currently available within a commercially available GIS package.

To complement and add value to the comprehensive point-level databases created for various service sectors, a large-scale survey of every sparsely populated community in Wales has recently been initiated providing a wealth of data on a range of publicly and privately supplied services at the aggregate community level. Questionnaires were sent to community council clerks in the selected communities (615 of the 866 communities in Wales) covering a wide range of services including shops and other services (including post offices, banks, petrol stations, mobile services and recycling facilities), childcare, education and day-care services, medical services, information and recreation services (including libraries, sports facilities and meeting places), emergency and security services, places of worship and public transport services. Comments were also invited with respect to current service levels and, additionally, in relation to recent changes in service provision levels. The aim has been to make the questionnaire as detailed as possible covering numerous sectors and service facilities. A response rate of 80 per cent has compared favourably with other surveys of this nature.

The survey is comparable in methodology to the work carried out by the RDC (1992, 1995) into service supply in rural parishes in England. There are, however, important enhancements associated with the present survey. The HEFCW survey is concerned, for example, with closures, or openings, of service facilities over a period of time, rather than a snapshot of the situation, and it is specific in inviting comments on the quality of service supply in the locality. The real advantage that the survey has over previous research, however, is the opportunity to combine the data with the point-level facility databases already constructed within the GIS, and the subsequent ability to perform sophisticated spatial analysis upon the various datasets. The survey, by drawing attention to the relationship between population size and service provision in rural areas, will also provide important insights into government policies based on concentrating new development and service provision in key settlements, as evidenced in Moseley and Packman's (1985) study which revealed major gaps in provision in smaller rural settlements of less than 500 population.

It is also envisaged that such surveys can feed into community-based studies such as those of Day and Murdoch (1993) in mid Wales and the Rural Lifestyles project in England (Cloke *et al.*, 1994). In particular such case study approaches could involve studying the use of such services by different sectors of the community. McLaughlin (1986), for example, found that there was a distinct differential use of such facilities with deprived groups within rural communities less likely to take up certain forms of professional services (with obvious implications for the viability of such services). Clearly the baseline survey of services could not provide the level of detail at the local level to test such hypotheses but further research will be needed to address questions of social (as well as physical) accessibility, consumer choice and service supply/demand. This inevitably needs to be tied into studies of the nature of socio-economic restructuring at the local level. In particular there is a need for detailed studies of individuals and groups of individuals who are experiencing social as well as physical isolation through household level surveys such as those carried out in Scotland (Shucksmith *et al*, 1996). Different communities will be subject to various forms of demographic changes which may have major knock on effects for the use of facilities. Evidence from mid Wales (Green and Owen, 1988), for example, suggests that the population increase in the decade 1971–81 was attributable solely to in-migration and that such trends were replicated in population projections to the end of the century suggesting older age groups will be disproportionately represented in such communities with younger, generally well-educated, groups forming the bulk of the out-migrants from parts of Powys, Dyfed and Gwynedd. The implications for service use have been under-researched but the increase in elderly, more affluent, groups within these communities, when combined with a declining birth rate, could be anticipated to affect the viability of village schools, for example, as well as having major implications for health care in rural areas (e.g. RDC, 1994). Next we highlight methods by which GIS can be used to explore such issues.

Developing a GIS-based model of survey provision for rural communities in Wales

In a previous paper we describe the survey of public services in Wales in more detail (Higgs and White, 1996). At the simplest level we can begin to use the survey as a basis for cross-tabulating provision ratios for a range of different services (health, education, transport, etc.) with government-based indicators (such as the Index of Local Conditions) and variables taken from the census. The analysis presented in the previous section suggests that these indicators are not effective in identifying rural deprivation and that an approach based on measures of service provision may, as identified in previous studies (e.g. Bochel and Chapman, 1995), be more appropriate. It should be possible, given temporal changes in services, to find out if the communities with the greatest level of disadvantage in Wales (based on such indicators) are also the ones that are losing in services. Are changes in the deprivation levels, for example, also being reflected in changes in service provision ratios and how does this, in turn, relate to the socio-economic restructuring taking place in such communities? Plots of all those census tracts beyond user specified distances of services will permit an analysis of those communities which are consistently under-served in terms of facilities and estimates of the proportion of the population potentially affected in order to investigate the potential for an overall indicator of public service provision in Wales.

Following on from this it should be possible, at the aggregate level, to identify the socio-economic characteristics of those communities (and within the confines of the ecological fallacy, the characteristics of the population within these census tracts) at specified distances – straight-line or travel-time – of service centres and hence identify 'gaps' in provision. Bochel and Chapman (1995), for example, used the Rural Facilities Information System (RUFIS) to calculate the number of service facilities, or lack of facilities, within a specified radius around a population centre. Another approach under investigation in the current project is to analyse accessibility to services such as shops, GPs and housing through a detailed study of available transport opportunities. This will involve investigating the distribution of the car-owning population at an aggregate level as determined from census information with the locations of services. However, as previous studies have identified, car ownership can be a poor proxy for accessibility where it is often the availability of a car to household members that is most important (e.g. Midwinter *et al.*, 1988).

In order to investigate changes in access to facilities, our research is also focusing on the use of the disaggregate (point) data of supply (e.g. for post offices and schools) in conjunction with population-weighted centroids (as demand points) to examine changing accessibility to services in rural Wales (White *et al.*, 1997). GIS can be used to calculate if the average distance to facilities has changed over time and to illustrate how changes in services compare with the demographic characteristics of such areas, and specifically variations in the elderly, unemployed and the young. The use of GIS for analysing and displaying this information has major advantages in that it enables a combination of point- and area-based analysis to be carried out. Data for services in the Grampian Region, for example, were used to compare the distribution of services in relation to settlement size in order to gauge the extent to which services are being concentrated in larger towns at the expense of rural areas (Bochel and Chapman, 1995).

Our future work will involve devising methods by which to incorporate and extend existing measures. We propose to build on the point- and area-based survey of facilities in Wales to incorporate accessibility measures and to examine the feasibility of applying such techniques at a variety of spatial scales in a range of policy environments. Using a combination of GIS and spatial statistics the aim is to propose a methodology of incorporating GIS-derived accessibility measures into an overall index of deprivation which is more sensitive to the true nature of disadvantage in rural areas. This will form the basis of future research efforts.

CONCLUSIONS

This paper has, firstly, been concerned with documenting the ways in which deprivation indicators are being used by UAs in Wales, and their perceived limitations, as well as the availability of alternative census- or non-census-based data sources. A major conclusion from this part of the research is that area-based measures, even accounting for their known limitations, are being used by local authorities faced with the task of deriving indexes of socio-economic conditions in the light of central government and European funding allocation processes.

Following on from this, the second section of the paper has been concerned with analysing spatial patterns in deprivation at the community level in Wales using four such area-based measures. This has revealed a relative consistency in the identification of the most deprived communities in Wales with some communities in the urban conurbations consistently appearing in the most deprived quartiles on each measure. The indicators are less adequate in highlighting deprivation in rural areas. Previous studies in Wales (e.g. Cloke and Davies, 1992; Cloke and Milbourne, 1992; Cloke *et al.*, 1995b), however, have identified rural communities which are experiencing declining levels of service provision, lack of job and housing opportunities, and low wages resulting in 'hidden' pockets of deprivation. The results from the analysis presented in this paper re-emphasize concerns over the use of current area-based indicators in the identification of particular aspects of deprivation in rural contexts and this, in turn, has drawn attention to the data sources available to researchers. This study has focused on one aspect of rural deprivation, namely changes in service provision and on the implications in terms of accessibility to such facilities for potentially vulnerable groups within such communities in Wales.

The latter part of the paper has been concerned with advocating the use of GIS approaches. GIS can be used to create a baseline survey of services with which to monitor the impacts of proposed policies such as the introduction of a new rate relief scheme targeted at general stores and post offices. Furthermore, the spatial analytical capabilities of such systems presents a methodology whereby we can begin to examine accessibility to services and to incorporate such variables in standard policy indicators used for targeting resources in rural areas. Forces that impact on service provision such as an ageing population, economic forces (financial constraints, commercial pressures), specialization in services (and the importance of new technologies and teleworking) and government policies (as espoused in the Rural White Papers) are likely to have far-reaching consequences for less mobile sections of rural communities. A number of policy documents have been produced which outline the types of policy initiatives likely to be required to improve the current situation with regard to service provision including the need to take into account the needs of rural dwellers and the importance of the planning system (RDC, 1994). It is the assertion of this paper that we need to be able not only to monitor the impacts of such forces through the kinds of spatial analytical techniques outlined, but also, given that area-based approaches to resource allocation are unlikely to be replaced entirely through a move to household welfare-based, measures, to adapt existing indicators to reflect the differential accessibility of vulnerable groups to changing services and the dispersed nature of rural deprivation. Our ongoing work will build on the 1995–6 survey of facilities in rural Wales in order to investigate the use of such measures in rural planning and policy making.

NOTE

The 'GIS in Public Service Provision' project (1994–6) was sponsored by the Higher Education Funding Council for Wales (HEFCW). The Rural Deprivation Project is sponsored by the ESRC (Grant Number R000221827). The opinions expressed in this paper are solely those of the authors and do not necessarily reflect those of the participating agencies.

APPENDIX 1
Most deprived 50 communities in Wales on Townsend Index

Community code	Community name	Unitary authority	Townsend Index	Rank
SW027	Tredegar Park	Newport	12.84	1
TT026	Townhill	Swansea	12.4	2
TT018	Penderry	Swansea	11.12	3
TE004	Gurnos	Merthyr Tydfil	11.03	4
TN002	Butetown	Cardiff	10.81	5
TD009	Pen-y-waun	Rhondda, Cynon, Taff	10.79	6
SW020	Pillgwenlly	Newport	10.65	7
TN008	Ely	Cardiff	9.42	8
SK007	Caia Park	Wrexham	9.24	9
TG014	Tylorstown	Rhondda, Cynon, Taff	8.7	10
SR003	Caldey and St Margarets Island	Pembrokeshire	8.68	11
TN001	Adamsdown	Cardiff	8.54	12
SX015	Trevethin	Torfaen	8.01	13
SW004	Bettws	Newport	7.6	14
TN022	Riverside	Cardiff	7.58	15
SK008	Cefn	Wrexham	7.55	16
SW022	Ringland	Newport	7.27	17
TG005	Maerdy	Rhondda, Cynon, Taff	6.82	18
SS008	Nantyglo and Blaina	Blaenau Gwent	6.81	19
TH012	Rhymney	Caerphilly	6.68	20
SW026	Stow Hill	Newport	6.58	21
TN017	Llanrumney	Cardiff	6.53	22
TH014	Van	Caerphilly	6.45	23
TS006	Glyncorrwg	Neath & Port Talbot	6.36	24
TT003	Bonymaen	Swansea	6.35	25
TN027	Splott	Cardiff	6.23	26
TT004	Castle	Swansea	6.22	27

Community code	Community name	Unitary authority	Townsend Index	Rank
TN003	Caerau	Cardiff	6.1	28
TN011	Grangetown	Cardiff	6.09	29
TN019	Plasnewydd	Cardiff	6.06	30
SZ002	Bangor	Gwynedd	5.9	31
TD008	Penrhiwceiber	Rhondda, Cynon, Taff	5.78	32
TJ001	Gilfach Goch	Rhondda, Cynon, Taff	5.73	33
TN029	Trowbridge	Cardiff	5.71	34
TS011	Sandfields West	Neath & Port Talbot	5.71	35
TH005	Darran Valley	Caerphilly	5.64	36
TH010	New Tredegar	Caerphilly	5.56	37
SX004	Cwmbran Central	Torfaen	5.55	38
TE008	Penydarren	Merthyr Tydfil	5.52	39
SS007	Llanhilleth	Blaenau Gwent	5.47	40
TC010	Holyhead	Anglesey	5.44	41
TE003	Dowlais	Merthyr Tydfil	5.41	42
SX016	Upper Cwmbran	Torfaen	5.36	43
SW002	Alway	Newport	5.2	44
TE006	Pant	Merthyr Tydfil	5.16	45
TH002	Bargoed	Caerphilly	5.11	46
SX014	Pontymoile	Torfaen	5.07	47
SM003	Aberystwyth	Ceredigion	5	48
TH001	Aber Valley	Caerphilly	4.95	49
TC039	Trewalchmai	Anglesey	4.92	50

APPENDIX 2
Most deprived 50 communities in Wales on Welsh Office
Index of Socio-economic Conditions

Community code	Community name	Unitary authority	Welsh Office Index	Rank
SJ007	Rhyl	Denbighshire	15.143	1
TP001	Barry	Vale of Glam.	14.184	2
TK033	Treflys	Powys	13.226	3
TN029	Trowbridge	Cardiff	12.13	4
TJ008	Pontypridd	Rhondda, Cynon, Taff	11.93	5
TN022	Riverside	Cardiff	11.898	6
TG014	Tylorstown	Rhondda, Cynon, Taff	10.554	7
TN008	Ely	Cardiff	10.497	8
SW020	Pillgwenlly	Newport	9.955	9
TT026	Townhill	Swansea	9.75	10
TN019	Plasnewydd	Cardiff	9.521	11
TD008	Penrhiwceiber	Rhondda, Cynon, Taff	9.211	12
TF013	Maesteg	Bridgend	9.101	13
SK007	Caia Park	Wrexham	9.068	14
TN011	Grangetown	Cardiff	8.722	15
TG001	Cwm Clydach	Rhondda, Cynon, Taff	8.695	16

Community code	Community name	Unitary authority	Welsh Office Index	Rank
TT018	Penderry	Swansea	8.651	17
TN001	Adamsdown	Cardiff	8.629	18
SW004	Bettws	Newport	8.21	19
SP004	Llanelli	Carmarthenshire	8.093	20
SW026	Stow Hill	Newport	7.837	21
TT004	Castle	Swansea	7.83	22
TH002	Bargoed	Caerphilly	7.797	23
TH012	Rhymney	Caerphilly	7.539	24
TN027	Splott	Cardiff	7.523	25
TG005	Maerdy	Rhondda, Cynon, Taff	7.379	26
SX015	Trevethin	Torfaen	7.371	27
TD001	Aberaman	Rhondda, Cynon, Taff	7.289	28
TT027	Uplands	Swansea	7.261	29
TF009	Garw Valley	Bridgend	7.26	30
TE004	Gurnos	Merthyr Tydfil	7.25	31
TG012	Treherbert	Rhondda, Cynon, Taff	7.197	32
SY012	Llandudno	Conwy	7.166	33
TJ010	Tonyrefail	Rhondda, Cynon, Taff	7.109	34
TD009	Pen-y-waun	Rhondda, Cynon, Taff	7.104	35
TN005	Castle	Cardiff	6.996	36
TC010	Holyhead	Anglesey	6.976	37
SS009	Tredegar	Blaenau Gwent	6.898	38
TF016	Ogmore Valley	Bridgend	6.679	39
SM003	Aberystwyth	Ceredigion	6.584	40
TK002	Bronllys	Powys	6.553	41
TH010	New Tredegar	Caerphilly	6.538	42
SS001	Abertillery	Blaenau Gwent	6.534	43
TD002	Abercynon	Rhondda, Cynon, Taff	6.488	44
TT010	Landore	Swansea	6.477	45
TN002	Butetown	Cardiff	6.431	46
TJ001	Gilfach Goch	Rhondda, Cynon, Taff	6.4	47
TF001	Brackla	Bridgend	6.355	48
TC039	Trewalchmai	Anglesey	6.276	49
TT003	Bonymaen	Swansea	6.166	50

APPENDIX 3
50 communities in Wales with highest SMRs 1990–1992

Community code	Community name	Unitary authority	SMR	Observed deaths	SMR rank
TN005	Castle	Cardiff	388.59	12	1
SK001	Abenbury	Wrexham	240.56	11	2
SN021	Myddfai	Carmarthenshire	223.97	10	3
TL022	Llanerfyl	Powys	215.33	11	4
SQ050	Walwyns Castle	Pembrokeshire	201.03	9	5
SR024	Slebech	Pembrokeshire	177.81	5	6

Community code	Community name	Unitary authority	SMR	Observed deaths	SMR rank
TH008	Maesycwmmer	Caerphilly	176.82	52	7
SR015	Manorbier	Pembrokeshire	170.43	31	8
SW020	Pillgwenlly	Newport	169.71	134	9
SQ014	Freystrop	Pembrokeshire	167.08	11	10
TD009	Pen-y-waun	Rhondda, Cynon, Taff	166.20	84	11
TL029	Llangynog	Powys	164.31	9	12
SL037	Pendine	Carmarthenshire	163.38	8	13
TC039	Trewalchmai	Anglesey	162.78	21	14
TL041	Pen-y-Bont-Fawr	Powys	161.85	9	15
TF005	Coychurch Higher	Bridgend	161.48	19	16
TK002	Bronllys	Powys	161.06	19	17
SH003	Bryneglwys	Denbighshire	160.51	10	18
SL013	Llanarthney	Carmarthenshire	157.51	19	19
TG001	Cwm Clydach	Rhondda, Cynon, Taff	156.02	74	20
TE004	Gurnos	Merthyr Tydfil	155.18	132	21
SX015	Trevethin	Torfaen	155.00	107	22
TN001	Adamsdown	Cardiff	153.74	126	23
SN013	Llanfihangel Aberbythych	Carmarthenshire	153.54	25	24
TG005	Maerdy	Rhondda, Cynon, Taff	153.50	92	25
TK029	Talybont-on-Usk	Powys	152.57	17	26
SQ017	Herbrandston	Pembrokeshire	152.34	8	27
TF014	Merthyr Mawr	Bridgend	151.17	7	28
TC001	Aberffraw	Anglesey	148.78	18	29
SW018	Nash	Newport	148.54	6	30
TG004	Llwyn-y-pia	Rhondda, Cynon, Taff	147.52	60	31
TL038	Mochdre	Powys	147.06	12	32
TN022	Riverside	Cardiff	146.75	212	33
TR010	Onllwyn	Neath & Port Talbot	146.30	30	34
SQ025	Manordeifi	Pembrokeshire	146.21	11	35
SS004	Cwm	Blaenau Gwent	145.69	83	36
SW021	Redwick	Newport	143.39	4	37
TJ001	Gilfach Goch	Rhondda, Cynon, Taff	143.24	64	38
SE009	Queensferry	Flintshire	143.14	40	39
SY010	Henryd	Conwy	142.97	16	40
TN027	Splott	Cardiff	142.53	207	41
TG014	Tylorstown	Rhondda, Cynon, Taff	141.54	125	42
SG010	Leeswood	Flintshire	141.18	38	43
SM032	Llanrhystyd	Ceredigion	140.75	17	44
TH005	Darran Valley	Caerphilly	140.70	50	45
SY007	Dolgarrog	Conwy	140.57	10	46
TF022	Ynysawdre	Bridgend	140.24	55	47
TN002	Butetown	Cardiff	139.74	70	48
TP019	St Donats	Vale of Glam.	139.71	6	49
SK017	Llay	Wrexham	139.40	89	50

APPENDIX 4
Most deprived 50 communities in Wales on DoE's Index of Local Conditions

Community code	Community name	Unitary authority	DoE Index of Local Conditions	Rank
TN022	Riverside	Cardiff	15.07	1
TG014	Tylorstown	Rhondda, Cynon, Taff	14.55	2
SJ007	Rhyl	Denbighshire	13.99	3
TN011	Grangetown	Cardiff	13.53	4
TN001	Adamsdown	Cardiff	13.46	5
SW020	Pillgwenlly	Newport	13.40	6
TN019	Plasnewydd	Cardiff	13.38	7
TT004	Castle	Swansea	12.01	8
SW026	Stow Hill	Newport	11.96	9
TN002	Butetown	Cardiff	11.81	10
TN003	Caerau	Cardiff	11.48	11
TN027	Splott	Cardiff	10.75	12
TT027	Uplands	Swansea	10.58	13
TN006	Cathays	Cardiff	9.82	14
TE003	Dowlais	Merthyr Tydfil	9.75	15
SZ002	Bangor	Gwynedd	9.09	16
SM003	Aberystwyth	Ceredigion	8.93	17
SW004	Bettws	Newport	8.63	18
SW028	Victoria	Newport	8.53	19
TN029	Trowbridge	Cardiff	8.46	20
TJ008	Pontypridd	Rhondda, Cynon, Taff	8.42	21
SR019	Pembroke Dock	Pembrokeshire	8.39	22
SW022	Ringland	Newport	8.10	23
TH012	Rhymney	Caerphilly	8.07	24
TD008	Penrhiwceiber	Rhondda, Cynon, Taff	8.06	25
TS006	Glyncorrwg	Neath & Port Talbot	8.05	26
TE004	Gurnos	Merthyr Tydfil	8.04	27
TD001	Aberaman	Rhondda, Cynon, Taff	7.97	28
TG008	Porth	Rhondda, Cynon, Taff	7.83	29
SK007	Caia Park	Wrexham	7.80	30
TN008	Ely	Cardiff	7.38	31
TN017	Llanrumney	Cardiff	7.30	32
SY012	Llandudno	Conwy	7.22	33
TG012	Treherbert	Rhondda, Cynon, Taff	7.19	34
SR018	Pembroke	Pembrokeshire	7.06	35
TG002	Cymmer	Rhondda, Cynon, Taff	7.06	36
TD007	Mountain Ash	Rhondda, Cynon, Taff	7.04	37
TT018	Penderry	Swansea	7.02	38
SQ029	Milford	Pembrokeshire	6.90	39
TH010	New Tredegar	Caerphilly	6.87	40
TG005	Maerdy	Rhondda, Cynon, Taff	6.77	41
TE005	Merthyr Vale	Merthyr Tydfil	6.68	42
TG001	Cwm Clydach	Rhondda, Cynon, Taff	6.52	43
SX014	Pontymoile	Torfaen	6.41	44
TT026	Townhill	Swansea	6.36	45

Community code	Community name	Unitary authority	DoE Index of Local Conditions	Rank
TF009	Garw Valley	Bridgend	6.34	46
SW027	Tredegar Park	Newport	6.33	47
TD004	Cwmbach	Rhondda, Cynon, Taff	6.29	48
TH002	Bargoed	Caerphilly	6.26	49
TB004	Barmouth	Gwynedd	6.25	50

APPENDIX 5
Most deprived 50 communities in Wales on the Breadline Index

Community code	Community name	Unitary authority	Breadline Index	Rank
SW027	Tredegar Park	Newport	43.3973	1
SR003	Caldey and St Margarets Island	Pembrokeshire	42.9317	2
TT026	Townhill	Swansea	42.7168	3
TE004	Gurnos	Merthyr Tydfil	40.774	4
TD009	Pen-y-waun	Rhondda, Cynon, Taff	40.2252	5
TT018	Penderry	Swansea	39.819	6
TN002	Butetown	Cardiff	38.2937	7
SK007	Caia Park	Wrexham	37.0533	8
SW020	Pillgwenlly	Newport	36.2753	9
SX015	Trevethin	Torfaen	33.8961	10
TN008	Ely	Cardiff	33.8722	11
TG014	Tylorstown	Rhondda, Cynon, Taff	33.8055	12
TG005	Maerdy	Rhondda, Cynon, Taff	33.2008	13
SW022	Ringland	Newport	33.1003	14
SK008	Cefn	Wrexham	32.8791	15
TH012	Rhymney	Caerphilly	32.8736	16
TS011	Sandfields West	Neath & Port Talbot	32.4941	17
TN001	Adamsdown	Cardiff	32.3128	18
TS006	Glyncorrwg	Neath & Port Talbot	31.8403	19
SW004	Bettws	Newport	31.6784	20
TS010	Sandfields East	Neath & Port Talbot	31.0812	21
SS008	Nantyglo and Blaina	Blaenau Gwent	30.8388	22
TH014	Van	Caerphilly	30.7216	23
TE008	Penydarren	Merthyr Tydfil	30.7135	24
TE003	Dowlais	Merthyr Tydfil	30.5382	25
SS007	Llanhilleth	Blaenau Gwent	30.4412	26
TT004	Castle	Swansea	29.6079	27
TN027	Splott	Cardiff	29.527	28
TJ001	Gilfach Goch	Rhondda, Cynon, Taff	29.4559	29
SX016	Upper Cwmbran	Torfaen	29.3185	30
SX004	Cwmbran Central	Torfaen	29.2946	31
TN003	Caerau	Cardiff	29.0222	32

Community code	Community name	Unitary authority	Breadline Index	Rank
TN017	Llanrumney	Cardiff	28.6197	33
TN022	Riverside	Cardiff	28.5393	34
TH010	New Tredegar	Caerphilly	28.4642	35
TC010	Holyhead	Anglesey	28.3267	36
TH005	Darran Valley	Caerphilly	28.3172	37
TR010	Onllwyn	Neath & Port Talbot	28.3155	38
TJ003	Llanharry	Rhondda, Cynon, Taff	28.3023	39
TT003	Bonymaen	Swansea	28.2634	40
SZ002	Bangor	Gwynedd	28.1705	41
TH002	Bargoed	Caerphilly	28.1536	42
ST004	Cefn Fforest	Caerphilly	28.1034	43
SS005	Ebbw Vale	Blaenau Gwent	28.0811	44
SW026	Stow Hill	Newport	27.9779	45
TG012	Treherbert	Rhondda, Cynon, Taff	27.9123	46
TF009	Garw Valley	Bridgend	27.8446	47
SS009	Tredegar	Blaenau Gwent	27.7741	48
TG004	Llwyn-y-pia	Rhondda, Cynon, Taff	27.7677	49
TE005	Merthyr Vale	Merthyr Tydfil	27.739	50

REFERENCES

Bochel, M. and Chapman, P. (1995). *Assessing Deprivation in Rural Scotland*, Paper presented at the Annual Meeting of the Institute of British Geographers, University of Northumbria, Newcastle.

Bradford, M., Robson, B. and Tye, R. (1995). 'Constructing an urban deprivation index', *Environment and Planning A* 27, 519–33.

Bruce, A., Gordon, D. and Kessell, J. (1995). 'Analysing rural poverty', *Local Government Policy Making* 22, 16–23.

Carstairs, V. (1995). 'Deprivation indices: their interpretation and use in relation to health', *Journal of Epidemiology and Community Health* 49, S3–S8.

Chapman, P. and Shucksmith, M. (1996). 'The experience of poverty and disadvantage in rural Scotland', *Scottish Geographical Magazine* 112, 70–5.

Cheshire County Council (1994). *Economic Disadvantage in Cheshire: Rural Disadvantage in Cheshire 1991.* Available from Research and Intelligence Unit, Resources Group, Cheshire County Council.

Clark, D.M. and Woollett, S. (1990). *English Village Services,* A report by ACRE for the Rural Development Commission, London.

Cloke, P. and Davies, L. (1992). 'Deprivation and lifestyles in rural Wales: I. Towards a cultural dimension', *Journal of Rural Studies* 8, 349–58.

Cloke, P. and Milbourne, P. (1992). 'Deprivation and lifestyles in rural Wales: II. Rurality and the cultural dimension', *Journal of Rural Studies* 8, 359–71.

Cloke, P., Milbourne, P. and Thomas, C. (1994). *Lifestyles in Rural England,* A Research Report to the Department of the Environment and the Economic and Social Research Council and the Rural Development Commission.

Cloke, P., Goodwin, M., Milbourne, P. and Thomas, C. (1995a). 'Deprivation, poverty and marginalization in rural lifestyles in England and Wales', *Journal of Rural Studies* 11, 351–65.

Cloke, P., Goodwin, M. and Milbourne, P. (1995b). '"There's so many strangers in the village now": marginalization and change in 1990's Welsh rural lifestyles', *Contemporary Wales* 8, 47–74.

Coombes, M. G., Raybould, S. R., Wong, Y. C. L. and Openshaw, S. (1995). 'Towards an index of deprivation: a review of alternative approaches', in *1991 Deprivation Index: A Review of Approaches and a Matrix of Results* (Department of the Environment) HMSO, London.

Cullingford, D. and Openshaw, S. (1982). 'Identifying areas of rural deprivation using social area analysis', *Regional Studies* 16, 409–18.

Day, G. and Murdoch, J. (1993). 'Locality and community – coming to terms with place', *Sociological Review* 41, 82–111.

Department of the Environment (1983). *Urban Deprivation Information Note 2*, Inner Cities Directorate, DoE, London.

Department of the Environment (1994). *Index of Local Conditions*, DoE, London.

ERI (Economic Research and Information) (1993). *Economic and Social Deprivation in Wales*, Economic Development and Strategic Planning Services, South Glamorgan County Council, Cardiff.

ERI (Economic Research and Information) (1996). *Indicators of Poverty: Welsh Unitary Authorities*, Research report commissioned by the National Local Government Forum Against Poverty, Cardiff Research Centre, Cardiff County Council.

Folwell, K. (1995). 'Single measures of deprivation', *Journal of Epidemiology and Community Health* 49, S51–S56.

Gordon, D. (1995). 'Census based deprivation indices: their weighting and validation', *Journal of Epidemiology and Community Health* 49, S39–S44.

Gordon, D. and Forrest, R. (1995). *People and Places II: Social and Economic Distinctions in England*, SAUS, University of Bristol.

Gordon, D. and Pantazis, C. (eds.) (1995). *Breadline Britain in the 1990s*, Report to the Joseph Rowntree Foundation, York, Joseph Rowntree Foundation.

Green A. and Owen, D. (1988). *Population and Labour Market Change in Mid Wales*, Report for Mid Wales Development Board, University of Warwick, Institute for Employment Research.

Hale, Rita and Associates (1996). *Fair Shares for Rural Areas ? An Assessment of Public Resource Allocation Systems*, Rural Research Report No. 22, Rural Development Commission, London.

Henderson, R. (1994). *Identifying local conditions: A critique of the proposals of the Department of the Environment*, BURISA (The British Urban and Regional Information Systems Association) Newsletter 115, 5–8.

Herbert, D. T. (1980). 'Urban deprivation and urban policy', in Rees, G. and Rees, T. L. (eds.) *Poverty and Social Inequality in Wales*, London, Croom Helm.

HMSO (1995). *Rural England: A Nation Committed to a Living Countryside*, Department of the Environment and the Ministry of Agriculture, Fisheries and Food, Cm 3016, HMSO, London.

HMSO (1996). *A Working Countryside for Wales*, Welsh Office Cm 3180, HMSO, London.

Higgs, G. and White, S. D. (1996). *Using a Survey of Public Service Provision at the Community Level in Studies of Disadvantage in Rural Wales*, Papers in Environmental Planning Research No. 13, Department of City and Regional Planning, University of Wales, Cardiff.

Hirschfield, A. (1994). 'Using the 1991 Population Census to study deprivation', *Planning, Policy and Practice* 9, 43–54.

Hodge, I., Dunn, J. and Monk, S. (1996). 'Redefining the Rural Development Areas: The limits of spatial targeting', *Regional Studies* 30, 207–14.

Howes, D.A., Green, M. and Kurtz, T. (1993). *Issues in the Assessment of Rural Deprivation in England*, Paper presented at AGI '93, Birmingham. AGI, London.

Lee, P., Murie, A. and Gordon, D. (1995). *Area Measures of Deprivation: A Study of Current Methods and Best Practices in the Identification of Poor Areas in Great Britain*, Centre for Urban and Regional Studies, University of Birmingham.

Lowe, P., Bradley, T. and Wright, S. (eds.) (1986). *Deprivation and Welfare in Rural Areas*, Norwich, Geobooks.

Mackay Consultants (1989). *Changes in Rural Service Provision in Scotland*, A report for the Scottish Consumer Council, Highlands and Islands Development Board and Scottish Development Agency.

McLaughlin, B. (1986). 'The rhetoric and reality of rural deprivation', *Journal of Rural Studies* 2, 291–307.

Martin, D., Senior, M. and Williams, H. (1994). 'On measures of deprivation and the spatial allocation of resources for primary health care', *Environment and Planning A* 26, 1911–29.

Mason, S. and Taylor, R. (1990). *Tackling Deprivation in Rural Areas: Effective Use of Charity Funding*, Action with Communities in Rural England (ACRE), Cirencester.

Midwinter, A., Mair, C. and Moxen, J. (1988). *Rural Deprivation in Scotland: An Investigation Into the Case of a Rural Aid Fund*, University of Strathclyde, Glasgow.

Midwinter, A. and Monaghan, C. (1990). *The Measurement and Analysis of Rural Deprivation*, Report prepared for the Convention of Scottish Local Authorities.

Morgan, K. and Price, A. (1992). *Re-building Our Communities: A New Agenda for the Valleys*, Occasional Paper, Department of City and Regional Planning, University of Wales, Cardiff.

Moseley, M. J. and Packman, J. (1985). 'The distribution of fixed, mobile and delivery services in rural Britain', *Journal of Rural Studies* 1, 87–95.

Openshaw, S. (1984). *Concepts and Techniques in Modern Geography 38: The Modifiable Areal Unit Problem*, Norwich, Geo Books.

Pacione, M. (1995). 'The geography of deprivation in rural Scotland', *Trans Inst. British Geographers* 20, 173–92.

Phillimore, P., Beattie, A. and Townsend, P. (1994). 'Widening inequality of health in northern England, 1981–1991', *British Medical Journal* 308, 1125–8.

Rural Development Commission (1992). *1991 Survey of Rural Services*, RDC, London.

Rural Development Commission (1994). *Rural Services: Challenges and Opportunities*, RDC, London.

Rural Development Commission (1995). *1994 Survey of Rural Services*, RDC, London.

Scott, D., Shenton, N. and Healey, B. (1991). *Hidden Deprivation in the Countryside. Local Studies in the Peak District National Park.* A report commissioned by the Peak Park Trust from the Department of Social Policy and Social Work, University of Manchester.

Scottish Homes (1993). *Indicators of Disadvantage and the Selection of Areas for Regeneration.* A report to Scottish Homes. Research Report No. 26.

Shucksmith, M. (1990). *'The Definition of Rural Areas and Rural Deprivation'*, Research Report No. 2, Scottish Homes, Edinburgh.

Shucksmith, M., Chapman, P., Clark, G. and Black, S. (1994a). 'Social welfare in rural Europe', *Journal of Rural Studies* 10, 343–56.

Shucksmith, M., Chapman, P. and Clark, G.M. (1994b). *Disadvantage in Rural Scotland: How is it Experienced and How Can it be Tackled ?*, Summary Report, Rural Forum Scotland.

Shucksmith, M., Chapman, P. and Clark, G.M. (1996). *Rural Scotland Today: The Best of Both Worlds ?*, Aldershot, Avebury.

Simpson, S. (1996). 'Resource allocation by measures of relative social need in geographical areas: the relevance of the signed chi-squared, the percentage and the raw count', *Environment and Planning A* 28, 537-554.

The Sports Council for Wales (1991). *Changing Times – Changing Needs,* The Sports Council for Wales, Cardiff.

Townsend, P. (1987). 'Deprivation', *Journal of Social Policy* 16, 125–46.

Townsend, P., Phillimore, P and Beattie, A. (1988). *Health and Deprivation: Inequality and the North,* London, Croom Helm.

Walford, N. and Hockey, A. (1991). 'Sources for the study of social change in the countryside: the need for integration', in Champion, T. and Watkins, C. (eds.), *People in the Countryside: Studies of Social Change in Rural Britain*, London, Chapman.

Welsh Office (1994). *Summary of Deprivation Indices used in the Welsh Office,* Statistical Directorate, Welsh Office, Cardiff.

White, S.D. and Higgs, G.(1997). *The Application of Deprivation Measures at the Community Level in Wales: A Statistical and GIS-based Approach*, Papers in Planning Research 165, Department of City and Regional Planning, University of Wales, Cardiff.

White, S.D., Guy, C.M and Higgs, G. (1997). 'Changes in service provision in rural areas, Part 2: Changes in Post Office provision in Mid Wales: A GIS based evaluation', *Journal of Rural Studies* forthcoming.

7. A MORE SEPARATE EDUCATION SYSTEM FOR WALES

Catherine M. Farrell and Jennifer Law

Education in England and Wales is frequently dealt with as one indivisible system. However, there are currently signs of an emerging Welsh education system which is more separate from England than historically has been the case. There are, for example, an increased number of educational institutions which are unique to Wales. In addition, the impact of a number of key educational reforms such as grant-maintained schools has been more limited in Wales due to a distinctive cultural and social environment. There are also proposals to develop specific initiatives such as the Welsh Baccalaureate. With the election of a Labour government, educational differences between England and Wales may be further extended, for example, with the recent White Paper for Wales and when the proposals to establish a Welsh Assembly are enacted.

This paper examines the distinctive nature of Welsh education. It is divided into three parts. Part one examines the historical development of education in Wales. Part two considers education reforms which have been introduced since 1979 and highlights the features unique to Wales. Part three focuses on the distinctive characteristics of education in Wales. Conclusions are drawn on the extent to which education in Wales differs from that of England.

THE WELSH EDUCATION SYSTEM EMERGES

The 1870 Education Act which established elementary (primary) schools and School Boards to administer education applied equally to Wales and England. However, post-elementary level education was slower to develop in England than Wales. The passing of the 1889 Welsh Intermediate Education Act produced a system of secondary schooling, provided in intermediate schools, which was unique to Wales. These schools were funded by government assistance and local rates and represent government support for post-elementary schooling which was not available at this time in England. The Central Welsh Board was established in 1896 to inspect and act as an examining body for intermediate schools. In the period 1896–1902, Wales had a separate system of secondary education in the shape of the intermediate schools which was administratively and financially distinctive from England (Jones, 1990: 4). Not only was the system in Wales quite separate, but it was considered to be so in advance of England, that it increased the pressure for similar developments in England.

Pressure to develop post-elementary education ensued in England, and as Curtis (1967) argues 'whilst affairs in Wales were being reduced to order and system, educational administration in England was growing more unwieldy'. School Boards, which had been established under the 1870 Education Act, wished to provide education for children after elementary school. In addition, England was becoming increasingly industrialized with demands for new skills and training. The Education Act 1902 allowed local education authorities in England and Wales to build secondary schools. The effect of this Act meant that in Wales, there were two types of secondary school – the intermediate county grammar schools administered by the Central Welsh Board and secondary schools administered by local education authorities and the Board of Education. Jones (1990: 27) highlights the advancement of secondary education in Wales compared with England: in 1931 the proportion of schoolchildren entering secondary schools in Wales was 19.3 per cent compared with 9.6 per cent in England. Of the number receiving secondary education in Wales, 61 per cent were educated without fees whilst in England only 44.6 per cent of children received free secondary education. Jones argues that whilst the development of secondary education in Wales prior to England demonstrated that Welsh communities were committed to its provision, the success of the initiative, however, was dependent on the response of the government based in England: 'paradoxically, only if developments in Wales meshed with political imperatives in England would these be tolerated by central government' (Jones, 1990: 32).

A Welsh Department of the Board of Education based in Whitehall was established in 1907. The establishment of the Welsh Department represented the first significant step in the advancement of the Welsh language and Welsh culture in schools within Wales (Randall, 1975: 469). Paradoxically, the promotion of 'Welshness', both in terms of the language itself and the cultural aspects of Wales, did not come from the Central Welsh Board, nor from local authorities, parents or teachers in Wales, but from the Welsh Department in London (Davies, 1973, Williams, 1988). The Department's position, argued strongly by Chief Inspector O. M. Edwards, was that the school curriculum in Wales neglected the language, literature and history of Wales. Jones (1988: 88) argues that 'parents generally deemed an examination course in French to be "superior" to one in Welsh'. The establishment of the Welsh Department served to promote the Welsh language and Welsh identity in the school curriculum.

In the post-war period, however, the uniqueness of education in Wales started to diminish. The 1944 Education Act introduced free compulsory secondary education provided in secondary modern and secondary technical schools throughout England and Wales, whilst also retaining the grammar schools. The Welsh intermediate schools were integrated into an all-England and Wales system with the repeal of the Welsh Intermediate Education Act in 1948. The integration of intermediate schools into a national system meant that the position of the Central Welsh Board was undermined. In 1947, its function as an examining body was taken over by the Welsh Joint Education Committee (WJEC). This Committee, established by Statutory Order, was constituted partly by representatives of the LEA Education Committees in Wales. All responsibility for education policy-making in Wales was retained by the Ministry of Education, while the Welsh department within the Ministry was responsible for overseeing the actual delivery of the service by LEAs.

Over time, there was growing dissatisfaction with the tripartite system (grammar, secondary modern and secondary technical) of schooling introduced in 1944. The failure of the system to achieve equality of opportunity for all children was stressed. Nationally, this led to demands for the establishment of a comprehensive system of education. In Wales, comprehensive schools were wholly encouraged in some areas, for example, Anglesey (P .E. Jones, 1988), but in other more industrial areas, such as the Rhondda Valley, the change was not welcomed. It was felt in some areas that equality of opportunity already existed in Wales. Once required to, however, education in Wales did conform to national guidelines.

Meanwhile, in the wider sphere of Welsh political and social life, campaigners in Wales argued for greater autonomy for Wales and, in 1964, the Welsh Office was established; but the Welsh Office did not gain responsibility for education until its relocation to Cardiff in 1971. Morgan (1981: 389) argues that at this stage the Welsh Office 'was really a co-ordinating department in Wales for policies conceived elsewhere'. Whilst education policies may have been formulated by the Ministry of Education, Hopkins (1989: 61) stresses that they 'have been well directed to the needs of Wales and have counted as high Welsh priorities – raising the school leaving age, dealing with pupil underachievement, examination reform, improving teacher quality'.

This examination of the development of education in Wales has revealed that in the first century of publicly provided education, the only 'exclusively Welsh' legislation was the Welsh Intermediate Education Act 1889. With the repeal of this Act in 1948, education in Wales was incorporated into an all-England and Wales education system. The existence of the Welsh Office and the position of the Welsh language and cultural tradition in the curriculum in Wales were the major factors which distinguished education in Wales from education in England.

REFORMING EDUCATION IN WALES, 1979–1997

The all-England and Wales education system existed until the major reforms in education in the mid 1980s. It was in this period that differences began to emerge in both the content and the impact of education policies between England and Wales. The agenda for educational reform in both England and Wales had been established during the 1970s. There was a perceived need for the school curriculum to focus more clearly on basic skills (Chitty, 1989: 75). This was supported by a number of so-called 'black papers' (Cox and Dyson, 1969) in this period which were influential in the creation of a new consensus on the need for educational reform. Their impact in Wales provides the focus for this section. The period has seen as an intensive phase of educational reorganization.

The Education Acts of 1980 and 1986 applied equally to England and Wales. The 1980 Act enhanced parental rights in relation to choice and involvement in schools. The Education Act II 1986 changed the constitution of school governing bodies and gave them more discretion over budgets. Since 1986, six further Education Acts have been passed: the Education Reform Act 1988; the Further and Higher Education Act 1992; the Education (Schools Performance) Act 1992; the Education (Schools) Act 1992; the Education Act 1993 and the Education Act 1994. The Education Reform Act 1988 transformed the whole system of education in England and Wales and introduced the idea of a market place with consumer choice as its chief selling point (Walford, 1994). The purpose of this was to 'bring about an improvement in the quality of educational provision by creating a system in which high quality provision is financially rewarded' (Bartlett, 1993: 125). The Act introduced a national curriculum with associated staged tests, local management of schools, open enrolment, new status schools – grant-maintained schools and city technology colleges – and placed publicly funded further and higher education within a national framework. As such, this was probably the most far-reaching of the six Education Acts.

A number of aspects of the 1988 reforms have been specific to Wales. The national curriculum, for example, is different in Wales. In broad terms, the curriculum is distinctive in two ways – the Welsh language and the Welsh 'orientation' of the curriculum. The national curriculum made Welsh a core subject in all 'Welsh-speaking' schools (schools in which more than half the basic curriculum subjects, other than English and Welsh, are taught wholly or partly in Welsh). In all other schools, Welsh is a foundation subject. As Baker (1993) has argued, the national curriculum elevated the status of the Welsh language in schools. The Welsh Office, for the first time, could insist that Welsh was taught in all schools in Wales. The requirement has been controversial in schools which are in predominantly English-speaking areas. For example, the case of three comprehensive schools which delayed the introduction of the Welsh language into the curriculum has been reported (Wenham, 1995). The statutory requirement for schools to teach Welsh as a second language in the 14–16 years curriculum has been temporarily withdrawn (September 1995) due to a shortage in the supply of teachers of the language. However, the requirement may be reintroduced in 1999.

The second major difference between the curriculum in England and Wales is that in five out of eleven subject areas, the Welsh Office has the power to determine the nature of the curriculum for schools in Wales. The Welsh Office works closely with the Curriculum and Assessment Authority in these matters. In addition to Welsh as a first and a second language, the subjects where the national curriculum is distinctive in Wales are music, art and history. In these areas the cultural, social, geographical and historical traditions of Wales – 'Y Cwricwlwm Cymreig' – must be reflected. The early efforts made by the Welsh Department of the Board of Education in developing this aspect of the school curriculum continue to differentiate Wales from England.

The introduction of grant-maintained schools and city technology colleges represented two of the more controversial elements of the 1988 legislation. Grant-maintained (or opted-out) schools receive their funding from central government. Schools which are grant-maintained (GM) operate independently from the LEA in their area and are free to purchase services required by them from the LEA or elsewhere. While provisions for GM schools in the 1988 Act were the same for England and Wales, the impact of this policy initiative has been different in Wales. Only 16 of a possible 1,925 primary and secondary schools in Wales have become GM schools. The GM sector represents 0.8 per cent of all schools in Wales in comparison with 4.5 per cent in England.

City Technology Colleges (CTCs), funded through a combination of private- and public-sector funding, provide a technology-oriented curriculum. Again, whilst the provision for these institutions was the same in England and Wales, the impact has been different; there are no CTCs in Wales. Reynolds (1994: 205) highlights the case of one comprehensive in Wales which was interested in CTC status. The informal response with which the request was allegedly met by the Welsh Office was that these institutions 'would be troublesome and controversial in Wales'.

The Education Reform Act also removed the polytechnics and other large HE institutions from LEA control and placed responsibility for these organizations with the Polytechnic and Colleges Funding Council in England, and in Wales, with the Welsh Office. With the passing of the Further and Higher Education Act 1992, higher and further education and sixth-form colleges were incorporated into a system managed by the Further and Higher Education Funding Councils for England, with a separate body responsible for these sectors in Wales. Further education and sixth-form colleges became corporate bodies in April 1993. Unlike in England, although the Further and Higher Education Councils in Wales exist as separate bodies, their duties are formally the responsibility of one Chief Executive. This is largely because of the smaller size of these sectors in Wales.

School inspection arrangements are also different in Wales. The Office of Her Majesty's Chief Inspector of Schools (OHMCI) in Wales was established in 1992 to undertake this function. Responsibility for inspection in England lies with the Office for Standards in Education (OFSTED). Schools in Wales operate on a five-year inspection plan and not four years as in England. The relationship between the head of OHMCI, Roy James, and the teaching profession in Wales is reported to be more 'friendly' than the sometimes antagonistic relations between Chris Woodhead and schools in England. The Chief Inspector for Wales has provided positive criticism and support to teachers but has not become involved in conflict with the profession. Under OHMCI's new leadership, these constructive relationships are likely to continue.

The Education Act 1993 was concerned with the management of the GM sector. In England, the Funding Agency for Schools was created and in Wales, the Schools Funding Council gained responsibility for the funding arrangements of grant-maintained schools. The Schools Funding Council for Wales has not yet been established due to the small size of this sector in Wales. This function is currently undertaken by the Welsh Office. The 1993 Act also introduced 'Educational Associations'. These come into operation in schools which are identified as 'at risk' of failing to fulfil their commitment to the provision of an acceptable standard of education in an Inspector's report. Unlike England, Wales has not yet witnessed the establishment of an Educational Association to deal with 'failing' schools.

The 1994 Education Act placed responsibility for the training of teachers in England with the Teacher Training Authority (TTA). Initially in Wales, responsibility for teachers and related activities was shared between the Higher Education Funding Council, and the Welsh Office, with some aspects of teacher training also held by the TTA. More recently, a separate unit of the TTA has been established in Wales to undertake these duties.

The reforms which have been introduced in education have significantly changed the system in both England and Wales. Whilst Wales shared many of the reforms with England, some aspects of the reforms have been distinctive. In addition to differences in the content of education policies, the impact of some of the reforms has been different in Wales. It can be argued that education in Wales is more distinct in the post-reform era than at any stage since 1948. This trend is likely to continue in the future. In part, this may be due to the establishment of a range of new educational institutions which have a separate 'Welsh remit'.

SEPARATE INSTITUTIONS – POLICY DIFFERENCES?

The central question for this section of the paper is: in what respects do key institutions make education in Wales distinctive from England? One of the most important of these institutions is the Welsh Office. While part of the system of England and Wales, education in Wales is directed by the Welsh Office. Although Jones argues that the 'existence of the Welsh Office and its education department legitimises Welsh claims to some differences of treatment' (G.E. Jones 1988: 91), he also argues that in practice the 'circulars which emanate from the Department of Education and Science (DFE, now the Department for Education and Employment, DFEE) emerge simultaneously from Cathays Park, differently numbered and signed by a different hand, usually with a common content'. In line with the education service in England, education in Wales is locally administered by education departments within local authorities. The existence of the Welsh Office establishes a separate administrative structure for education in Wales.

Whilst it can be argued that the role of the Welsh Office is to apply the legislative reforms conceived in Westminster to Wales, the Welsh Office has some capacity to adopt separate education policies. According to Farrell and Law (1995), the Welsh Office has two roles in education: policy exclusion and policy development. The Welsh Office may exclude Wales from policies introduced in England on the basis that they are not appropriate for Wales. The decision not to introduce aspects of the Education Act 1993 in Wales provides an example of the capacity of the Welsh Office to reject some aspects of national policy in Wales. The requirement in the 1993 Act for schools to hold an annual ballot to consider GM status was not introduced in Wales. A complete reversal of this decision came with the passing of the Education (Annual Consideration of Ballot on GM status (Wales)) Order 1994. It is not clear why the initial exclusion of Wales from the legislation was later reversed.

The role of the Welsh Office may also be one of developing separate education policies in Wales. Two recent policy initiatives introduced by the Welsh Office provide examples of Welsh Office activity in developing separate education policies in Wales. The first of these is *People and Prosperity: An Agenda for Action in Wales* (January 1995) – the 'Popular Schools' initiative, concerned with the provision of additional capital resources to schools which are achieving good examination results. These resources are intended to enable school expansion. Schools, through their LEAs, are required to bid competitively for these funds. The second initiative, *A Bright Future: Getting the Best for Every Pupil in Wales* (April 1995), proposes clear targets for pupil achievement. Under this initiative, every school has to announce to parents its targets for improving the performance of its pupils. Initially the Welsh Office had not imposed attainment targets on schools, rather schools were responsible for identifying these. However, the new Government has announced that it will set literacy and numeracy targets for schools in England and Wales. Peter Hain, the Welsh Education Minister, has stressed that Wales would have its own 'tough, but realistic targets' (Dalingwater, 1997a). Both the 'Popular Schools' initiative and 'A Bright Future' are directed to the promotion of the market in education in Wales – one through the provision of resources and the other via information to parents. In relation to the 'Popular Schools'

initiative, the DFEE, in contrast to the Welsh Office, is pursuing a strategy
of supporting the 'weakest' schools, rather than the 'best', with additional
finance. The separate White Paper (Welsh Office 1997) for education
indicates that the new Government seeks to develop further the uniqueness
of education in Wales. As highlighted by Peter Hain (1997):

> Education here [in Wales] is different. Solutions tailored for big English cities
> are not always right for our schools. Wales has its own culture and its own
> needs. We have a proud heritage of commitment to education. We have our
> own language which must be nurtured at every opportunity. We have close
> communities where schools can thrive.

The development of education institutions in Wales has been particularly
marked since the Education Reform Act 1988. The reforms have provided
the opportunity for the Welsh Office to adopt administrative structures in
Wales separate from bodies with responsibilities for England and Wales. All
of the organizations established are 'quangos' accountable to the Secretary
of State for Wales for a range of education activities. Some of these took on
new responsibilities, such as those relating to the curriculum in Wales
(Curriculum and Assessment Authority). Others gained responsibility for
aspects of education which had either been the responsibility of LEAs in
Wales, or which had not been held previously in Wales. LEAs in Wales have
lost responsibility for sixth-form, further and some elements of higher
education to the Further and Higher Education Funding Councils. In terms
of new powers, the transfer of responsibility for higher education in Wales
from the DFEE to the Higher Education Funding Council meant that Wales
gained responsibility for this area of education. Reynolds (1994: 204) refers
to these developments as the 'emerging Welsh education polity'. These
institutions have a role in ensuring that education policies delivered in Wales
meet 'Welsh' objectives. For example, the Chair of the Curriculum and
Assessment Authority in Wales, whilst supporting the Dearing recommendations on the national curriculum in England, commented that 'we are
concerned, however, to make sure that we are meeting the particular
conditions in Wales' (Plaut, 1994). The Authority has consulted widely with
the teaching profession in Wales on its recommendations on the national
curriculum (Reynolds, 1995).

The development of these new institutions has added to the already
existing policy community in Wales. Due, in part, to its small size, relations
within the education community are closer than those that exist in England.

For example, the relationship between the Welsh Office and LEAs is relatively informal. As argued by Osmond (1985: 253) 'it is possible for the Welsh Office civil servants to establish personal relationships and acquire detailed knowledge of just 45 councils in a way that it is much more difficult for Department of the Environment officials who have to deal with hundreds of local authorities in England'. These close and informal relationships are likely to be further enhanced with the reported consultation between the new Welsh Office Ministers and teaching unions on the issue of education standards (Dalingwater, 1997b).

The establishment of the new institutions is likely to have a major impact on education in Wales. As they develop their roles, these bodies are likely to strengthen the emerging differences in education between England and Wales. Reynolds (1996:15) states that 'although we do not at present have in place very distinctive Welsh policies, it is important to realise that we do have in place a distinctive organizational infrastructure to implement them'. A number of recent education policies have been criticized for not sufficiently meeting the needs of Wales. Plaid Cymru, for example, has accused the Government of 'continuing its policy of imposing solutions to English educational problems on the people of Wales' (cited in Dalingwater, 1997c). The party is critical of proposals from the Curriculum and Assessment Authority for Wales relating to the future of A Levels. Another example is the introduction of nursery education vouchers. This policy was particularly controversial in Wales. The National Association of Head Teachers, for example, opposed the vouchers on the basis that nursery education is already offered to 90 per cent of four-year-olds in Wales (cited in Wightwick, 1995). The nursery voucher scheme has already been abolished in Wales, in advance of similar action in England. Given the Welsh electorate's support for the Government's proposals for a Welsh Assembly, additional institutional change may very well occur now. Since one of the aims of the Assembly is to ensure that the 'actions of government in Wales match the priorities of the people of Wales' it is likely that education policies will be further differentiated from those in England (Labour Party 1997: 5). An example of a policy that the Assembly could develop is the Welsh Baccalaureate which has been proposed by David and Jenkins (1994) and supported by the Institute of Welsh Affairs. The development of this curriculum and examination system would undoubtedly further enhance the differences between education in England and Wales.

CONCLUSION

This paper has examined the development of education in Wales and the educational reforms which have been introduced by successive Conservative administrations. The distinctive characteristics of the education service in Wales have been highlighted. The separate nature of education in Wales was removed by the Education Act 1944 which brought intermediate secondary education in Wales into the national system of England and Wales. Between 1944 and 1988, education in Wales operated within the national England and Wales framework of education. Educational reform since 1988 has created some differences in both the content and impact of education policies in Wales. It has also established a number of new educational institutions which have the potential to contribute to the development of more specifically 'Welsh' policies. As a consequence, whilst part of the system of England and Wales, education in Wales has become more separate in the post-Reform Act era. Separate policies for Wales, more focused on needs in Wales, are likely to develop with the establishment of a Welsh Assembly.

NOTE

The Joseph Rowntree foundation has supported this project as part of its programme of research and innovative development projects, which it hopes will be of value to policy makers and practitioners. The facts presented and views expressed in this paper are, however, those of the authors and not necessarily those of the Foundation.

REFERENCES:

Baker, C. (1993). 'Bilingual education in Wales', in H. B. Beardsmore (ed.), *European Models of Bilingual Education,* Clevedon, Multilingual Matters Ltd.

Bartlett, W. (1993). 'Quasi-markets and educational reforms', in J. Le Grand and W. Bartlett (eds.), *Quasi Markets and Social Policy,* Basingstoke, Macmillan.

Chitty, C. (1989). *Towards A New Education System – The Victory of the New Right?,* London, The Falmer Press.

Cox, C. B. and Dyson, A. E. (eds.) (1969). *Fight for Education: A Black Paper.* London, The Critical Quarterly Society.

Curtis, S. J. (1967). 'History of education in Great Britain', in J. A. Davies (1973), *Education in A Welsh Rural County 1870–1973,* Cardiff, University of Wales Press.

Dalingwater, A. (1997a). 'Wales will set its own numeracy targets, says Hain', *Western Mail,* 14 May.

Dalingwater, A. (1997b). 'Hain asks for union help to lift standards', *Western Mail,* 16 June.

Dalingwater, A. (1997c). 'Clash over future of A Levels', *Western Mail*, 12 February.

David, J. O. and Jenkins, D. D. O. (1994). 'Welsh Baccalaureate Cymru' paper presented at the Institute of Welsh Affairs Conference, March 1995.

Davies, J. A. (1973). *Education in A Welsh Rural County 1870-1973*, Cardiff, University of Wales Press.

Farrell, C. M. and Law, J. (1995). *Educational Accountability in Wales*, York, York Publishing Services for the Joseph Rowntree Foundation.

Hain, P. (1997). 'Crusade for the best schools', *Western Mail*, 8 July.

Hopkins, K. (1989). 'Educational administration and policy making 1889–1989', Conference on Centenary of Welsh Intermediate Education Act 1889.

Jones, G. E. (1988). 'What are schools in Wales for? Wales and the Education Reform Act', in G. Day and G. Rees (eds.), *Contemporary Wales*, 2.

Jones, G. E. (1990). *Which Nation's Schools? Direction and Devolution in Welsh Education in the Twentieth Century*, Cardiff, University of Wales Press.

Jones, P. E. (1988). 'Some Trends in Welsh Secondary Education 1967–1987' in G. Day and G. Rees (eds.), *Contemporary Wales*, 2.

Labour Party (1997). *New Labour because Wales Deserves Better*, Manifesto.

Morgan, K. O. (1981). *Wales, Rebirth of a Nation 1800–1980*, Cardiff, University of Wales Press.

Osmond, J. (1985). 'The dynamic of institutions', in J. Osmond, *The National Question Again – Welsh Political Identity in the 1980s*, Dyfed, Gomer.

Plaut, R. (1994). The Curriculum Council for Wales *Newsletter,* March, Cardiff, Curriculum Council for Wales.

Randall, P.J. (1975). 'The origins and establishment of the Welsh Department of Education', *The Welsh History Review*, Vol.7, No.4, 450–71.

Reynolds, D. (1994). 'Building our national identity: education policy and a Welsh parliament', in J. Osmond, *A Parliament for Wales*, Dyfed, Gomer.

Reynolds, D. (1995). 'Education policies in Wales 1978–1994: from problems to policies?', in W. Bellin, J. Osmond and D. Reynolds, *Towards an Education Policy for Wales*, Cardiff, Institute of Economic Affairs.

Reynolds, D. (1996). 'Creating an education system for Wales', *Welsh Journal of Education*, Spring No.1, 4–21.

Walford, G. (1994). *Choice and Equity in Education*, London, Cassell.

Welsh Office (1995) *People and Prosperity: An Agenda for Action in Wales*, Cardiff, HMSO.

Welsh Office (1995). *A Bright Future: Getting the Best for Every Pupil in Wales*, Cardiff, HMSO.

Welsh Office (1996). *A Bright Future: More Self-Government for Schools in Wales*, Cardiff, HMSO.

Welsh Office (1997). *Building Excellent Schools Together*, Cardiff, HMSO.

Wenham, L. (1995). 'Rage over last schools to teach Welsh', *Western Mail*, 7 August.

Wightwick, A. (1995). 'Headteachers reject nursery scheme', *Western Mail*, 18 December.

Williams, T. I. (1988). 'Language, religion, culture', in T. Herbert and G. E. Jones, *Wales 1880–1914*, Cardiff, University of Wales Press.

8. THE FATE OF THE WELSH CLERGY: AN ATTITUDE SURVEY AMONG MALE CLERICS IN THE CHURCH IN WALES

Susan H. Jones and Leslie J. Francis

INTRODUCTION

Listening to the morale of the clergy may well prove to be a good indicator of the health of religion toward the end of the twentieth century. It is surprising, therefore, that so little recent attention has been given to this area by sociologists of religion, apart perhaps from research concerned particularly with the role of women clergy, like the studies conducted in the USA by Carroll, Hargrove and Lummis (1983) and Lehman (1985), in the UK by Nason-Clark (1984) and Lehman (1987), or in New Zealand by Pym (1992). A more broadly based approach to researching the Anglican clergy in England was pioneered in the 1960s by two British sociologists, Robert Towler and Anthony Coxon in a book, published a decade after the empirical research had been conducted, with the provocative title *The Fate of the Anglican Clergy* (Towler and Coxon, 1979). This initiative was followed by a second study in England by Ranson, Bryman and Hinings (1977) comparing the responses of Anglicans, Methodists and Roman Catholics under the simple title, *Clergy, Ministers and Priests*. There was also a study by Blaikie (1979), under the more dramatic title of *The Plight of the Australian Clergy*. More recent and more narrowly focused studies of clergy in England have concentrated on issues concerned with rural ministry (Davies, Watkins and Winter, 1991), the ordination of women (Aldridge, 1989), liturgical change (Aldridge, 1986), stress (Fletcher, 1990), role (Rutledge, 1994; Francis and Rodger, 1994a) and personality (Francis, 1991; Francis and Rodger, 1994b; Francis and Kay, 1995; Francis and Robbins, 1996a).

The clergy of the Church in Wales had almost entirely escaped empirical research until a few studies initiated during the 1990s began to map their attitudes towards issues like baptismal policy (Thomas, 1994), pastoral provision (Harris and Startup, 1994, 1996), poverty and social need in their parishes (Gregory, 1995), and women in ministry (Francis and Robbins, 1996b). These clergy, however, are a particularly interesting group among whom to base research for at least four reasons. To begin with, the Church in Wales is a comparatively small, but autonomous, province of the Anglican church. The whole province is divided into just six dioceses and supports fewer than 700 stipendiary clergy (Brierley and Hiscock, 1993). Second, the province gives the impression of generating a tightly knit network among the clergy. While firmly rooted in the Anglican communion, there is a clear sense of not being part of the Church of England since disestablishment in 1920 (Walker, 1976; Price, 1990). Third, while being disestablished, there is a clear sense of identity between the Church in Wales and being Welsh. The liturgical, pastoral and administrative life of the Church in Wales is firmly rooted in a bilingual community which is committed to promoting the Welsh language. Fourth, while currently trying to assert its rootedness in Welsh language and culture, the history of the English roots of the Anglican church in Wales continues to distinguish the Church in Wales from the indigenous strands of the Welsh independent churches.

In an earlier study published in *Contemporary Wales*, Francis and Robbins (1996b) provided an in-depth study of women clergy in the Church in Wales immediately prior to the Governing Body's decision to ordain women to the priesthood. It traced the experiences of women clergy from the onset of their call to ministry, through the selection and training processes, into their work in parish ministry, and explored the attitudes of women clergy to issues like collaborative ministry, inclusive language and the distinctive contribution which women may make to the total ministry of the church. Throughout this study attention was focused on the voice of women clergy, while the voice of men clergy was silent. The aim of the present study, therefore, is to redress the balance by reporting the findings of a research project involving an attitude survey among male clergy ordained in the Church in Wales since 1971.

NATURE OF THE RESEARCH

The present study developed from a concern expressed by the Board of Ministry of the Church in Wales regarding the proportion of clergy selected, trained and ordained in the province who subsequently cease to function as clergy within the Church in Wales. As a consequence of this initiative, the project received the full support and backing of the Secretary of the Board of Ministry and of the Chair of that Board, the Archbishop of Wales. While the study has its roots in a practical concern expressed by the Board of Ministry, the design of the research, the analysis of the data, and the interpretation of the findings were properly left to the independent responsibility of the present authors.

Sample

In view of the specific question raised by the Board of Ministry, the sample was defined as all clergy ordained in the Church in Wales over the twenty-two-year period between 1971 and 1992. The ordination lists of the six dioceses produced 708 names of men and women ordained to both stipendiary and non-stipendiary ministry. The current addresses of these individuals were identified mainly from information held by the Church in Wales or recorded in *Crockford's Clerical Directory*, with the informal grape-vine, so well developed in a small province, filling many of the gaps. Of the 708 originally ordained, 33 had died and only three others proved untraceable. This left a mailing list of 672 names.

Questionnaires were mailed to all 672 identified clergy, including those who had retired, left ministry for secular employment, moved to active ministry in another Anglican province or in another denomination, and even a few who were serving time in prison. The questionnaire was accompanied by a letter of commendation from the Archbishop of Wales and a prepaid return envelope. Each questionnaire was numbered to enable follow-up of non-respondents. Over a period of time, 550 questionnaires were thoroughly and carefully completed, making a satisfactory response rate of 82 per cent. In addition, a few partially completed questionnaires were returned, with one or more sections left incomplete. It was decided to treat such questionnaires as an indicator of an unwillingness to co-operate fully in the project and they were not included in calculating the response rate or in the final analysis.

The comments the clergy made about receiving and completing the questionnaire reveal a wide range of opinion. Some of the comments were clearly affirmative about the whole concept of the research project. One cleric wrote: 'I am glad the Church in Wales is sufficiently concerned about the feelings and needs of clergy to undertake a survey of this nature.' Other clergy, however, were less supportive of the project, as illustrated by one cleric who wrote: 'It is all very nice for these questionnaires to provide you with data to fill in your day's work, but I would be grateful if you could tell me something of its worth.' Overall the data demonstrated that a quarter (24.5%) of those ordained in the Church in Wales between 1971 and 1992 were serving in another part of the Anglican communion or had taken up secular employment. Moreover, the majority of those who move away from ministry in the Church in Wales do so within the first four years after ordination. Within this period 15 per cent of clerics were recorded as having left the Church in Wales.

Questionnaire
The questionnaire employed in the survey was designed almost entirely to avoid using open-ended questions. All the questions, therefore, involved the use one of three main types of pre-coded response formats. The questionnaire contained five main sections.

The first part was constructed to discover information about the clergy's background, including issues like: where they were born and educated; where they lived before ordination; how often they and their parents attended church and chapel while they were growing up. Questions were asked about their selection for training, about their ordination, first curacy and current ministry. The majority of these questions were in multiple-choice format. Part two was designed to discover the attitudes of the clergy towards a wide range of experiences associated with ministry in the Church in Wales. This section contained 146 clearly formed attitudinal statements, rated on a five-point Likert scale: *agree strongly, agree, not certain, disagree* and *disagree strongly*. The third section of the questionnaire contained the short form of the Revised Eysenck Personality Questionnaire (Eysenck, Eysenck and Barrett, 1985). This instrument provides four scales, of twelve items each, designed to measure extraversion, neuroticism and psychoticism and to produce a lie scale. Each item is rated on a dichotomous scale: *yes* and *no*. Part four of the questionnaire contained a specifically modified form of the Maslach Burnout Inventory (Maslach and Jackson, 1986), shaped for use among British clergy. This modified instrument provides three scales, of ten items each, designed to measure emotional exhaustion, depersonalization and personal accomplishment. Each item is rated on a five point scale: *agree strongly, agree, not certain, disagree* and *disagree strongly*. The final section provided the opportunity for some more discursive open-ended responses.

The questionnaire was constructed after a series of conversations with Church in Wales clergy, to ensure that the right range of questions was being asked in appropriate language. The penultimate draft of the questionnaire was given to a sample of six clergy who were asked to respond to the questions and to help develop the questionnaire. In particular they were asked to comment on the difficulties they encountered in answering the questions and the amendments they felt should be made. The questionnaire was revised in the light of these comments.

SURVEY RESULTS

From this enormously rich database, the present analysis aims to profile the attitudes of one important subgroup of clergy. These are the male clergy, ordained in the Church in Wales between 1971 and 1992, who are currently active in full-time stipendiary parochial ministry within the Church in Wales. This subgroup contained 309 individuals. It is on the basis of the replies of these 309 individuals that the rest of this paper is constructed. This is a crucial group for understanding the morale of the Church in Wales for two reasons. First, the parochial stipendiary ministry provides the backbone for the Church in Wales. These are the clergy who are in day-to-day contact with both the pastoral work and the mission of the Church in Wales. Second, the clergy who have been ordained in the Church in Wales and decided to stay in active parochial ministry within the province may be assumed to be those best able to know the strengths and weaknesses of the Church in Wales as viewed from the inside.

In studying the attitudes of this particular subgroup of clergy, it is necessary to keep in mind what, by very definition, they do *not* represent. Because the database did not begin until the cohort ordained in 1971, clergy ordained before 1970 are excluded. Because the focus of the analysis is on perceptions of ministry in Wales, those who have ceased to minister in Wales are excluded. Because the concern is with full-time stipendiary parochial ministry, those who have retired or are engaged in non-stipendiary or non-parochial ministry are excluded. Because the ministry of women remains so different from the ministry of men, female deacons are excluded. In addition, at the time when the research was undertaken the Church in Wales had not yet ordained women to the priesthood. Because the interest of the study is with those ordained in the Church in Wales, clergy ordained elsewhere, for example in the Church of England, and who have moved into the Church in Wales are excluded. Having defined carefully both what the subgroup represents and what it does not represent, for the sake of economy the respondents will be referred to henceforth simply as *the clergy*.

The following analysis profiles the attitudes of the male clergy, ordained in the Church in Wales between 1971 and 1992, who are currently active in full-time stipendiary parochial ministry, under twelve main headings, described as follows: (i) an overview of the clergy's impressions of working in the Church in Wales; (ii) an examination of attitudes to living in Wales; (iii) the question of the Welsh language; (iv) views on how well theological colleges prepared the clergy for ministry in Wales; (v) overall satisfaction with ministry; (vi) perceptions of the provincial structures; (vii) an examination of the place of churchmanship in the Church in Wales; (viii) attitudes towards the liturgy of the Church in Wales; (ix) the clergy's views regarding their bishops; (x) the issue of the pastoral care of the clergy; (xi) the contrast in clergy attitudes to the Church of England and to the Church in Wales; (xii) the level of exhaustion experienced by the clergy.

The Church in Wales: an overview
The data clearly reveal a love-hate relationship between the clergy and the Church in Wales as a whole. The vast majority of the clergy (76%) agree that they feel a great loyalty to the Church in Wales. This is perhaps understandable given the fact that these are the very individuals who have decided to stay. None the less, many of them are not slow in voicing criticisms of the present Church structures. Three areas in particular come in for major criticism. The first concerns the overall mood of conservatism within the Church in Wales. Nearly three-fifths (56%) of the clergy complain that the Church in Wales is too conservative. The second area concerns the way in which appointments are made to parishes. Again some three-fifths (60%) of the clergy complain that the patronage system in the Church in Wales needs reform. The third area concerns the whole problem of operating in such a small province.

    While only a small number of clergy (17%) feel that in principle the Church in Wales is too small to maintain a full provincial structure, many more are very conscious of the dangers and difficulties of working in such a tightly knit community. For example, two-fifths (41%) of the clergy feel that the Church in Wales is too incestuous, while nearly half (47%) complain that everybody knows everybody else's business in the Church in Wales. Against this negative view, 45 per cent maintain that there is a helpful feeling of intimacy in the Church in Wales, and only a quarter (23%) would go so far as to say that the Church in Wales is too small to be healthy.

Living in Wales
For many of the clergy who choose to continue to work in the Church in Wales, some of the attraction is remaining part of the wider Welsh culture

and environment. Nearly two-thirds (63%) of the clergy express the view that Welsh culture is important to them. Nearly as many (55%) go so far as to say that they feel great loyalty to Welsh culture. Only a small minority of the clergy feel disadvantaged by living in Wales. Thus, 16 per cent say that they feel excluded by Welsh culture. Looking at specific aspects of life, 9 per cent feel socially deprived living in Wales, another 9 per cent feel intellectually deprived, 10 per cent feel culturally deprived, 12 per cent feel professionally deprived, and 13 per cent feel spiritually deprived living in Wales. The one major area of concern about living in Wales arises in connection with the educational opportunities for children. As many as two-fifths (41%) of the clergy express the view that insistence on the Welsh language in schools can limit educational opportunities for some children.

Welsh language

The clear commitment to the Welsh language can be seen both as a major strength and as a potential source of weakness. The strength lies in the unambiguous statements that the Church in Wales is not simply an extension of the Church of England into Wales and that the Church in Wales identifies with the Welsh language cause. The potential weakness may lie in the marginalization of significant numbers of monoglot laity and clergy. Overall, a higher proportion of clergy consider bilingualism to be a strength than consider it to be a weakness. While half (50%) of the clergy agree that bilingualism is a major strength in the Church in Wales, the proportion falls to just over a third (36%) of the clergy who agree that bilingualism is a major problem in the Church in Wales.

The clergy themselves are well aware of the significant dangers in the emphasis placed on the Welsh language. As many as one in four (24%) of the clergy feel that the Church in Wales makes non-Welsh-speaking clergy feel excluded. A similar proportion (24%) feel that it is too difficult for non-Welsh-speaking clergy to establish themselves in the Church in Wales. The proportion rises to two in five (40%) who feel that the Church in Wales puts too much emphasis on the clergy's ability to speak Welsh, while 42 per cent feel that it is too difficult for non-Welsh-speaking clergy to move post freely in the Church in Wales. The proportion rises even further to well over a half (55%) who feel that it is too difficult for non-Welsh-speaking clergy to be accepted in senior posts of responsibility in the Church in Wales.

On the other hand, there is a significant proportion of clergy for whom the Welsh language is personally important or who feel that the Church in Wales should put greater emphasis on the Welsh language. Nearly half

(46%) of the clergy agree that the Welsh language is important to them, while a quarter (26%) of the clergy agree that the Church in Wales should put more emphasis on the clergy's ability to speak Welsh. What is also clear from the data is that the vast majority of the clergy appreciate the need for more Welsh-speaking clergy. Thus, over three-quarters (78%) of the clergy agree that the Church in Wales needs more Welsh-speaking clergy. At the same time, very little resentment is shown towards the appointment of monoglot clergy in appropriate places. Only 6 per cent of the clergy take the view that the Church in Wales gives too many posts to non-Welsh-speaking clergy.

Initial training

Before being ordained in the Church in Wales, the majority of clergy currently serving in full-time stipendiary parochial ministry will have attended a full-time residential theological college. Many will have trained in Wales at St Michael's College, Llandaff, or, prior to the decision to close this institution in the summer of 1976, at Burgess Hall, Lampeter. Others will have been trained at one of the theological colleges in England.

The clergy's views of the adequacy of their initial training varies greatly from one area of ministry to another. There is general consensus that theological college prepared them well for taking Sunday services, but less consensus that theological college did such a good job in certain other areas. The following statistics show the proportions of clergy who feel their theological college prepared them well for specific areas of ministry: conducting Sunday services (84%), hospital visiting (73%), preaching (65%), work with the bereaved (65%), pastoral visiting (63%), work with schools (42%), work with children (40%), marriage counselling (36%), work with teenagers (26%) and parish administration (25%). In addition to these general areas of ministry, the clergy were less confident that their theological college had prepared them well for certain aspects of ministry *in Wales*. For example, while 46 per cent felt their theological college had prepared them well for ministry in urban Wales and 44 per cent felt their theological college had prepared them well for ministry in suburban Wales, only 22 per cent felt they had been prepared well for ministry in the Welsh industrial valleys. Only 12 per cent felt their theological college had prepared them well for ministry in rural Wales. It is significant that the Church in Wales has a large number of rural parishes.

The clergy also generally felt inadequately prepared for life in Wales itself. Only one in five (20%) of the clergy felt their theological college had prepared them well for becoming part of the local Welsh community, with a similar proportion (20%) thinking that their theological college had prepared them well for conducting bilingual liturgy. One in seven (14%) of the clergy felt their theological college had prepared them well for working in bilingual communities and only one in twelve (8%) felt their theological college had prepared them well for pastoral work in Welsh-speaking communities.

Satisfaction in ministry

Overall, the majority of the clergy ordained in the Church in Wales who have decided to stay in full-time stipendiary parochial ministry in the province report that they have found their ministry rewarding. They are clear, however, that they have found their ministry more rewarding in some areas than in others. The clearest consensus is that they have found the experience of ministry in the Church in Wales *personally* rewarding. There is less consensus that their ministry has been *spiritually* rewarding and less consensus still that it has been *professionally* rewarding. Considerably fewer clergy have found their ministry *intellectually* rewarding. More than three-quarters (77%) of the clergy say that their experience of the Church in Wales has been personally rewarding. The proportion falls to two-thirds (66%) who say that their experience of the Church in Wales has been spiritually rewarding, and to three-fifths (61%) who say that their experience of the Church in Wales has been professionally rewarding. Less than two-fifths (37%) of the clergy feel that their experience of the Church in Wales has been intellectually rewarding.

Provincial structure

The way in which the Church in Wales attempts to maintain a full provincial structure may be seen as both a strength and a weakness, viewed from different perspectives. The strength would be found in guaranteeing that a distinctive Welsh perspective could be brought to matters like liturgy and doctrine. The weakness would be found if, in practice, such aims were not properly realized. Overall the clergy remain very doubtful about the success of many aspects of the provincial structure. Thus, less than one in five feel that the Church in Wales's doctrine commission is effective (17%) or that the Church in Wales's liturgical advisory commission is effective (18%). The main boards of the Church have also failed to generate confidence. Only one in eight (13%) of the clergy feel that the ministry committee (now the Board of Ministry) is effective, while somewhere between one in three and one in four (30%) feel that the Board of Mission is effective. Views on the capability of the Church in Wales in areas of specialist ministry vary considerably from area to area. While only 19 per cent of the clergy feel that the Church in Wales has developed effective specialist ministries in education, the proportion rises to 43 per cent who feel that the Church in Wales has developed effective specialist ministries in social concerns. One in five (20%) of the clergy feel that the Church in Wales has developed effective specialist ministries in its Cathedrals and one in four (27%) feel that the Church in Wales provides adequate in-service training for clergy.

Churchmanship orientation

The Anglican communion is characterized by a wide range of churchmanship orientations, from the Evangelical to the Catholic ends of the spectrum. In recent years the Anglican communion has also been significantly influenced by the Charismatic renewal. The Church in Wales reflects these differences within the wider Anglican communion. Inevitably some clergy feel that some aspects of the churchmanship continuum flourish more readily in the Church in Wales than others. The research data, however, suggest that all aspects of the spectrum feel almost equally disadvantaged. Thus just under a quarter (24%) of the clergy feel that there are insufficient opportunities for Evangelical Anglicans in the Church in Wales. At the same time, 29 per cent of the clergy feel that there are insufficient opportunities for Catholic Anglicans in the Church in Wales and 25 per cent feel that there are insufficient opportunities for Charismatics.

One of the major areas of difference between the Evangelical and Catholic perspectives concerns the structure of liturgy. Both Catholics and Evangelicals regard the current liturgical provision within the Church in Wales as less than satisfactory. One in six (16%) of the clergy complain that the liturgy of the Church in Wales is too Catholic, while one in three (33%) of the clergy complain that the liturgy of the Church in Wales is not Catholic enough.

Liturgy

The autonomy of the Church in Wales is expressed clearly through its decision to develop its own liturgy and prayer book. For this reason *The Alternative Service Book 1980*, developed by the Church of England, is not authorized for use in the Church in Wales. Four years after the Church of England authorized its new book of services, the Church in Wales published its own new service book in 1984, *The Book of Common Prayer*. This book is different from *The Alternative Service Book 1980* in three important ways. All the services are available through the medium of Welsh as well as through the medium of English. The structure of the communion service is much closer to that of the 1928 revision prepared by the Church of England. God is addressed in the archaic second person singular. A clear majority of the clergy (61%) feel that *The Book of Common Prayer* (1984) used in the Church in Wales is too traditional. Over half (56%) of the clergy say that they feel frustrated with *The Book of Common Prayer* and just under a half (49%) of the clergy say that the liturgy of the Church in Wales does not meet their spiritual needs.

At the same time as publishing *The Book of Common Prayer* in 1984, the Church in Wales also produced a second slim volume under the title, *The Holy Eucharist in Modern Language*. Opinion varies regarding the quality of this liturgy. While the majority of clergy are critical of *The Book of Common Prayer*, over half (52%) say that they feel thoroughly at home with it. The proportion falls to 29 per cent who feel thoroughly at home with *The Holy Eucharist in Modern Language*.

Discontent with the authorized liturgy of the Church in Wales encourages a significant proportion of clergy to look elsewhere for liturgical resources. Nearly half (46%) of the clergy prefer *The Alternative Service Book 1980* to the liturgy of the Church in Wales and almost a third (31%) of the clergy prefer the Roman Catholic liturgy to the liturgy of the Church in Wales.

What is also clear from the data is that the majority of clergy appreciate the benefits and advantages of a bilingual liturgy. Nearly two-thirds (63%) of the clergy feel that bilingual liturgy is an asset to the Church in Wales, compared with less than a fifth (17%) who feel that bilingual liturgy is a liability to the Church in Wales. More than a third (36%) of the clergy feel that Welsh-language liturgy contributes to growth in the Church in Wales, compared with less than a sixth (15%) who feel that Welsh-language liturgy contributes to decline in the Church in Wales. At the same time, many of the clergy are sensitive to the fact that Welsh-language liturgy may present a special barrier to some categories of worshippers. Thus, 43 per cent of the clergy say that Welsh-language liturgy deters active participation in the Church in Wales among incomers to Wales, and 46 per cent of the clergy say that Welsh-language liturgy deters active participation in the Church in Wales among visitors.

Bishops
Since the dioceses in the Church in Wales are relatively small, it is in theory possible for clergy to know their bishop quite well. Given relatively simple

diocesan structures, the bishops may be seen to be involved in many of the day-to-day matters of their dioceses, and as the bishops are elected to office, it is reasonable to suppose that those so elected are well known in the province. What, then, do the clergy feel about the calibre of their bishops?

First and foremost, the clergy in the Church in Wales see their bishops as pastors. Even on this point, however, a higher proportion of the clergy is critical of the bishops than uncritical of them. Thus, 45 per cent of the clergy regard most bishops in the Church in Wales as good pastors, with the other 55 per cent less confident about this. The clergy in the Church of Wales also see their bishops as leaders. However, while 45 per cent of the clergy regard most bishops in the Church in Wales as good pastors, the proportion falls to 36 per cent who regard most bishops in the Church in Wales as providing good leadership to the church, with the other 64 per cent less confident on this issue. While 36 per cent of the clergy regard most bishops in the Church in Wales as providing good leadership to the church, the proportion falls further to 30 per cent who regard most bishops in the Church in Wales as providing good leadership to society. The other 70 per cent are less confident about this. Confidence in the bishops falls even further when it comes to matters of skills in administration or in theology. Just over a quarter (28%) of the clergy agree that most bishops in the Church in Wales are good administrators, and slightly over a fifth (22%) of the clergy agree that most bishops in the Church in Wales are good theologians. The lowest level of confidence expressed in the bishops concerns their competence in deploying the clergy. Only one in seven (14%) of the clergy regard bishops in the Church in Wales as good at *assessing* clergy potential, while a similar proportion (13%) of the clergy regard bishops in the Church in Wales as good at *nurturing* clergy potential. The proportion falls further to one in eleven (9%) who regard bishops in the Church in Wales as good at clergy deployment. Given the influence and power of bishops in this area of ministry, the lack of confidence expressed by the clergy would seem to be a highly significant indicator of clergy morale.

Clergy care

While a key aspect of the clerical role involves extending pastoral care to others, it is widely recognized that clergy themselves often need pastoral care. As such, a crucial question to be faced by the churches is that of who cares for the carer. A major finding from the present survey concerns the extent to which clergy feel unsupported by the church they serve. At the top of their list comes the concern that the Church in Wales fails to provide adequate support for clergy who experience problems in their professional ministry. Three-fifths (61%) of the clergy complain that the Church in Wales does not show enough care for clergy who experience difficulties in the parish. Three-fifths (61%) of clergy complain that the Church in Wales does not show enough care for clergy who suffer from work-related stress. The clergy are also concerned that the Church in Wales fails to provide adequate support for clergy who experience problems in their personal lives, especially in areas of family life and sexuality. Nearly half (48%) of the clergy complain that the Church in Wales does not show enough care for clergy who experience marriage breakdown and almost two-fifths (37%) of the clergy complain that the Church in Wales does not show enough care for clergy who experience sexual problems. Nearly a third (30%) of the clergy complain that the Church in Wales does not show enough care for clergy who have problems with their children. Over a quarter (27%) of the clergy complain that the Church in Wales does not show enough care for clergy who have homosexual relationships, and one in six (17%) of the clergy complain that the Church in Wales does not show enough care for clergy who have affairs with parishioners. Two other significant areas of concern involve crises of faith and alcohol. Over two-fifths (42%) of the clergy complain that the Church in Wales does not show enough care for clergy who experience crises of faith. Just under two-fifths (38%) of the clergy complain that the Church in Wales does not show enough care for clergy who experience alcohol problems.

Viewing this same set of issues from a different perspective, very few clergy criticize the Church in Wales for being too lenient with clergy who experience problems. Only a handful of clergy feel that the Church in Wales treats too leniently clergy who experience problems with their children (1%), crises of faith (2%), work-related stress (3%), marriage breakdown (6%), alcohol problems (7%), or difficulties in the parish (7%). The proportion begins to rise, however, in some areas related to sexuality. One in ten (10%) of the clergy feel that the Church in Wales is too lenient with clergy who experience sexual problems, one in seven (15%) of the clergy feel that the Church in Wales is too lenient with clergy who have affairs with parishioners, and one in five (20%) of the clergy feel that the Church in Wales is too lenient with clergy who have homosexual relationships.

Looking to England
Until 1920 what is now the Church in Wales was part of the Church of England. For many Anglican clergy serving in Wales, England is not too

many miles distant. A number of these clergy were trained in England; some have spent part of their ministry in England before returning to Wales; some have close friends working in the Church of England; some work alongside clergy in neighbouring parishes who were ordained in England and then moved to Wales; and many read the *Church Times* or *Church of England Newspaper*. Inevitably clergy make comparisons with life the other side of Offa's Dyke, and the data demonstrate that the comparison is none too flattering for the Church in Wales.

To begin with, many of the clergy feel that there are better career prospects for clergy in England, particularly in specialist ministries and especially for women. Thus, 43 per cent of the clergy feel that the Church of England provides better career opportunities for its clergy than the Church in Wales. Half (49%) of the clergy feel that the Church of England has more opportunities for female clergy than the Church in Wales, and two-thirds (67%) of the clergy feel that the Church of England provides more opportunities for specialist ministries than the Church in Wales. Second, the majority of the clergy feel that the Church of England is less conservative and more open to change than the Church in Wales, with three-fifths (60%) of the clergy believing that the Church of England is more open to change than the Church in Wales. Third, a significant number of clergy consider that the Church of England is a better employer than the Church in Wales. This point is demonstrated by the facts that 31 per cent of the clergy believe that the Church of England houses its clergy better than the Church in Wales, 30 per cent of the clergy believe that the Church of England pays its clergy better than the Church in Wales; and 21 per cent of the clergy believe that the Church of England cares for its clergy better than the Church in Wales. In addition a fifth (21%) of the clergy believe that the Church of England manages patronage better than the Church in Wales. Finally, a significant number of clergy consider that the Church of England is better led, better informed and more spiritually alive than the Church in Wales. This point is demonstrated by the facts that 42 per cent of the clergy claim the Church of England to be more theologically aware than the Church in Wales, 31 per cent of the clergy claim the Church of England to be more spiritually alive than the Church in Wales, and 26 per cent of the clergy claim the Church of England to be better led than the Church in Wales.

Exhaustion
The items from the emotional exhaustion subscale of the burnout inventory highlight the stress and strain under which this group of clergy are working.

Nearly half (47%) of the clergy feel 'used up' at the end of the day in parish ministry, and some two-fifths (41%) of the clergy feel that they are working too hard in their parish. A third (36%) of the clergy feel frustrated with their parish ministry, with a quarter (25%) feeling that working with people all day is a real strain for them. A fifth (22%) say that they feel emotionally drained from their parish ministry, and slightly less (18%) say that they feel fatigued when they get up in the morning and have to face another day in the parish. In all 15 per cent of the clergy say that they feel 'burned out' from their parish ministry. One in ten (9%) feel that they have reached the 'end of their tether'. One in seventeen (6%) claim that they would feel a lot better if they could get out of parish ministry.

CONCLUDING REMARKS

This study has profiled the attitudes of clergy ordained in the Church in Wales between 1971 and 1992 working in full-time stipendiary parochial ministry within the Church in Wales. On the surface there are some very positive and encouraging signs for the future of the Church in Wales. These clergy are, by and large, thoroughly committed to what they are doing and to the context in which they are doing it. The majority of them feel a high level of loyalty to Wales, to the Church in Wales, and to ministry in Wales. Given this level of commitment among the professional leadership, there are good indicators of a promising future for Anglicanism in Wales.

Looking beneath the surface, however, these data also provide some clear warning signs for the future of the Church in Wales. First, it needs to be recalled that as many as one in four of the clergy ordained within the Church in Wales during the period under review, between 1971 and 1992, had ceased to minister within the Church in Wales. This represents a considerable wastage among those individuals whom the Church in Wales had selected and trained for ministry. Many of those who had ceased to minister within the Church in Wales, either by leaving ministry for secular employment or by moving to ministry in England, may by this very action be signalling a somewhat less positive attitude toward the Church in Wales. Second, many of those clergy who remain in active ministry within the Church in Wales show significant signs of dissatisfaction with this ministry. Many are feeling stressed and burnt out by their ministry. Many feel inadequately prepared by their initial training for the job that faces them. Many feel unsupported by the church they serve. Many lack confidence in the bishops and in the provincial structures to provide the leadership and support which they recognize they need. These are no easy matters to address in an age when many churches struggle for survival in an increasingly secular and post-Christian society. Yet the warning signs are there and it would be clearly irresponsible for the Church in Wales to ignore them.

Against this background the Church in Wales is currently making a helpful and appropriate response by investing resources in promoting the personal and professional development of the clergy. The portfolio of continuing ministerial education has been enhanced in recent years by a programme of mid-ministry consultations and by the introduction of a peer-assisted programme of ministry review relevant to clergy at all stages of their career.

The present survey deserves replication in a decade's time to monitor how such investment in personal and professional development has been reflected in changes in the morale of the clergy. At the same time, any such replication will need to give serious consideration to assessing the impact of the ordination of women to the priesthood on the morale of male clergy. Anecdotal evidence suggests that for some male clergy the ordination of women to the priesthood in January 1997 generated a significant boost to morale, as a development for which they had longed was finally realized. For other male clergy, however, the selfsame ordination symbolized an unforgivable departure from tradition and lowered confidence in the future of the Church in Wales. Evidence of this nature, however, provides no firm basis on which to assess the long-term significance of such an important and far-reaching decision in the life of the Church. Replication of the present study could provide a much more secure foundation on which to base proper evaluation and future developments.

REFERENCES

Aldridge, A. (1986). 'Slaves to no sect: the Anglican clergy and liturgical change', *Sociological Review*, 34, 357–80.

Aldridge, A. (1989). 'Men, women, and clergymen: opinion and authority in a sacred organisation', *Sociological Review*, 37, 43–64.

Blaikie, N. W. H. (1979). *The Plight of the Australian Clergy*, Brisbane, University of Queensland Press.

Brierley, P. and Hiscock, V. (1993). *UK Christian Handbook: 1994/95 Edition*, London, Christian Research Association.

Carroll, J. W., Hargrove, B. and Lummis, A. T. (1983). *Women of the Cloth: A New Opportunity for the Churches*, San Francisco, Harper and Row.

Davies, D., Watkins, C. and Winter, M. (1991). *Church and Religion in Rural England*, Edinburgh, T. and T. Clark.

Eysenck, S. B. G., Eysenck, H. J. and Barrett, P. (1985). 'A revised version of the psychoticism scale', *Personality and Individual Differences*, 6, 21–9.

Fletcher, B. (1990). *Clergy Under Stress: A Study of Homosexual and Heterosexual Clergy*, London, Mowbray.

Francis, L. J. (1991). 'The personality characteristics of Anglican ordinands: feminine men and masculine women?', *Personality and Individual Differences*, 12, 1133–40.

Francis, L. J. and Kay, W.K. (1995). 'The personality characteristics of Pentecostal ministry candidates', *Personality and Individual Differences*, 18, 581–94.

Francis, L. J. and Robbins, M. (1996a). 'Differences in the personality profile of stipendiary and non-stipendiary female Anglican parochial clergy in Britain and Ireland', *Contact*, 119, 26–32.

Francis, L. J. and Robbins, M. (1996b). 'A woman's voice in a man's world: listening to women clergy in the Church in Wales before the vote', *Contemporary Wales*, 9, 74–90.

Francis, L. J., and Rodger, R. (1994a). 'The influence of personality on clergy role prioritisation, role influences, conflict and dissatisfaction with ministry', *Personality and Individual Differences*, 16, 947–57.

Francis, L. J., and Rodger, R. (1994b). 'The personality profile of Anglican clergymen', *Contact*, 113, 27–32.

Gregory, D. (1995). 'Welsh clergy speak! A study of clergy's experiences of poverty and social need in their parishes', unpublished paper presented to British Sociological Association Study of Religion Group conference, Lincoln.

Harris, C. C. and Startup, R. (1994). 'The Church in Wales: a neglected Welsh institution', *Contemporary Wales*, 7, 97–116.

Harris, C. C. and Startup, R. (1996). 'Clergy activities in the Church in Wales', *Research in the Social Scientific Study of Religion*, 7, 109–26.

Lehman, E. C. (1985). *Women Clergy: Breaking Through Gender Barriers*, New Jersey, Transaction Inc.

Lehman, E. C. (1987). *Women Clergy in England*, Lampeter, Edwin Mellen Press.

Maslach, C. and Jackson, S. (1986). *The Maslach Burnout Inventory*, 2nd edition, Palo Alto, California, Consulting Psychologists Press.

Nason-Clark, N. (1984). 'Clerical attitudes towards appropriate roles for women in church and society: an empirical investigation of Anglican, Methodist and Baptist clergy in southern England', unpublished Ph.D. dissertation, London School of Economics and Political Science.

Price, D. T. W. (1990). *A History of the Church in Wales in the Twentieth Century*, Penarth, Church in Wales Publications.

Pym, R. (1992). 'Crumbs from the mitre: a comparison of the ministry experiences of ordained women and men in the Church of the Province of New Zealand', unpublished MA dissertation, University of Auckland.

Ranson, S., Bryman, A. and Hinings, B. (1977). *Clergy, Ministers and Priests*, London, Routledge and Kegan Paul.

Rutledge, C. J. F. (1994). 'Parochial clergy today: a study of role, personality and burnout among clergy in the Church of England', unpublished M.Phil. dissertation, University of Wales, Lampeter.

Thomas, T. H. (1994). 'An examination of the attitudes of the clerics in the Church in

Wales to Christian Initiation', unpublished M.Th. dissertation, University of Oxford.

Towler, R. and Coxon, A. P. M. (1979). *The Fate of the Anglican Clergy*, London, Macmillan.

Walker, D. (1976). *A History of the Church in Wales*, Penarth, Church in Wales Publications.

9. YOUNG PEOPLE'S USE OF WELSH: THE INFLUENCE OF HOME AND COMMUNITY

Heini Gruffudd

At a time when both the number of pupils in Welsh-medium schools, and the number of Welsh-speaking children and young people is increasing, English is replacing Welsh in domains favoured by young people. In spite of an increase in individual bilingualism, the consequent lack of diglossia in society's use of language presents certain difficulties for Welsh as a threatened language (Ferguson, 1959, Fishman, 1972). It could make it superfluous to those who do not use it as their symbol of identity, or as a mark of attachment to a particular ethnic or cultural group (Lambert, 1967). In a world where Anglo-American mass media hold sway over young people, how does the apparent decrease in opportunity to use the threatened language in various domains affect the language habits of young people? How does its use in various domains and situations differ? Which young people succeed in using it as their first or main language? What are the effects of region, class and gender on language use and which other factors are at work in language choice? Are there differences between attitude towards the threatened language and actual use of the language? C. H. Williams (1987) has noted the dearth of evidence on these issues in Wales.

Research undertaken by the Department of Adult Continuing Education at the University of Wales Swansea has attempted to answer some of these questions (Gruffudd, 1996), with an emphasis on use rather than attitude (compare Thomas and Williams, 1976, 1977). Our study involved bilingual young people aged 16–17 in the area of south Wales between Cross Hands in the west and Port Talbot in the east, and up to Llandeilo and the heads of the Amman, Tawe, Neath and Afan valleys in the north. The area of study was divided into five regions: the Gwendraeth valley; Llanelli; the Amman valley; Tawe/Neath; and Swansea/Port Talbot, according to the catchment areas of the bilingual and Welsh-language secondary schools. This region includes some of the most Welsh-speaking parts of Wales, and also some of the most English-speaking. It is an area where the struggle between Welsh and English for domination of various domains has been steadily shifting westwards during this century, and is thus of great significance for the future of Welsh (Aitchison and Carter, 1994: 97).

HOME LANGUAGE

One initial aim was to look at the linguistic nature of families, and the language patterns of communication between parents; parents and children; and siblings. Significant correlations were found between the patterns of language use among young people and the language patterns of the home. Fishman (1991) has emphasized the home as the main centre of any attempt at language transmission, as it is central in the child's experience. The linguistic importance of the home is commonly accepted in Wales (Jones, 1994), in the past often to the detriment of developing the use of Welsh in other domains. It has also been acknowledged that children's positive attitude to Welsh is closely linked to the use of Welsh in the home (C. H. Williams, 1987), while on the other hand it has been argued that peer pressure and popular culture are stronger influences than home and school in shaping attitudes towards Welsh (Baker, 1992). The influence of home, peers and adults has been found to affect children at differing ages, with adults and the community holding sway after 14 (Jones, 1997).

A first difficulty is to determine what is a Welsh-speaking home. In our sample of 329 young people (around 60 per cent of the relevant age group of bilingual young people) the linguistic ability in Welsh of their parents was surprisingly high. As many as 84.2 per cent claimed that their parents had at least an 'average' knowledge of Welsh, and 54.1 per cent thought that their parents' ability in Welsh was 'very high'. Nevertheless, actual patterns of language use among Welsh speakers can vary substantially, according to place, topic discussed, who is addressed and in which company. Hallam (1978) has suggested that the language of the home is likely to turn to English where one parent's ability in Welsh is not strong, and the same suggestion is made by Harrison and others (1981). Because of this tendency, we paid particular attention to how the language use of young people was connected specifically to 'very high' Welsh-language ability among parents.

Questionnaire answers were obtained relating to the ability in Welsh of parents, and of the wider family, and on the use of Welsh among parents and with children. It became apparent immediately that most young people,

TABLE **9.1**
Welsh-language ability of parents according to area: percentages

	Gwendraeth	Llanelli	Amman	Tawe/Neath	Swansea
None	3.8	12.9	5.5	11.0	6.8
Very weak	0.0	1.6	0.0	6.8	8.5
Weak	0.0	3.2	3.6	8.2	8.5
Fair	5.0	8.1	16.4	9.6	27.1
Strong	15.0	11.3	21.8	12.3	30.5
Very strong	76.3	62.9	52.7	52.1	18.6

even in English-speaking areas, had a certain amount of Welsh within their broader families. Within the whole sample only 3 per cent of the families, which included parents and grand-parents, had no Welsh at all, and this percentage was fairly similar in all areas. The greatest difference was to be found in the percentages of families who had a 'very high' knowledge of Welsh. This varied from 63.3 per cent in the Welsh-speaking heartland areas of the Gwendraeth valley in Carmarthenshire to 16.9 per cent in the more anglicized areas of Swansea/Port Talbot. This linguistic pattern of the broader family resembled fairly closely the linguistic ability of the parents in these areas (Table 9.1): there was no vast difference between the linguistic ability of mothers and fathers, except in the Tawe/Neath areas (65.8 per cent of mothers fluent, 47.2 per cent of fathers), but on the whole mothers tended to be more fluent in Welsh than fathers, with 64 per cent considered to be fluent, compared to 57 per cent of fathers.

Although the linguistic ability of the families in the Welsh-speaking areas generally reflected the linguistic pattern of the area, the Welsh-language ability of parents in the anglicized areas was significantly higher than the percentage of Welsh speakers in the community. Due to the anglicizing influence of any discrepancy between parents in Welsh language ability, just 39 per cent of all parents use mainly Welsh with each other where no non-Welsh-speaking person is present (Table 9.2).

To appreciate the pattern of language use in the home, the use of language among parents was compared with their declared ability in the language. It was seen that almost all parents who spoke Welsh, or mainly Welsh, with each other had a 'very high' ability in Welsh. In all other groups, where parents were of mixed ability, i.e. where one parent had a lower ability in Welsh than the other, it was clear that English was the dominant language. This clearly suggests that linguistic erosion among Welsh speakers occurs in

TABLE **9.2**
The use of language among parents

	Number	Percentage
English only	139	42.6
Mainly English	35	10.7
Half Welsh, half English	25	7.7
Mainly Welsh	38	11.7
Welsh only	89	27.3
No response	3	–
	329	100

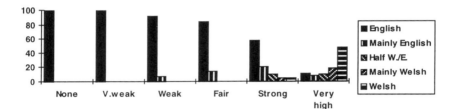

FIGURE **9.1**
Language spoken by parents with each other

the home environment. It will be seen that actual use of Welsh among parents, and between parents and children, was a more influential factor in encouraging Welsh language use among young people than simply ability in the language.

The weakened position of the Welsh language between parents at home, compared with language ability, is seen in all areas, but is particularly prominent in anglicized areas. Whereas just 27.6 per cent of parents in the Gwendraeth valley speak English or mainly English, 81.3 per cent of parents in the Swansea/Port Talbot area do so. The figure in all other areas is around 50 per cent. Nevertheless, parents spoke more Welsh with their children than with each other. Mothers were more likely to use Welsh with the young people, with 54.3 per cent doing so at least most of the time, compared with 47.5 per cent of fathers. There was also a greater tendency to use solely Welsh with young people: 42.2 per cent of mothers spoke only Welsh with their children, and 39.1 per cent of fathers did likewise,

TABLE 9.3
Use of Welsh among siblings

	Number	Percentage
English only	80	26.8
Mainly English	57	19.1
Half Welsh/English	39	13.1
Mainly Welsh	32	10.7
Welsh only	90	30.2
Missing	31	
	329	100

compared with just 27.3 per cent of parents who spoke only Welsh to each other. This varied very much according to the linguistic nature of the localities. In the Gwendraeth valley, 75 per cent of parents spoke Welsh with children; 53.2 per cent in the Llanelli area, 38 per cent in Tawe/Neath, 36.3 per cent in the Amman valley and 21.1 per cent in the Swansea/Port Talbot areas. The disappointing figure here is the Amman valley, which is considerably more Welsh-speaking than Tawe/Neath.

A crucial consideration for this study was the use of Welsh made by siblings, all of whom were bilingual, and most of whom had received a substantial degree of Welsh-medium education: 54 per cent of siblings used Welsh at least half the time with each other (Table 9.3). The patterns of language use reflected the linguistic usages of parents. Table 9.4 shows the comparison between the use of Welsh by parents with children, and the use

TABLE 9.4
Use of Welsh among siblings, compared with the language spoken to them by their parents – numbers and percentages

Amount of Welsh spoken by parents:	English only		Mainly Eng.		Equal Eng./Welsh		Mainly Welsh		Welsh only	
	no.	%	no.	%	no.	%	no.	%	no.	%
None	51	75.8	13	19.7	3	4.5	0	0	0	0
Rarely	13	43.3	15	50.0	2	6.7	0	0	0	0
A little	4	22.2	10	55.6	2	11.1	2	11.2	0	0
Fair amount	4	11.1	14	38.9	7	19.4	5	13.9	6	16.7
A lot	4	11.1	2	5.6	10	27.8	8	22.2	12	33.3
Always	4	3.6	3	2.7	15	13.5	17	15.3	72	64.9

of Welsh among siblings and it is clear that the language spoken among siblings is closely associated to the language spoken to them at home. When no English is spoken in the home, 93.7 per cent of siblings speak Welsh at least half the time with each other. Similarly, when no Welsh is spoken to siblings at home, 95.5 per cent speak mainly English to each other. The overwhelming influence of the language spoken to siblings at home is seen in other situations of language use, and this should be a major consideration in any attempt at reversing language shift.

This link between home language and language use was confirmed in interviews with young people from various areas. (All quotations are translated.) A brother and a sister from a Welsh-speaking family in a fairly anglicized part of Swansea regarded Welsh as their first language. The brother's opinion was that 'home life has more influence on children than school life'. Referring to friends from English-speaking homes, he said 'When they are at home, English influences them more than Welsh.' A daughter of Welsh-speaking parents in Swansea said 'almost all who have parents who speak Welsh to them speak Welsh'. A sister from a Welsh-speaking home in the Neath valley said, 'Well, of the people I know who are sort of Welsh, but the parents don't speak Welsh anyway, then it's more usual for them to speak English, but I would say that most of the Welsh people who speak Welsh at home speak Welsh to each other.'

Complicated patterns of language use emerged among siblings where the two languages were spoken at home. A son of an English-speaking mother and a Welsh-speaking father in the Gwendraeth valley said, 'I'm more used to speaking English with my mother, and I speak more Welsh with my father . . . I speak Welsh and English, half and half . . . I speak a lot of English in the house – at home – and a lot of English at school.' He felt that English was his first language, and this choice, made through instinct or habit, is one that young people have to face in many circumstances, according to the linguistic nature of their surroundings.

Contrary to expectations based on previous research suggesting that girls have a more positive attitude than boys towards Welsh (Sharp *et al.*, 1973: 82; Baker 1992: 120), males were not less likely to use Welsh than females. A total of 28.8 per cent of sisters spoke only Welsh to a brother or sister, while 31.9 per cent of brothers used Welsh only. Only 6.3 per cent of girls spoke mainly Welsh, compared to 15.9 per cent of boys, and 21.9 per cent of sisters spoke more English, compared with 15.9 per cent of brothers, while 26.9 per cent of sisters spoke English only, compared to 26.8 per cent of brothers.

TABLE 9.5

Use of Welsh and English among siblings, according to area: percentages

	Amman valley	Gwendraeth valley	Swansea/ Port Talbot	Llanelli	Tawe/Neath
English only	45.1	15.7	28.3	18.2	30.4
Mainly English	15.7	10.0	41.5	20.0	13.0
Half W./E.	9.8	21.4	9.4	14.5	8.7
Mainly Welsh	11.8	5.7	7.5	21.8	8.7
Welsh only	17.6	47.1	13.2	25.5	39.1

Although the Gwendraeth valley was the only area of the study where more than half of the siblings spoke mainly Welsh to each other (Table 9.5), this was considerably less than the proportion of parents who had either a 'strong' or 'very high' level of Welsh-language use at home. In other areas, the percentage of Welsh-speaking siblings was nearer to Welsh-language use by parents. This suggests a worrying language shift in the Welsh heartland, but a heartening consolidation of language patterns in anglicized and urban areas among siblings where parents wish to speak Welsh. This is an essential development in language maintenance (Hindley 1990: 242–7).

The one area that appeared to be a particular cause of concern was the Amman valley, an area still considered to be traditionally Welsh, but where the percentage of Welsh speakers has fallen below 70 per cent in many parts. The persistently disappointing language use scores in this area confirm the negative attitudes towards the threatened language in areas with between 40 and 70 per cent Welsh speakers (Williams 1979). The percentage of siblings using only English with each other was far higher than in all other areas, including anglicized Swansea, and the percentage speaking mainly Welsh with each other was far below the neighbouring Gwendraeth valley. Siblings in the Amman valley who had attended the English stream of a comprehensive school, rather than the Welsh stream, showed a particular tendency towards using English with each other. Of these 56.3 per cent spoke English only with their brothers and sisters, while a further 18.8 per cent spoke mainly English, making a total of 75.1 per cent who tended towards English. In the case of these siblings, 45.7 per cent had parents who spoke only English with each other, and a further 20 per cent had parents who spoke mainly English. It seems that a combination of anglicized homes in this area, and English-medium education, has a detrimental effect on the use of Welsh.

THE LANGUAGE OF SOCIETY

A further aim of the study was to gauge what use of Welsh and English was made by these young people among bilingual friends and peers. The language choice of young people in various situations could be influenced by several factors, such as the dominant language in the location, the language generally associated with the subject discussed, the initial language of relationship between individuals, the perceived trendiness of a particular language, the influence of individuals strongly linked to a particular language and a reaction against a language associated with authority. The combination of these factors resulted in interesting and possibly unexpected language patterns.

TABLE **9.6**

Use of Welsh among bilingual young people

	Number	Percentage
Never/very little	56	17.0
Less than half	67	20.4
Half Welsh/half English	72	21.9
More than half	70	21.3
Almost all Welsh/always	64	19.5

There was no overall tendency towards using English when these siblings spoke to bilingual peers. It could be claimed that there was a greater tendency to use Welsh, as 62.7 per cent of the young people spoke Welsh at least half the time to each other. What is seen, however (Table 9.6) is less weighting towards the use of only English or only Welsh. Just 19.5 per cent of young people now spoke only Welsh and 17 per cent spoke only English. In this context greater variety is seen according to area, with the Welsh-speaking heartland of the Gwendraeth valley showing the most positive results for Welsh. Apart from the Amman valley, where patterns of language use among young people is a clear source of worry, it was seen that language patterns vary predictably according to the linguistic nature of the community. Of young people in the Welsh-heartland region 87.6 per cent spoke Welsh at least half the time with bilingual peers, compared with 42.3 per cent in Swansea/Port Talbot and 40 per cent in the Amman valley.

Other factors which we studied to add to the overall pattern included (i) the language spoken to a Welsh-speaking best friend; (ii) the number of close friends who are Welsh-speaking; (iii) the language used with other age groups; (iv) the overall amount of Welsh spoken by the young people daily.

TABLE **9.7**

Use of Welsh with closest bilingual friend

	Number	Percentage
Never or almost never	84	25.5
Less than half	94	28.6
About half	38	11.6
More than half	28	8.5
Almost always or always	85	25.8

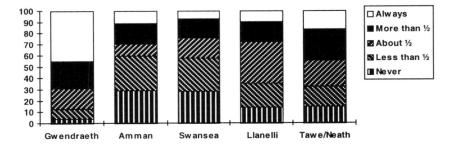

FIGURE **9.2**

Use of Welsh among bilingual young people, according to area

As would be expected, in most instances these new factors increased the amount of English used by young people outside the Welsh heartland.

The language spoken to a best Welsh speaking friend (Table 9.7) is likely to reveal if Welsh is used as the main language of the young person concerned. Interest in making the threatened language the main personal language is a concern in Catalonia (Fuster 1993). To attempt to make the threatened language the chief language of homes and of young people, a campaign is currently afoot in the Basque country under the title *of 'Ahoz aho, belaunez belaun'* (by word of mouth from generation to generation) (Euskararen Berripapera 1996: 4).

In close interpersonal relationships, Welsh was seen to be weaker than English among these bilingual young people. The only area where the majority spoke Welsh at least half the time to a closest friend was in the Gwendraeth valley, where 75 per cent did this. The corresponding percentages for other areas were: Amman 31, Swansea/Port Talbot 37.3, Llanelli 32, Tawe/Neath 43.8. When asked how many of the young people's six closest friends were Welsh-speaking, it was expected that the language patterns would more closely reflect the linguistic nature of the society. Although this was true to some extent, it became clear that the Welsh- medium schooling that most of these young people had received had played a major role in the formation of friendships, as only 37 out of the 329 young people had a majority of non-Welsh-speaking close friends. Close associations formed during schooling present a hopeful platform for the expansion of use of Welsh in activities outside the education field.

Among 63.8 per cent of the young people of the Gwendraeth valley, all the friends were bilingual and surprisingly this high proportion was repeated in Llanelli (66.1 per cent) and Tawe/Neath (60.3 per cent). The two areas with substantially weaker percentages were Swansea/Port Talbot (23.7 per cent) and the Amman valley (16.7 per cent). Overall 88.7 per cent had three or more bilingual close friends. The percentages were 98.7 in the Gwendraeth valley, 96.8 in Llanelli, 91.8 in Tawe/Neath, 79.6 in the Amman valley and 71.2 in Swansea. It is clear that Welsh-speaking friendship networks can be maintained in English-speaking areas, although they are more likely to be strong in the Welsh heartland.

It was expected that a stronger use of Welsh with the older age group, associated with a weaker use of Welsh with their own age group, would be another sign of continuing language shift towards English. It was found that the age of those addressed did contribute to a change in language use, and there were significant differences between the various age groups. Nevertheless, the pattern was not one of continuous language shift. Substantially more Welsh was spoken to older people, and the use of Welsh diminished according to the age of those addressed, with the weakest category being the young people themselves; but the level of use of Welsh increased once more when younger people and children were talked to. It could be argued that Welsh is seen on the one hand as the language of old people, and also as the language of children, having less relevance for the daily lives of the young people themselves. If this is true, this should be one of the central issues faced by those interested in language shift in Wales today (Dafis 1992: 15). As young people become released from the education system, they enter a world with very different language values, where the weight of English is likely to be much stronger than during their childhood. Where the school could be a microcosm of a Welsh-speaking world, wider society does not provide this linguistic shelter, and a shift towards English becomes apparent.

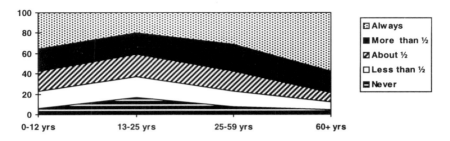

FIGURE 9.3
Use of Welsh with bilingual speakers of different age groups

The main socializing centres for young people throughout the area were clubs and pubs, dances and discos, the cinema and sports clubs, and in all these domains, English was on the whole the dominant language. This was particularly true of almost all such establishments in anglicized areas, and of dances and discos in every area. In order to change the language used by young people amongst each other, it is fairly evident that more Welsh needs to be introduced to these socializing domains. It was also clear that *yr Urdd*, the Welsh League of Youth, fails to attract young people of this age group to its weekly activities, and its influence on the language spoken by young people was therefore negligible.

The decline in Welsh-language use could possibly confirm the observations of Fishman (1991: 23) on the way it is seen as a symbol of past values rather than of modern life. Baker (1992: 188) comes to the conclusion that the attitude of children in the 12–16 age group towards Welsh deteriorates with age. Nevertheless, one should not discard the possibility that young people revert to speaking Welsh after a period of anti-authoritarian rebellion during school age. There was a tendency for the young people in the study to use more Welsh at 16+ than they had done previously (Gruffudd 1996: 88). There is also a need to explain why there was a tendency to use more Welsh with children, and to relate this to another extremely positive finding of the study, that only 4.3 per cent of the whole group would not wish their own future children to receive Welsh medium- education. It seems that a general positive attitude towards Welsh is reflected by willingness to use the language where it is seen, for whatever reason, to be acceptable and practical. In Figure 9.3, the peak corresponds to the higher use of English among young people, compared to a greater use of Welsh with all other age groups.

TABLE **9.8**
Proportion of Welsh used on a daily basis

	Number	Percentage
Almost none	50	15.2
Less than half	92	28.0
About half	93	28.3
More than half	75	22.8
Almost all	19	5.8
	329	100

When the figures are analysed according to area, once again it is the Welsh heartland which has by far the most positive influence on choosing to speak Welsh. Here young people spoke Welsh to older bilingual people at least half the time. In Llanelli 93.6 per cent did this, 89 per cent in Tawe/Neath, 76.3 per cent in Swansea/Port Talbot, and 74.6 per cent in the Amman valley. When speaking to bilingual children, 95 per cent in the Gwendraeth valley spoke Welsh at least half the time, compared to 83.9 per cent in Llanelli, 78.1 per cent in Tawe/Neath, 63.1 per cent in Swansea/Port Talbot and 58.2 per cent in the Amman valley. With the 26–59 age group, 93.7 per cent in the Gwendraeth valley spoke Welsh at least half the time, compared to 79.1 per cent in Llanelli, 78.9 per cent in Tawe/Neath, 65.3 per cent in the Amman valley and 61 per cent in Swansea/Port Talbot.

In order to gain a broad picture of total language use among young people, they were asked to judge how much Welsh they used daily. It was encouraging that only 15.2 per cent did not use any Welsh at all, and that it was possible for a substantial proportion of young people to use mainly Welsh as their means of daily communication. Once again, the Gwendraeth valley had a substantially higher proportion of young people who spoke Welsh at least half the time, and only 6.3 per cent in this area of Welsh heartland claimed to speak no Welsh.

In all areas there is a core of mainly Welsh speakers, and this varies according to the linguistic nature of the area, apart from the Amman valley, which once again shows a deteriorating pattern. There is also a substantial proportion of young people for whom the opportunity to use Welsh and English is fairly equal. This can be interpreted as showing a language shift towards English in the Welsh heartland, but also the success of social and family networks in anglicized areas in providing domains for Welsh speakers. This phenomenon of equal bilingualism has been regarded as a

TABLE **9.9**

Proportion of Welsh used on a daily basis, according to area (percentages)

	Gwendraeth	Amman	Llanelli	Tawe/Neath	Swansea
Almost none	6.3	20.0	9.7	13.7	30.5
Less than half	13.8	40.0	35.5	27.4	28.8
About half	27.5	27.3	30.6	27.4	28.8
More than half	35.0	12.7	22.6	27.4	10.2
Almost all	17.5	0.0	1.6	4.1	1.7

stage of transition towards the dominant language in cases of language shift (Edwards, 1985), but the constancy of the percentage, between 27 per cent and 30 per cent in all areas, suggests that this phenomenon is at present widespread and substantial, if not yet permanent.

YOUNG PEOPLE'S VIEWS

The views of young people on their own language habits showed the influence of key individuals on the one hand, and the influence of belonging to different culture groups on the other. They also reveal the anglicizing effect of further education establishments, and of English-speaking newcomers to Welsh-speaking areas. A girl from the Welsh heartland said with emphasis that Welsh was the language she spoke to her friends, but at college in Ammanford, her language habits had significantly changed: 'The twenty of us who are in the class, we talk Welsh with one boy and one girl . . . that's all of us who speak Welsh.' She studied health studies at the college, 'it's all in English, there's nothing in Welsh.' A boy from the Welsh heartland who had a mixed language home said that he had spoken a lot of English at school. He had a girlfriend who 'speaks English with me, but if I go to the house, she speaks Welsh to her parents'. In the case of his own friends, he said, 'English was everything . . . some had English parents, coming from England, but they had learnt Welsh, but yet, they'd rather speak English together.' This boy then changed to English during the interview and said, 'If you talk to someone in Welsh [who is more used to talking English] you obviously won't make friends with that person because they think that you're a lot more Welsh at heart and that you would have a different set of interests perhaps.' To this boy Welsh was a symbol of a set of cultural values to which he did not wish to be seen to adhere. He had noticed at school that there were two distinct cultural groups 'Welsh people would speak Welsh all the time, speak about Welsh things, novels, go to see plays, go to the Welsh gigs, Welsh music . . . And the English friends then . . . speak Welsh and English, but mostly English. Read English novels, listen to English music, do English subjects like Chemistry, Physics and Biology. There was a clear rift.' The school taught sciences through the medium of English, and it seems that this arrangement had strengthened the tendency towards English among many of the pupils. This is a lesson to be learnt by many schools in traditionally Welsh areas which have a similar arrangement. It is not without purpose or success that many secondary schools in the anglicized parts of Wales have for years taught all subjects through the medium of Welsh.

Two sisters from the Welsh heartland had a strong commitment to Welsh, and they noticed that others would change their language to accommodate their language adherence. One said, 'if a boy speaks to me, he changes to speak Welsh . . . if you speak Welsh with a person, he changes.' Her sister reiterated this view, 'that's what I saw too: if someone spoke English to me, and I answered them back in Welsh, they would turn immediately and speak Welsh to me.' There is clearly a role for committed Welsh speakers, who are regarded as such by other bilingual people who will then change to Welsh. The sister's view was that speaking English was fashionable during school age. She had seen that young people were more likely to speak Welsh in the sixth form, 'when they come to sixth form they all turned to speak Welsh together . . . It was odd, and I thought, "O blinkin' 'eck", What's happening to them?' This could be confirmation of a trend towards Welsh among older teenagers when circumstances allow, and of the positive effect of continuing Welsh-medium education. It could also be a sign that English is transitionally fashionable for the younger 11–16 age group. Exactly the same opinion on the transient trendiness of speaking English was expressed by another girl of a Welsh-speaking family who said that 'there was a period when people thought it was trendy to speak English . . . or to speak mostly in English . . . [but] they change back.'

A girl from a Welsh-speaking home in an anglicized area commented that choice of language depended on the main language associated with various friends, and specific people, or the dominant language pattern of a group, 'It depends who you speak to . . . I have one friend with whom I'd never speak English . . . But yet, if she speaks with someone English [who tends to use English], she'd speak English to her.' Another of her friends had been an English influence, but she had now moved to a Welsh area, and 'speaks Welsh, because everyone there speaks Welsh.'

The initial language of friendship was seen to be formative in the case of a boy from a Welsh home in an anglicized area. 'I find that there are people with whom I've started speaking English, and I then find out that they can speak Welsh. I find it odd to communicate with them in Welsh after that.' An intricate pattern of language use is seen in the example of a girl from a Welsh-speaking family in an anglicized part of Swansea; the girl would speak Welsh with her parents and younger brother, mainly English with her closest friends, but Welsh without hesitation with a key Welsh-speaking peer.

LANGUAGE CHOICE

It has been seen that choice of language depended on location, family background, medium of education, attachment to culture group, and on the person or persons spoken to. These represent a complicated, changing web (Jones 1997: 43–74). The use of more than one language in these situations has been called situational code-switching (Wardhaugh 1993: 106). A widely known phenomenon in Wales is code-mixing, where both languages are used and mixed during a single utterance. A further type of code-switching is metaphorical code-switching where the language changes according to the topic discussed. All of these types of code-switching can reveal the extent to which a weaker language is being eroded by the stronger (Fishman 1991: 55).

It was found with young people that a considerable amount of metaphorical code-switching occurred. Their confidence in using Welsh in discussing different topics varied considerably according to the language they had mainly associated with those topics. There was, for example, a fair balance between Welsh and English when young people discussed topics relating to school and college education and religion, contexts where Welsh, in the lives of these young people, had been dominant or had generally had an equal share with English. On the other hand, there were many contexts where English was dominant (Table 9.10), and these included particularly the whole world of popular culture, with its various forms of musical and visual entertainment. For example, 74.4 per cent of the young people would favour English when discussing rock music, while just 4.9 per cent would favour Welsh.

Comparing various influences which could affect young people's confidence in using Welsh, the following displayed a differential factor between tendency to use Welsh and English. The figures show the difference between the percentage who favoured Welsh and the percentage who favoured English in each case; the larger the number, the larger the presumed association between the various factors and the use of Welsh or English:

TABLE **9.10**

The language preferred by young people when discussing various topics:
percentages

	Welsh preferred	No preference	English preferred
Religion	28.9	42.2	28.9
College work	22.2	48.3	29.5
Greeting	19.5	53.8	26.3
Literature	16.0	41.3	42.0
Food preparation	13.1	48.6	37.9
Current affairs	11.9	48.6	39.3
Jobs/business	10.3	42.6	46.8
Philosophizing	10.0	38.3	51.4
Sports	8.5	61.4	30.1
Courtship	8.2	37.7	54.1
Leg pulling	6.1	33.4	60.4
Television/films	5.2	35.6	59.1
Sex	4.3	31.9	63.8
Rock music	4.9	20.7	74.4
Bike/car repairs	3.3	36.2	60.2

1) Confidence/lack of confidence in linguistic literacy   48.1
2) Use of Welsh/use of English with friends   41.5
3) Parents speaking Welsh/English with children   41.0
4) Academic ability/Lack of academic ability in Welsh   31.1
5) Welsh-bilingual sixth form/English college   18.7
6) Living in the Welsh heartland/anglicized area   17.4
7) General academic ability/lack of ability   16.2
8) Girls/boys   8.3
9) Middle class/working class   6.6

It seems that constant use of Welsh with friends and speaking Welsh at home are the most powerful factors in giving young people confidence in using Welsh while discussing most topics. It can safely be argued that the use of Welsh at home is the most influential factor in securing the active use of Welsh among young people. When young people had been spoken to almost always in Welsh at home, it was found that the only topic that they would be happier to discuss in English would be rock music. The majority would just as happily discuss all other matters in Welsh. These topics included sports, television and films, current affairs, philosophizing, courting, business, practical work, literature and telling jokes. With young people who had been spoken to partly in English but mainly in Welsh at home, confidence in using Welsh was noticeably weaker. Sports, literature, current affairs, practical matters and business were the topics where the majority were equally comfortable in Welsh. In homes where there was less use of Welsh, the majority of young people would still be equally comfortable in discussing sports in Welsh. This may reflect the influence of sports teams at school, sports clubs in the community, and of the Welsh-language sports service on radio and television. In homes where no Welsh was spoken, young people would use English while discussing all of the above topics.

STEPS FORWARD

Some attention has been given to ways of encouraging the use of Welsh among young people (Ioan 1993, Jones 1992). There seems, however, to be a need for a major determined attempt to convince Welsh-speaking parents to use Welsh as the main language of the home, to encourage at least one parent within mixed-language marriages to use Welsh with children, and to encourage English-speaking parents who send children to Welsh schools to learn Welsh and to use it at home. This could be within the scope of the Welsh Language Board were it to adopt a more creative role as a language planning body. Young people could also be made aware of their possible role as key language speakers within their friendship groups. The majority of young people conformed to the dominant language of their surroundings, and young Welsh speakers could have a very positive influence on group language patterns.

As close friendships networks consisted mostly of Welsh speakers, they could be used as a base for Welsh social, sporting and other popular activities, with particular emphasis on public houses, clubs and discos. This work could be an important part of the role of the increasing number of *Mentrau Iaith*, the Welsh Language Initiatives, of which three, *Menter Cwm Gwendraeth*, *Menter Aman Tawe* and *Menter Llanelli* already operate in the area concerned. *Yr Urdd*, the Welsh League of Youth, would be well advised to target this age group and to move away from its strong associations with younger age groups within the education world in order to exploit young people's newly found anti-authoritarian freedom in pubs and discos. The possibilities for arranging Welsh or bilingual events, according to the linguistic nature of the area, in popular centres of entertainment are exciting. Welsh television and Welsh radio need to find the right recipe to attract young people, and there is no reason why detailed market research, associated with originality and creativeness, would not succeed in finding the ingredients necessary for success. Welsh rock music, with emphasis on active local participation, must be an essential part of a growing Welsh youth culture. Although this scene is intrinsically anti-authoritarian, adequate support must be given to it, just as support in Wales is given to almost all other art forms. The Welsh Language Board, in association with the Welsh Arts Council, could set up a Youth Rock Body which would operate independently, emulating a similar venture in Catalonia. Eventually the Welsh rock scene needs to be accepted on an equal footing to the Anglo-American scene, so that Welsh young people will belong on the one hand to the world-wide youth culture, but also have their own means of cultural expression and identity.

The Welsh heartland, as the only area where Welsh is thriving, must receive special attention from government agencies concerned with the economy, training and education as linguistic survival is intrinsically connected to economic prosperity. Language planning strategies should not only be the concern of language movements and agencies, schools and homes but also of agencies connected with economic development. Recent criticism, for example, that inward investment to Wales has been concentrated in eastern parts of the country should be heeded. It should not be forgotten by those who have viewed the attempts to reverse language shift in Wales pessimistically that the overall view of Welsh held by the young people in both Welsh- and English-speaking areas, and rural and urban areas was almost unanimously positive. Where circumstances and linguistic background are favourable, young people on the whole use Welsh willingly.

REFERENCES

Aitchison, J. and Carter, H. (1994). *A Geography of the Welsh Language 1961–1991*, Cardiff, University of Wales Press.

Baker, C. (1992). *Attitudes and Language*, Clevedon, Multilingual Matters.

Dafis, Cynog (1992). 'Pobl ifanc a'r iaith', *Barn*, 351, April, 13–16.

Edwards, J. (1985). *Language, Society and Identity*, Oxford, Blackwell.

Euskararen Berripapera, August 1996, IV, 1.

Ferguson, C. A. (1959). 'Diglossia', *Word*, 15, 325–40.

Fishman, J. A. (1972). *The Sociology of Language*, Rowley, Mass, Newbury House.

Fishman, J.A (1991). *Reversing Language Shift*, Clevedon, Multilingual Matters.

Fuster, Emili Boix (1993). *Triar no és trair, Identitat i llengua en els joves de Barcelona*, Barcelona, edicions 62.

Gruffudd, G. H. (1996). *Y Gymraeg a Phobl Ifanc*, Adran Addysg Barhaus Oedolion, Prifysgol Cymru Abertawe.

Hallam, P. R. (1978). 'Dylanwad cefndir cymdeithasol a ieithyddol y cartref a'r ysgol ar ymlyniad plentyn wrth y Gymraeg', unpublished M.Ed. dissertation, University of Wales Swansea.

Harrison, G. *et al.* (1981). *Bilingual Mothers in Wales and the Language of Their Children*, Cardiff, University of Wales Press.

Hindley, Reg (1990*). The Death of the Irish Language*, London, Routledge.

Ioan, G. (1993). *Hen wlad fy nhadau?*, Aberystwyth, Urdd Gobaith Cymru/Y.M.C.A..

Jones, B. (gol.) (1992). *Iaith Ifanc*, Aberystwyth, CYD.

Jones, I. G. (1994). *Ar Drywydd Hanes Cymdeithasol yr Iaith Gymraeg*, Prifysgol Cymru Aberystwyth, Aberystwyth.

Jones, R. O. (1997). *Hir Oes i'r Iaith*, Cardiff, University of Wales Press.

Lambert, W. E. (1967). 'A social psychology of bilingualism', *Journal of Social Issues*, 23, 91–109.

Sharp, D. *et al.* (1973). *Some Aspects of Welsh and English in the Schools of Wales*, Basingstoke, Macmillan.

Thomas, C. J. and Williams, C. H., (1976, 1977). 'A behavioural approach to the study of linguistic decline and nationalist resurgence, a case study of the attitudes of sixth-formers in Wales', Part I, *Cambria* III, 102–24; Part II, *Cambria* IV, 152–73.

Wardhaugh, Ronald (1993). *An Introduction to Sociolinguistics*, Oxford, Blackwell.

Williams, C. H. (1979). 'An ecological and behavioural analysis of ethnolinguistic change in Wales', in Giles, H. and Saint-Jacques, B. (eds.*), Language and Ethnic Relations*, Oxford, Pergamon, 27–55.

Williams, C. H. (1987). 'Location and context in Welsh language reproduction: a geographic interpretation', *International Journal of the Sociology of Language*, 66, 61–83.

Williams, G. (ed.) (1987). 'The sociology of Welsh', *International Journal of the Sociology of Language*, 66.

10. THE WELSH ECONOMY: A STATISTICAL PROFILE[1]

Stephen Drinkwater

INTRODUCTION

This profile follows the format of the corresponding feature which appeared in Volume 9 of *Contemporary Wales*.[2] The fifteen tables in the main text are arranged, with accompanying commentary, in five sections, covering Output, Income and Expenditure; Employment; Unemployment; Earnings; and House Prices. The tables are based on information made available prior to 1 July 1997 and, as noted in previous surveys, compilation and production lags with respect to certain official statistics mean that 'latest' figures sometimes date back two or three years.

In April 1997, Government Office Regions replaced Standard Statistical Regions as the primary unit of analysis for regional statistics in the UK. However, since much of the data were published before this date, the latter definition will continue to be employed whenever Wales is compared with the other regions. Similarly, due to the recent local government reorganization in Wales, some tables may not yet be available for the newly defined administrative areas. Therefore, the main body of the text retains information for the former counties, in an attempt to maintain consistency with previous surveys, wherever possible. An appendix containing key statistics and brief commentary for the new unitary authorities is also included.

OUTPUT, INCOME AND EXPENDITURE

Gross Domestic Product (GDP) is the most commonly used measure of the level of economic activity and welfare in an economy, and it is detailed for the regions of Great Britain in 1995 in Table 10.1. The figures indicate a further deterioration in terms of GDP per head in Wales relative to the rest of the UK. GDP per head in Wales was £8,440 in 1995, the second lowest of all regions. This amount represented 83.3 per cent of the UK average in 1995, a fall of 0.4 percentage points from a year earlier. The gap with the poorest region, Northern Ireland, is also narrowing rapidly. It stood at £30 in 1995, compared with £148 in 1994.

These figures are even more worrying when put into an international context. *Eurostat* data reveal that GDP per head in Wales fell from 85 per cent of the harmonized European Union (EU) average in 1987 to 84 per cent in 1993, even after taking account of the addition of East Germany in 1991. Dunford (1996) identifies two elements which can cause differences in GDP per head across regions. The first depends upon differences in productivity and the second upon differences in the employment rate or in the way in which human potential is mobilized. He accounts for Wales' poor GDP performance by a mixture of the two elements.

Further evidence of declining living standards in Wales relative to other countries is provided by OECD figures which estimated that GDP per head in the Republic of Ireland surpassed that of Great Britain in 1996. Ireland has the fastest growing economy in Western Europe, a fact illustrated by OECD figures for 1986, when GDP per head in Ireland was just 63 per cent of the British figure. The example of Ireland has provided ammunition for advocates of more independent decision making in Wales, who argue that Welsh prospects would be better served as a small country within the EU. It is said that Ireland has greater negotiating powers in Brussels than Wales by virtue of its independent status, enabling it to acquire far more EU money in terms of grants and subsidies.

Table 10.1 also gives details of income and expenditure in UK regions, showing that Wales has the lowest level of personal income per head in the UK by quite a considerable margin and that the gap with the other regions is widening. In 1995, personal incomes in Wales were only 84 per cent of the national average, down from 86.5 per cent a year earlier. Wales fared only slightly better when disposable income is considered as the Welsh incomes were equivalent to 86.3 per cent of the UK average using this definition. Given the fact that Wales has the lowest income levels in the UK, it is hardly surprising to find that Wales was ranked last in terms of consumers' expenditure. However, the figures reveal that individuals in Wales spend a higher proportion of their disposable income than the rest of the country, since Welsh consumers only spent 12.5 percentage points less than their UK counterparts.

TABLE 10.1
Regional accounts, 1995

	GDP per head		Personal income per head		Personal disposable income per head		Consumers' expenditure per head	
	£	% of UK	£	% of UK	£	% of UK	£	% of UK
South East	11775	116.2	12557	116.2	9708	113.2	8653	113.4
East Anglia	10226	100.9	10810	100.0	8632	100.7	7132	93.5
South West	9663	95.3	10284	95.2	8192	95.6	7184	94.1
West Midlands	9649	95.2	10245	94.8	8217	95.8	7230	94.7
East Midlands	9926	97.9	10276	95.1	8206	95.7	7470	97.9
Yorkshire & Humberside	9166	90.4	9920	91.8	7978	93.1	7220	94.6
North West	9181	90.6	9846	91.1	7928	92.5	7401	97.0
North	8932	88.1	9393	86.9	7596	88.6	6821	89.4
England	10324	101.8	10987	101.7	8678	101.2	7760	101.7
Scotland	9872	97.4	10498	97.2	8415	98.2	7210	94.5
Northern Ireland	8410	83.0	9440	87.4	8027	93.6	6806	89.2
WALES	8440	83.3	9073	84.0	7400	86.3	6678	87.5
UNITED KINGDOM	10137	100.0	10805	100.0	8573	100.0	7631	100.0

Note: Provisional figures.
Source: Office for National Statistics

Table 10.2 shows GDP per head in the former Welsh counties, along with figures for disposable household income. Since the *Office for National Statistics* (ONS) was not able to produce more up to date figures with respect to GDP at the sub-regional level, the discussion in this section is confined to the sub-regional differences in household income in Wales.[3] Amongst the counties, the wealthiest part of Wales in 1994 is found to be South Glamorgan, even though incomes had fallen relative to the UK average compared to 1992. Gwynedd was able to maintain relatively a high and stable level of income despite the problems encountered by those involved in agriculture. The situation in the poorest area of Wales, Mid Glamorgan, has not really improved since 1990, with household incomes remaining around 80 per cent of the UK average. Details about household expenditure are not available at the sub-regional level.

The position of industrial output in Wales is shown by the Index of Production and Construction, contained in Table 10.3. The index fell by 1.3 per cent between the fourth quarters of 1995 and 1996. There was also a slight reduction in output of 0.7 per cent between the third and fourth

TABLE 10.2
GDP per head, household income per head and household disposable income per head: Wales and former counties 1989–94

| | GDP per head | | | | | | Household income per head | | | | | | Household disposable income per head | | | | | |
| | 1989 | | 1991 | | 1993 | | 1990 | | 1992 | | 1994 | | 1990 | | 1992 | | 1994 | |
	£	% of UK	£	% of UK	£	% of UK	£	% of UK	£	% of UK	£	% of UK	£	% of UK	£	% of UK	£	% of UK
Clwyd	7060	93.0	7897	93.2	8830	89.9	7278	88.9	8049	87.9	8751	90.2	6037	91.2	6784	90.2	7461	93.0
Dyfed & Powys	5899	77.7	6459	76.2	7052	76.1	7235	88.3	7867	85.9	8391	86.5	5940	89.7	6695	89.0	7237	90.2
Gwent	6664	87.8	7203	85.0	7643	82.5	7115	86.9	8073	88.2	8414	86.7	6004	90.7	6864	91.2	7139	88.9
Gwynedd	6047	79.7	6581	77.7	7216	77.9	7281	88.9	8374	91.5	8983	92.6	6250	94.4	7310	97.2	7794	97.1
Mid Glamorgan	5762	75.9	5898	69.6	5792	62.5	6477	79.1	7298	79.7	7781	80.2	5440	82.1	6201	82.4	6621	82.5
South Glamorgan	8152	107.4	9500	112.1	10346	111.7	7696	94.0	9017	98.5	9509	98.0	6484	97.9	7690	102.2	7998	99.6
West Glamorgan	6547	86.3	7450	87.9	7736	83.5	7339	89.6	8335	91.1	8460	87.2	6248	94.3	7046	93.6	7318	91.2
WALES	6570	86.6	7242	85.5	7660	82.7	7162	87.5	8083	88.3	8549	88.1	6012	90.8	6878	91.4	7303	91.0

Source: Office for National Statistics

TABLE 10.3
Index of production and construction for Wales, (a) seasonally adjusted, (b) 1990 = 100

1992 SIC Section	Sub-section	Description	1990 weights per thousand	Annual indices 1995	Annual indices 1996	Quarterly 1995 Qtr 4	1996 Qtr 1	1996 Qtr 2	1996 Qtr 3	1996 Qtr 4	% change Prev. Qtr	% change Prev. Year
C-F		Production and construction	1000	108.7	107.3	107.8	106.1	105.2	109.3	108.5	-0.7	-1.3
C-E		Production industries (Revised Definition)	818	108.3	108.7	109.0	106.9	107.2	110.8	109.9	-0.8	0.4
C		Mining and quarrying	31	81.2	72.8	77.9	66.9	69.9	86.3	68.3	-20.9	-10.3
D		Manufacturing (revised definition)	710	110.8	110.5	111.8	108.8	109.5	112.4	111.3	-1.0	-0.3
	DA	Food products, beverages and tobacco	59	105	110	106	109	110	111	110	-1.3	4.8
	DB–DC	Textiles, textile products, leather and leather products	24	96	96	92	97	96	96	96	0.5	0.7
	DD	Wood and wood products	8	112	106	105	113	107	99	103	4.6	-5.9
	DE	Pulp, paper and paper products: printing and publishing	51	120	117	120	113	110	120	124	3.3	-2.9
	DF	Coke and refined petroleum products	59	110	126	130	121	124	130	129	-0.7	15.0
	DG	Chemicals, chemical products and man-made fibres	78	107	105	105	97	92	93	93	-0.4	-12.4
	DI	Other non-metallic mineral products	21	88	89	89	85	83	83	79	-4.2	-6.6
	DJ	Basic metals and fabricated metal products	162	116	114	115	110	113	121	116	-3.7	-1.1
	DK	Machinery and equipment not elsewhere classified	34	94	95	97	95	98	96	94	-2.1	2.3
	DL	Electrical and optical equipment	83	119	118	121	120	118	118	113	-4.3	-1.2
	DM	Transport equipment	71	112	111	111	113	114	118	126	6.4	4.6
	DH, DN	Other manufacturing (inc. rubber & plastic products)	60	110	108	107	105	110	106	103	-2.3	-3.7
E		Electricity, gas and water supply	76	95.6	106.2	94.6	104.8	101.4	105.1	113.4	7.9	11.0
F		Construction	182	110.4	100.8	110.2	102.6	95.8	102.7	102.2	-0.4	-8.7
		Market sector analysis (c) — Consumer goods	148	110.1	110.1	110.2	109.8	109.5	107.8	105.8	-1.8	-1.7
		Market sector analysis (c) — Intermediate goods	559	107.0	106.2	106.7	104.5	107.0	109.2	107.6	-1.4	0.1
		Market sector analysis (c) — Investment goods	110	112.5	112.7	113.6	114.8	115.2	118.1	121.9	3.2	4.4

Notes: a Revisions to the series are normally made each quarter to take account both of more recent information and improved seasonal factors.

      b All series are seasonally adjusted unless otherwise stated in the notes.

      c The weights have been revised. The construction industry (Weight 182) is excluded from this analysis.

Source: Welsh Office

TABLE 10.4

Identifiable general government expenditure: 1995–1996

| | £ per head | | | | | As percentage of UK identifiable expenditure per head | | | |
	England	Scotland	Wales	Northern Ireland	United Kingdom	England	Scotland	Wales	Northern Ireland
Agriculture, Fisheries, Food and Forestry	49	101	83	163	58	84	173	142	281
Trade, Industry, Energy and Employment	79	131	106	293	91	87	144	116	322
Roads and Transport	173	164	160	112	170	102	97	94	66
Housing	68	142	133	145	80	85	178	166	182
Other Environmental Services	150	264	261	186	166	90	158	157	112
Law, Order and Protective Services	246	267	197	627	256	96	104	77	245
Education[a]	588	791	625	867	616	96	128	101	141
National Heritage	48	55	31	–	47	103	119	66	–
Health and Personal Social Services	806	989	917	924	831	97	119	110	111
Social Security	1536	1676	1814	1785	1569	98	107	116	114
Miscellaneous[b]	–	34	26	36	6	–	567	433	600
TOTAL	3743	4614	4352	5139	3889	96	119	112	132

Notes:　a Expenditure on national heritage in Northern Ireland is included with education.
　　　　　b Expenditure includes the costs of central administration of the offices of the Secretaries of State of the territorial departments.

quarters of 1996. The cause of the contraction, compared with a year earlier, can be pin-pointed to the construction industry, where output fell by 8.7 per cent over the period, while the production industries experienced a small rise of 0.4 per cent. Output in mining and quarrying was 10.3 per cent lower than it had been a year earlier. The index in this industry, relative to its 1990 level, had recovered from 66.9 in the first quarter to 86.3 in the third quarter of 1996, only to suffer another large drop in the fourth quarter (68.3). Manufacturing output fell by 0.3 per cent over the year, despite the strong showings of coke and refined petroleum products, food products and transport equipment. The electricity, gas and water supply sector was the best performer over the period, with an increase in output of 11 per cent. Turning to analysis of the market sector, two sectors achieved a positive growth rate between the final quarters of 1995 and 1996, intermediate goods (0.1 per cent) and investment goods (4.4 per cent), while output declined by 1.7 per cent in consumer goods.

Identifiable government expenditure per head in Wales was 16 per cent higher than in England for the financial year 1995/6, as shown in Table 10.4. However, an average government spending equivalent to £4,352 per head of the Welsh population was the lowest of the three Celtic regions. Wales' position is further weakened by the fact that identifiable expenditure excludes spending on defence, since it is estimated that Wales gets only 1.5 per cent of UK defence procurement, compared with 55 per cent in the South East of England. The activities which gained most in Wales relative to average UK expenditure per head were agriculture, fisheries, food and forestry, housing, and other environmental services. The only departments to acquire a less than proportional share of the government's spending budget were roads and transport, law, order and protective services, and national heritage.

EMPLOYMENT

Tables 10.5 and 10.6 give details of the change in employment in Wales and Great Britain between December 1996 and twelve months earlier. Table 10.5 compares the absolute numbers of male and female employees in the British regions on these two dates, while Table 10.6 breaks down the overall number of employees into industrial groupings for Wales and Great Britain.[4] The most striking statistic in Table 10.5 is that female employees now out-number males in Wales, one of only three regions where this is true. The reason for this occurrence can be found in Table 10.6 which shows that

TABLE **10.5**

Employment: Wales, Great Britain and regions, employees in employment, thousands, not seasonally adjusted, December 1995 and 1996

	1995			1996		
	Male	Female	Total	Male	Female	Total
South East	3643	3576	7218	3712	3592	7304
East Anglia	429	381	810	430	388	817
South West	869	881	1750	897	906	1803
West Midlands	1080	977	2057	1095	998	2092
East Midlands	801	778	1579	786	781	1567
Yorkshire & Humberside	963	930	1893	969	931	1900
North West	1174	1166	2341	1205	1183	2389
North	528	538	1066	544	545	1088
Scotland	980	1009	1988	967	1004	1971
WALES	478	472	949	475	477	952
GREAT BRITAIN	10945	10706	21651	11079	10805	21884

Source: Department for Education and Employment

female employment grew by just over 1 per cent over the period, whilst male employment contracted by 0.63 per cent, leading to a small overall expansion in employment in Wales (0.32 per cent). These trends were reversed for Britain as a whole, where male employment growth exceeded that of females, producing an overall growth of 1.08 per cent. It is interesting to note that the growth in female employment in Wales was achieved by an increase in the number of part-time employees coupled with a fall in the number of full-time workers. The number of male part-time employees also increased, but this growth was not as great as that seen in the remainder of the country.

Given the small employment changes witnessed in Wales over the period, one might have expected employment in the different industries to have remained relatively stable, but Table 10.6 shows that this is not entirely correct. Both manufacturing and services experienced an expansion in employment, with the growth in manufacturing employment (2.42 per cent) greater than that of services (0.15 per cent). One of the most successful manufacturing industries in Wales is the automotive sector, which now consists of around 150 companies employing 25,000 workers, making Wales a leading region in the UK car industry, along with the West Midlands. Nationally, manufacturing employment shrunk but service sector employment rose by a much larger amount (1.72 per cent) than that seen in Wales. The relatively sluggish performance of Wales's service sector can be

TABLE 10.6
Employees in employment ('000s) in Great Britain and Wales, by industry (SIC92), December 1995 and 1996

	Great Britain			Wales		
	Dec. '95	Dec. '96	%Δ	Dec. '95	Dec. '96	%Δ
Agriculture, hunting, forestry and fishing (A,B)	247	242	–2.02	18	19	5.56
Mining and quarrying (C)	65	63	–3.08	5	3	–40.00
Manufacturing (D)	3981	3955	–0.65	207	212	2.42
Electricity, gas and water supply (E)	158	123	–22.15	9	7	–22.22
Construction (F)	810	830	2.47	37	37	0
Wholesale, retail, trade and repairs (G)	3722	3784	1.67	145	147	1.38
Hotels and restaurants (H)	1186	1254	5.73	52	59	13.46
Transport, storage and communication (I)	1273	1306	2.59	41	39	–4.88
Financial intermediation (J)	1006	998	–0.80	25	24	–4.00
Real estate, renting and business activities (K)	2709	2803	3.47	80	79	–1.25
Public administration and defence: compulsory social security (L)	1341	1307	–2.54	74	74	0
Education (M)	1798	1785	–0.72	88	87	–1.14
Health and social work (N)	2440	2497	2.34	128	124	–3.13
Other community, social and personal activities (O–Q)	915	937	2.40	40	42	5.00
Service industries (G–Q)	16389	16671	1.72	673	674	0.15
Total Male	10945	11079	1.22	478	475	–0.63
Male part-time	1206	1286	6.63	47	49	4.26
Total Female	10706	10805	0.92	472	477	1.06
Female part-time	4898	4943	0.92	222	228	2.70
TOTAL	21651	21884	1.08	949	952	0.32

Source: Department for Education and Employment

put down to falls in employment in the majority of its component industries, including transport, storage and communication, financial intermediation, and health and social work. A final observation from the table, is that some of the former main employers in the Welsh economy now account for a very small proportion of the total workforce. More specifically, it is estimated that only 3,000 workers are currently employed in mining and quarrying and 7,000 are involved in electricity, gas and water supply.

A well documented feature of the Welsh economy over the past decade has been the increasing proportion of the workforce employed by foreign-owned companies. In 1995, 73,500 manufacturing workers were employed in foreign-owned factories, an increase of 8.4 per cent on the previous year's total. These employees were distributed amongst 364 manufacturing plants, which was eleven more than there was in 1994. In 1996, the inward investment scene in Wales, and in the UK for that matter, was dominated by one announcement, the news that Lucky Goldstar (LG) of South Korea would be investing £1.7 billion in an semi-conductor factory in Newport. This was the largest single foreign investment ever made in Europe. It is estimated that this development will create 6,100 jobs on its own and as many as 15,000 additional jobs could be created within the Welsh economy because of its positive employment effects on support industries, including an estimated 2,000 construction workers needed to build the plants. The LG investment has helped transform south-east Wales into the best place in Britain to get a job according to a recent *Mori* survey. They forecast that up to 22,000 jobs could be created in the area, 60 per cent of which would be in the service sector.

In contrast, job opportunities in south-west Wales are becoming increasingly scarce, with little inward investment flowing into the area and the announcements of further redundancies, including major job losses at oil refineries in Milford Haven. However, the Pembrokeshire economy was not as badly affected as first thought by the *Sea Empress* disaster. Nevertheless, a Cardiff Business School report estimated that the oil spill cost the fishing industry £5 million and the tourist industry £21 million. The impact of the BSE crisis on agriculture cannot be fully quantified at present, but the continuing EU ban on British beef means that prospects in the industry are bleak.

Apart from LG, many other foreign companies decided to invest in Wales in 1996, making it a record year for inward investment, with more than 15,000 jobs being created. The new investments included 300 jobs by Halla forklift trucks in Merthyr, 300 at Matsushita electronics in Cardiff, a further 1,000 by the Sony corporation at Bridgend and 300 by the Bertrand Faure Group who manufacture car seats in Tredegar. These successes suggest the gloomy forecasts that Wales would attract a lower share of inward investment have yet to materialize, but notice of the threat posed by low-wage Eastern European countries was served by the decision of Lucas SEI to transfer its operations from Neath to Poland. However, the whole strategy of bidding for inward investment has been put under increased scrutiny. In an interesting survey, Yoshimoto (1996) argues that Japanese companies would have come to the UK without government aid because the strong yen forced companies to produce outside Japan in order to maintain international competitiveness. Foreign investors are also attracted to the UK by its cultural and economic advantages, such as the language and the high profit to labour cost ratio. The precise location for the investment has then been largely determined by which region can offer the largest grant to the potential investor. For example, it is estimated that grants equivalent to £30,000 per job were provided to attract LG to Wales. This prompted the view that these funds could have been directed to other job-creating projects.

It has long been recognized that small businesses make a vital contribution to the overall healthiness of an economy. However, it is estimated that small firms contribute less to the Welsh economy than they do to any of the other regions. Less than a quarter of Welsh manufacturing output is produced by firms with less than 100 employees, whereas the UK average is around a third. This has led to a call for selective support to be given to small businesses in certain important strategic sectors, such as research and development.

UNEMPLOYMENT

One of the apparent major successes of the Welsh economy, and that of the UK in general, in recent years has been the reduction in unemployment rates. Table 10.7 tracks the time series of unemployment rates in the UK regions over the 10 years preceding 1996. Although in absolute terms the unemployment rate in Wales has continued to fall (8.2 per cent in 1996), it is once again beginning to creep up relative to the UK average (7.5 per cent), whereas the two rates had been equal in 1994. The return to its historical position of above average unemployment rates is a worrying trend for Wales and one hopes that the large differentials seen in the mid-1980s are not to reappear. Compared with other UK regions, only Northern Ireland and the North had higher average unemployment rates than Wales during the course of 1996.

Table 10.8 reports official government figures for the actual numbers out of work in the UK regions. Even though the number of male and female claimants fell substantially in Wales in the year to April 1997, both of these reductions were lower than the percentage falls seen in the UK; 20.7 per cent compared with 23.7 per cent for males and 25.8 per cent compared with 26.5 per cent for females. Furthermore, a most important question to ask at this point is whether these changes represent a true fall in the numbers out of work or are the result of the introduction of the Jobseekers Allowance (JSA) in October 1996. It is estimated that the JSA removed over 160,000

TABLE 10.7

Annual average unemployment rates, Wales, United Kingdom and regions.
Males and females combined, seasonally adjusted, 1987-1996

	1987	1988	1989	1990	1991	1992	1993	1994	1995	1996
South East	7.1	5.3	3.9	3.9	6.9	9.2	10.2	9.0	7.9	7.0
East Anglia	7.3	5.1	3.5	3.7	5.8	7.6	8.1	7.1	6.3	5.8
South West	8.0	6.0	4.3	4.2	6.9	9.2	9.5	8.1	7.0	6.2
West Midlands	11.3	8.8	6.5	5.7	8.4	10.3	10.8	9.9	8.3	7.4
East Midlands	8.9	7.1	5.4	5.1	7.2	9.0	9.5	8.7	7.6	6.8
Yorkshire & Humberside	11.3	9.3	7.3	6.6	8.7	9.9	10.2	9.6	8.7	8.0
North West	12.4	10.3	8.4	7.6	9.3	10.6	10.7	10.0	8.7	8.0
North	13.9	11.8	9.8	8.7	10.3	11.1	11.9	11.6	10.8	9.9
Scotland	13.1	11.2	9.4	8.2	8.8	9.4	9.7	9.3	8.1	7.9
Northern Ireland	16.4	15.0	14.0	12.8	12.9	13.8	13.8	12.6	11.4	10.9
WALES	12.1	9.9	7.3	6.7	9.0	10.0	10.3	9.3	8.7	8.2
UNITED KINGDOM	9.9	8.0	6.2	5.8	8.0	9.7	10.3	9.3	8.2	7.5

Source: Department for Education and Employment

TABLE 10.8

Unemployment: Wales, United Kingdom and regions. Claimants, thousands,
seasonally adjusted, April 1996 and 1997

	1996			1997		
	Male	Female	Total	Male	Female	Total
South East	498.8	169.5	668.3	365.1	123.5	488.6
East Anglia	45.8	15.7	61.5	34.6	11.7	46.3
South West	114.2	39.1	153.3	81.9	27.6	111.3
West Midlands	147.2	48.0	192.5	111.8	34.5	146.3
East Midlands	105.0	33.6	138.6	77.4	24.0	101.4
Yorkshire & Humberside	152.1	44.8	196.9	119.6	33.9	153.5
North West	186.0	53.2	239.2	147.0	40.1	187.1
North	111.2	29.3	140.5	86.5	22.0	108.5
Scotland	151.6	45.8	197.4	126.2	35.8	162.0
Northern Ireland	66.6	19.4	86.0	51.2	13.6	64.8
WALES	81.5	24.0	105.5	64.6	17.8	82.4
UNITED KINGDOM	1659.9	522.5	2182.4	1267.2	384.2	1651.4

Source: Department for Education and Employment

claimants from the UK unemployment register in the six months immediately after its introduction. Therefore, the JSA is likely to have had a significant distorting influence on Welsh unemployment statistics.

TABLE 10.9
Unemployment by duration and age: Wales, United Kingdom and regions, April 1997

| | Percentage of total unemployed | | |
	Unemployed for over one year	Unemployed for over five years	In 18-24 age group
South East	39.5	7.2	22.1
East Anglia	31.5	5.9	24.9
South West	33.3	6.3	24.2
West Midlands	37.5	9.8	26.3
East Midlands	34.4	8.1	25.8
Yorkshire & Humberside	33.9	7.6	26.6
North West	33.8	8.0	27.8
North	37.9	9.2	26.6
Scotland	31.1	6.8	25.5
Northern Ireland	54.5	21.9	24.3
WALES	33.6	6.8	27.6
UNITED KINGDOM	36.5	8.2	25.0

Source: National Online Manpower Information System (NOMIS)

Following claims that the claimant count figures underestimate the true number without a job, the present system is currently under review. Many favour a move to the International Labour Organisation definition of unemployment, an internationally consistent measure, which defines an individual as being unemployed if they do not have a paid job and have sought work in the previous four weeks and are available to work within the next two weeks. A further cause for concern is the uneven distribution of unemployment among different sections of the population. An Employment Policy Institute report claims that the gap between 'work rich' and 'work poor' households is widening. The percentage of UK households without a wage earner had risen from 17.5 per cent in 1992 to 19.3 per cent in 1996, whilst the percentage of dual income households is also on the rise.

Whilst UK unemployment has fallen considerably over the past few years, the percentage who are described as long term unemployed (unemployed for over 52 weeks) has remained relatively constant across the regions. The most recent unemployment statistics broken down by different durations are reported in Table 10.9. Wales is following the national trend of having a rising percentage of very long term unemployed (those individuals unemployed for five or more years), which increased from 4.8 per cent in April 1995 to 6.8 per cent in April 1997. Amongst the twelve regions, Wales

TABLE **10.10**

Unemployment by former county: Wales, unadjusted, workforce base, April 1997

County	Male		Female		All	
	Number	Rate	Number	Rate	Number	Rate
Clwyd	7445	7.5	2113	2.8	9558	5.5
Dyfed	8294	9.4	2427	4.1	10721	7.3
Gwent	10149	9.4	2828	3.6	12977	7.0
Gwynedd	6807	11.3	1958	3.9	8765	7.9
Mid Glamorgan	12444	11.7	3097	3.6	15541	8.0
Powys	1451	4.8	540	2.0	1991	3.5
South Glamorgan	10458	8.7	2811	2.6	13269	5.8
West Glamorgan	8590	10.8	2212	3.3	10802	7.4
WALES	65638	9.5	17986	3.3	83624	6.7

Source: NOMIS

had the fourth lowest percentage of unemployed persons out of work for over one year and the third lowest out of work for over five years. An alternative way of considering the duration of unemployment is to examine the average length of time which an individual remains unemployed. Using January 1997 figures, it is found that, on average, Welsh claimants spend five weeks less on the unemployment register than their British counterparts, with the difference being greatest for the over fifty age group. Within Wales, the average unemployment durations for males and females was quite similar, 32 and 26 weeks respectively. Table 10.9 also reports the percentage of the total stock of unemployed persons accounted for by the 18–24 age group. The problem of youth unemployment is more severe in Wales compared with other regions because this age group accounts for 27.6 per cent of the total number of unemployed persons, compared with a UK average of 25 per cent. The only region to rank above Wales in this category was the North West. The new government policies designed to tackle youth unemployment should hopefully help to alleviate the situation in Wales.

The relative unemployment rankings of areas within Wales have been greatly altered over the past decade. The traditional view that unemployment blackspots are almost exclusively confined to the South Wales Valleys is no longer accurate. Unemployment remains a serious problem in some valley communities but other parts of Wales are also beginning to emerge as areas where unemployment is equally as high. Table 10.10 reveals that Mid Glamorgan still has the highest unemployment rate at

8 per cent, but four of the other former Welsh counties were within a percentage point of this rate in April 1997. The only former counties to experience lower unemployment rates than the Welsh average were Powys, Clwyd and South Glamorgan. Of these counties, Powys has by far the lowest rates for males, females and in total.

The finer breakdown provided by the former counties still conceals fairly large variations in unemployment within each area. Travel to Work Areas (TTWAs), the smallest areas to approximate local labour markets and, therefore, for which official unemployment rates can be calculated, can be used to examine Welsh unemployment in greater detail. For example, within Mid Glamorgan, the highest rate is found in the Aberdare TTWA at 10.8 per cent in April 1997. This is despite the fact that there has been a considerable reduction in the unemployment rate in Aberdare over the last few years (a decrease of over 6 percentage points since April 1993). Further confirmation of the changing geography of unemployment in Wales is given by the fact that Aberdare no longer has the highest unemployment rate in Wales. This rather dubious distinction now belongs to Holyhead, where the rate is 12 per cent, which is sufficient to place it fifth amongst all 334 TTWAs in the UK. In contrast, only 2.1 per cent of the workforce were unemployed in Newtown, one of the lowest rates in the UK.

EARNINGS

As in previous surveys, the bulk of the earnings information is provided by the *New Earnings Survey* (NES), the most comprehensive and detailed source available at the regional and sub-regional level for Great Britain. Table 10.11 summarizes the broad earnings picture in Wales and the other regions in April 1996. Once again, Wales appears at the foot of the earnings table for all employees, at just 89 per cent of the British average. An average weekly wage of £313.1 represents a 3.9 per cent increase on the previous year's figure, the third lowest increase amongst the 11 regions. The Northern region was able to leapfrog Wales at the bottom of the earnings table by virtue of a 5.5 per cent increase in its overall earnings.

Further light may be shed on the poor earnings performance by examining the components of the overall figure. Welsh males have the lowest weekly earnings of any region (£345.5), whereas it is only in the East Midlands where females earn less than they do in Wales (£250.5). This contrasts sharply with 1995, when Welsh females had risen to fifth in the regional rankings. The source of the decline appears to stem from the

TABLE 10.11

**Average gross weekly earnings: Wales, Great Britain and regions, £'s.
All industries and services. Full-time employees on adult rates, April 1996**

	Manual males	Non-manual males	All males	Manual females	Non-manual females	All females	All employees
South East	320.9	528.7	457.5	218.3	343.9	327.5	407.2
East Anglia	297.6	418.8	357.5	187.1	285.5	265.7	325.5
South West	282.7	431.4	364.8	185.5	277.0	261.1	326.5
West Midlands	297.1	425.0	360.1	191.5	276.4	256.9	324.3
East Midlands	294.1	413.1	352.9	181.8	271.1	248.7	317.9
Yorkshire & Humberside	292.8	410.0	350.7	182.6	270.4	252.5	316.4
North West	300.0	430.0	367.8	191.3	281.1	265.3	330.0
North	301.9	408.3	350.7	184.8	270.7	251.9	315.6
Scotland	290.9	434.0	363.6	189.7	282.8	262.0	324.9
WALES	295.0	406.8	345.5	184.8	270.4	250.5	313.1
GREAT BRITAIN	301.3	464.0	391.3	195.2	302.4	283.0	351.5

Source: New Earnings Survey, 1996

TABLE 10.12

**Distribution of gross weekly earnings: Wales, Great Britain and regions, £'s.
All industries and services. Full-time employees on adult rates, April 1996.
Percentage with weekly earnings less than £170 for males and less than
£130 for females**

	Manual males	Non-manual males	All males	Manual females	Non-manual females	All females
South East	7.6	2.8	4.4	10.4	1.7	2.8
East Anglia	6.7	4.9	5.8	20.3	3.1	6.6
South West	11.1	5.2	7.8	17.5	3.9	6.3
West Midlands	8.3	4.5	6.4	15.5	4.0	6.6
East Midlands	10.1	4.4	7.3	19.2	3.9	7.8
Yorkshire & Humberside	9.7	5.7	7.7	20.5	4.0	7.4
North West	8.7	4.7	6.6	16.3	3.4	5.6
North	9.7	5.4	7.7	20.0	4.7	8.0
Scotland	9.7	4.8	7.2	17.1	4.0	6.9
WALES	11.1	6.1	8.8	18.9	4.4	7.8
GREAT BRITAIN	9.0	4.1	6.3	16.0	3.1	5.4

Source: New Earnings Survey, 1996

Table 10.13
Average gross weekly earnings by broad industry and occupational groupings: Wales and Great Britain, £'s
Full-time employees on adult rates, April 1996

	Manual males			Non-manual males			Manual females			Non-manual females			All males			All females		
	Wales	GB	% GB	Wales	GB	% GB	Wales	GB	% GB	Wales	GB	% GB	Wales	GB	% GB	Wales	GB	% GB
All industries and services	295.0	301.3	97.9	406.8	464.0	87.7	184.8	195.2	94.7	270.4	302.4	89.4						
All index of production industries	326.1	327.4	99.6	456.9	487.3	93.8	205.7	205.0	100.3	272.0	295.0	92.2						
All manufacturing industries	323.8	323.6	100.0	452.4	479.6	94.3	205.7	205.0	100.3	268.1	289.4	92.6						
All service industries	256.3	277.3	92.4	386.2	458.9	84.2	158.7	187.9	84.5	270.4	304.0	88.9						
All occupations													345.5	391.3	88.3	250.5	283.0	88.5
All manual occupations													295.0	301.3	97.9	184.8	195.2	94.7
All non-manual occupations													406.8	464.0	87.7	270.4	302.4	89.4

Source: New Earnings Survey, 1996

earnings of manual females, where earnings actually fell by 0.3 per cent between 1995 and 1996, the only category in the table where such a reduction in earnings took place between these two dates. Neither was the performance of non-manual females sufficient to compensate for this shortfall, since Wales was the only region to experience less than a 3 per cent growth in total female earnings over the year.

Table 10.12 takes a slightly different emphasis, by reporting the percentage of employees who earn below a specified threshold. The worrying trend observed for females in the previous table is again evident, with the gains achieved in 1995 being reversed. The percentage of females earning less than £130 a week actually increased from 7.5 per cent in 1995 to 7.8 per cent in 1996, with the result that only the Northern region had a greater proportion of its females with earnings below this level. On the other hand, the percentage of males earning less than £170 per week was reduced quite significantly, from 10.5 per cent in 1995 to 8.8 per cent in 1996, but this was not enough to enable Wales to overtake any of the other regions in this respect.

Compared with the other regions, Wales has traditionally had lower earnings in non-manual occupations, and in the service sector in particular. As these sectors account for an ever larger proportion of the workforce, it is not surprising that relative earnings in Wales are on a downward trend. Table 10.13 reveals that Welsh earnings in non-manual occupations have continued to deteriorate compared with the rest of the country. Not only is it the non-manual occupations where Wales suffers, since manual females in service industries earn less than 85 per cent of their British counterparts and nominal earnings had dropped by around £12 a week from their 1995 figure. On the positive side, both manual males and females in the production industries continue to earn more than the national averages, but as the manual/non-manual earnings differential becomes ever wider, this is scant consolation, and in any case, the advantage Wales possesses over Britain in these categories has diminished over time.

Substantial earnings variation within Wales is another cause for concern, as demonstrated in Table 10.14, which reports average earnings, broken down by occupation and gender, in the former counties in 1996. Earnings are lowest in the three predominantly rural counties of Dyfed, Gwynedd and Powys, the only places where employee earnings were less than £300 a week. Dyfed suffers mainly with respect to female earnings, which are just 85 per cent of the Welsh average, whereas in Gwynedd, males do only slightly better in relative terms, with earnings of 90 per cent of the Welsh average.

TABLE **10.14**
Average gross weekly earnings: Wales and former counties, £'s.
All industries and services. Full-time employees on adult rates, April 1996

Former County	Manual Males	Non-Manual Males	All Males	Manual Females	Non-Manual Females	All Females	All Employees
Clwyd	309.9	440.6	359.8	197.1	261.9	242.6	322.9
Clwyd East	324.6	-	373.5	-	261.1	244.3	335.3
Dyfed							
(excl. Llanelli)	-	-	331.3	-	224.8	213.4	286.0
Gwent	300.0	399.3	340.8	186.4	259.3	238.8	311.9
Gwynedd	269.3	354.4	310.9	-	261.5	237.3	284.8
Mid Glamorgan	281.5	416.1	338.3	196.4	280.7	259.5	309.2
Powys	247.4	-	-	165.2	-	-	275.0
South Glamorgan	301.7	412.9	368.4	197.8	287.1	274.9	333.6
West Glamorgan							
(inc. Llanelli)	310.6	400.2	347.1	-	265.7	246.2	314.5
WALES	295.0	406.8	345.5	184.8	270.4	250.5	313.1

Note: – denotes not available as sample requirements were not met
Source: *New Earnings Survey,* 1996

The only earnings information published for Powys is for manual earnings, which are again very low for both males and females. Amongst the other former counties, male and female earnings are highest in South Glamorgan, but if Clwyd-East is considered, male earnings are highest in this area, which helps to elevate Clwyd into second place in the overall rankings.

A drawback with the NES data published in the tables is that they exclude part-time workers altogether and miss out many of those with low wages because they only cover full time workers who earn in excess of the lower earnings limit (£72.40 a week in 1996). This problem is exacerbated for Wales, where the proportion of part-time employees is higher and wages are lower than the national averages, and Wales' true position is therefore more likely to be affected by the tables' neglect of these factors. Reliable estimates of the extent of low pay are difficult to obtain, but the House of Commons Library estimates that 81,000 workers in Wales currently earn less than £3 an hour, over 21,000 of whom earn less than £2 an hour.

Low pay is currently a crucial issue in view of the debate about the desirability of a national minimum wage. The new Labour government is committed to introducing a minimum wage and they are thought to favour a simple nationwide wage, as opposed to one which varies by region. This should be to the advantage of Welsh employees. The responsibility for setting the value of the minimum wage will belong to a new body called the

Low Pay Commission. This will consist of a combination of unions, employers and independent experts. The level of the minimum wage is of vital importance to both employers and employees. Its exact amount has yet to be formally announced but the general consensus is that it will be somewhere in the range of £3.50 to £4 per hour. The minimum wage is likely to have its greatest impact on occupations such as hotels and restaurants, sewing machinists, industrial cleaners, hairdressers and care assistants. It is argued by some groups, such as the Low Pay Unit, that a minimum wage is vital for Wales, especially to protect those workers on temporary, seasonal and part-time contracts. On the other hand, many small traders oppose the imposition of a minimum wage, claiming that it will only reduce employment and raise prices, leading to a reduction in quality. For example, Welsh hoteliers argue that this is a crucial time in the development of the Welsh tourist industry, which employs, either directly or indirectly, around 9 per cent of the Welsh workforce and the imposition of a minimum wage will be harmful to its future prospects. However, the traditional view that a minimum wage necessarily reduces employment has recently been questioned, especially in the United States, where an influential study by Card and Krueger (1995) found that employment levels were not reduced in certain industries after increases in the minimum wage and were even raised in some. It is argued that tourism could be one such industry where such an occurrence might be observed because higher minimum wages might be expected to generate increased spending power within the economy.

HOUSE PRICES

The UK housing market has continued its recovery throughout 1996, to such a extent that there is little doubt that the slump witnessed in the early part of the 1990s is now over. Further evidence for this is given by the re-emergence of many of the features seen in the housing market of the late 1980s, the most notable of which is the North-South divide in house prices. Its return has been fuelled by different demand patterns in the two parts of the country. In the north, potential buyers are unwilling to pay inflated prices, while in the south, especially in London, the shortage of suitable properties has been reinforced by the willingness of buyers to bid up the price of properties, often by virtue of huge City bonuses. The divide can clearly be seen in Table 10.15, which reports average house prices, collected by the Halifax Building Society. House prices in Wales rose by 5.8 per cent in the year to March 1997 and even though this was a lower growth rate than

TABLE 10.15
Average house prices, first quarter 1997, Wales, United Kingdom, regions and former Welsh counties

Regions of the UK	£	Annual % Change	Welsh Counties[a]	£	Rank out of 58 counties[b]
South East	85662	9.1	South Glamorgan	65256	19
East Anglia	61572	5.3	West Glamorgan	53407	40
South West	67142	7.3	Mid Glamorgan	48716	49
West Midlands	65793	6.5	Gwent	48212	51
East Midlands	57094	6.9	Clwyd	46200	53
Yorkshire & Humberside	52852	3.4	Dyfed	40561	58
North West	54825	4.5	Gwynedd	n/a	n/a
North	51022	1.8	Powys	n/a	n/a
Scotland	59457	1.9			
Northern Ireland	52027	2.9			
WALES	54106	5.8			
UNITED KINGDOM	66899	7.2			

Notes: [a] Counties figures are average semi-detached prices.
[b] Excludes Northern Ireland.
Source: Halifax Building Society Price Index No.67

the UK average (7.2 per cent), Wales still managed to climb one place in the house price rankings, to eighth in the first quarter of 1997. These figures imply that Wales had the most buoyant housing market of any of the so-called 'northern' regions over this period.

House price information has not yet been provided by the Halifax Building Society for the new unitary authorities, so intra-regional variation continues to be analysed at the county level. Gwent was the only former county in Wales to improve on its UK ranking in 1997 compared with a year earlier. Rising house prices in this part of Wales could be associated with the opening of the second Severn crossing and this trend is likely to continue as housing shortages are forecast in the Newport area in the wake of the LG announcement. With other counties suffering a fall in their relative positions, Dyfed assumed its customary position at the foot of the table for the 58 UK counties for which house prices could be provided, and it was joined in the bottom ten counties by West Glamorgan, Mid Glamorgan and Clwyd. Neither Gwynedd nor Powys met the sample requirements necessary for publication, but it is assumed that house prices would also be low in these two areas. The figures for counties refer to average semi-detached house prices so they are not directly comparable with the regional figures which refer to seasonally adjusted prices for all houses and all buyers. The

UK average for semi-detached houses was £65,875, which is slightly in excess of the highest Welsh figure – South Glamorgan (£65,256).

There is evidence that the traditional determinants of house prices are no longer so potent and that new forces are starting to influence the housing market (*Observer*, 1996). The new factors relate to the character of the neighbourhood, which are thought to influence the quality of life, examples of which include school quality, crime rates and health indicators. Evidence in favour of these changes can be found by examining house price changes in more dis-aggregated areas. For example, Wales's fastest-growing towns in terms of house prices are found to be Cowbridge and Hay-on-Wye. On the other hand, according to a *HM Land Registry* survey covering the second and third quarters of 1996, Wales had seven out of the ten UK property black spots. The worst affected areas are found in the South Wales Valleys, where house prices are estimated to have fallen by 16.8 per cent in Merthyr Tydfil between 1995 and 1996, by 14.8 per cent in Rhondda, Cynon, Taff and by 8.2 per cent in Blaenau Gwent.

OVERVIEW

As a result of the vote in favour of devolution, Wales faces a number of important changes and challenges in the years ahead. The political agenda is likely to be dominated by discussions over the make-up and workings of the new assembly, with the precise role which the assembly has to play within the Welsh economy one of the important issues to be determined. The influence which the assembly is able to have on the Welsh economy will be dependent upon the powers awarded to it. Unlike the Scottish parliament, it is known that the assembly will not be able to vary taxes or make new laws, but with the Welsh Office budget at its disposal and all the quangos under its control, it may be able to channel the available resources more effectively. Whatever powers are eventually awarded to the Welsh Assembly, it will still have serious economic problems to address, the most notable of which is the ever deteriorating position of earnings and GDP in Wales, both relative to Great Britain and to the rest of the EU.

At the same time as Wales acquires greater control from Westminster, ties with Europe will become increasingly close as the projected start date for European Monetary Union and the introduction of a single European currency in 1999 draws ever nearer. Within Wales, businesses have a mixed view on the benefits of a European single currency. Only 45 per cent of Welsh firms interviewed as part of a Deloitte and Touche/*Western Mail* business confidence survey said that they would like to see Britain part of a single currency (*Western Mail*, 1997). There was some good news for the Welsh economy stemming from the EU, with its decision to name Cardiff as the location for a prestigious summit meeting for EU heads of states in 1998. This meeting is expected to have positive spin-off effects for the economy in south-east Wales, most notably for the tourist industry.

APPENDIX: UNITARY AUTHORITY DATA

Area and population statistics are displayed for all 22 Welsh Unitary Authorities (UAs) in Table A. Not surprisingly, the most densely populated Welsh authority is Cardiff, which had well over 2,200 persons per square kilometre in 1995. The next three most densely populated areas were all situated in the former county of Gwent (Newport, Torfaen and Blaenau Gwent), but each of these UAs had less than 725 persons per square kilometre. The most sparsely populated UA in Wales is Powys, with just 24 persons per square kilometre. The most rapidly expanding areas in terms of population growth are the mainly rural authorities of Monmouthshire and Ceredigion. At the other end of the scale, Anglesey lost the highest percentage of its population between 1991 and 1995. The lack of employment opportunities on the island, which leads people to move away from the area, is the most likely cause of this finding. Support for this explanation can be found if the components of the change are examined, because the entire loss of population is accounted for by migration and other factors.

The distribution of overseas-owned manufacturing units in the Welsh UAs and the associated number of employees is reported in Table B. Caerphilly, Flintshire and Rhondda, Cynon, Taff all had in excess of 40 foreign-owned manufacturing plants in 1995. The majority of the other UAs had more than ten such plants within their boundaries. Only four Welsh UAs had less than 1,000 workers in plants of this type, three of which were to be found in north Wales. This part of Wales did contain two UAs with more than 6,000 employees in foreign-owned companies (Wrexham and Flintshire), but the greatest concentration of workers in overseas-owned plants was found in south Wales. Rhondda, Cynon, Taff had the highest number of employees in foreign-owned plants, with 7,150, closely followed by Bridgend, which had 50 fewer.

TABLE A
Area statistics and population change in Welsh Unitary Authorities, 1991–95

	Area (sq. km.)	1995 population density (persons per sq. km.)	Mid year population estimates (thousands)		
			1991	1995	% Change
Blaenau Gwent	109	672	73.0	73.2	0.3
Bridgend	247	529	129.4	130.7	1.0
Caerphilly	278	611	171.5	169.9	−1.0
Cardiff	139	2226	300.0	309.4	3.2
Carmarthenshire	2390	71	170.5	169.5	−0.6
Ceredigion	1794	39	66.6	70.2	5.5
Conwy	1130	98	108.5	111.2	2.4
Denbighshire	844	109	91.7	91.6	−0.1
Flintshire	435	335	142.7	145.7	2.1
Gwynedd	2546	46	116.0	118.0	1.7
Isle of Anglesey	715	94	69.4	67.2	−3.2
Merthyr Tydfil	111	529	59.9	58.7	−2.0
Monmouthshire	851	101	80.4	85.6	6.6
Neath & Port Talbot	440	317	139.4	139.6	0.1
Newport	190	722	136.9	137.2	0.2
Pembrokeshire	1588	71	113.0	113.5	0.5
Powys	5197	24	120.1	122.3	1.8
Rhondda, Cynon, Taff	426	563	237.4	239.9	1.1
Swansea	377	612	231.6	230.6	−0.4
Torfaen	126	717	91.4	90.4	−1.1
The Vale of Glamorgan	335	355	119.2	118.8	−0.3
Wrexham	500	247	122.9	123.4	0.5
WALES	20766	140	2891.5	2916.8	0.9

Source: Office for National Statistics

Table C shows the numbers out of work and unemployment rates by UA. In April 1997, only the Isle of Anglesey and Blaenau Gwent had unemployment rates in excess of 10 per cent. The lowest rates were seen in Monmouthshire and Wrexham (4.8 per cent) and Powys (3.7 per cent). Female unemployment rates are particularly low throughout Wales, since no Welsh UA had more than 6 per cent of its female working population out of work. Male unemployment continues to be a problem in most areas, with unemployment rates in excess of 10 per cent in just under half of the UAs.

In 1996, earnings information was published below the county level for the first time. Earnings data are now available for the Training and Enterprise Councils (TECs), TTWAs, parliamentary constituency areas, local authority districts and UAs in Great Britain. However, in many cases the data are suppressed because these areas fail to meet the relevant

TABLE B

Employment in overseas-owned manufacturing plants in Wales, by Unitary Authority, 1995

	Plants	Employees
Blaenau Gwent	23	2650
Bridgend	19	7100
Caerphilly	43	6500
Cardiff	16	4250
Carmarthenshire	13	2650
Ceredigion	6	350
Conwy	–	700
Denbighshire	–	1750
Flintshire	42	6100
Gwynedd	–	700
Isle of Anglesey	5	750
Merthyr Tydfil	8	1650
Monmouthshire	6	1450
Neath & Port Talbot	15	4150
Newport	17	3600
Pembrokeshire	5	1450
Powys	9	2600
Rhondda, Cynon, Taff	41	7150
Swansea	16	3750
Torfaen	20	3400
The Vale of Glamorgan	11	3750
Wrexham	38	7050
WALES	364	73500

Notes: a – denotes the number of plants suppressed to avoid disclosure.
b Number of employees rounded to the nearest 50.

Source: Welsh Register of Manufacturing Employment

publication criteria (sample size of 10 or more; standard error 5 per cent or less than the estimate), a problem which affects Wales more than most other regions. Table D reports gross average weekly earnings for employees in UAs, but no data are available for 8 out of the 22 authorities. Earnings in all 14 of these UAs were below the national average and since the remaining authorities are mainly rural, this situation is unlikely to be reversed in the areas where the data were suppressed.

Industrial South Wales provides both the UAs with the highest and lowest earnings. In Neath and Port Talbot, weekly earnings of £338.9 may be the result of a high concentration of workers in high-paying manufacturing jobs, whereas in Blaenau Gwent, earnings were £255.1 a week, representing

TABLE C
Unemployment by Unitary Authority and Wales, unadjusted, workforce base, April 1997

	Male		Female		All	
	Number	Rate	Number	Rate	Number	Rate
Blaenau Gwent	2073	13.9	540	6.0	2613	10.9
Bridgend	2409	11.8	685	3.4	3094	7.6
Caerphilly	4032	12.9	956	4.0	4988	9.0
Cardiff	8189	8.3	2127	2.4	10316	5.5
Carmarthenshire	3713	9.6	1109	3.8	4822	7.1
Ceredigion	1193	7.2	377	3.5	1570	5.8
Conwy	2410	10.7	649	3.2	3059	7.2
Denbighshire	1900	9.9	511	3.0	2411	6.6
Flintshire	2271	5.9	697	2.9	2968	4.7
Gwynedd	3476	10.8	989	3.7	4465	7.5
Isle of Anglesey	2021	14.9	590	5.8	2611	11.0
Merthyr Tydfil	1583	12.8	361	3.3	1944	8.3
Monmouthshire	1188	6.6	417	2.7	1605	4.8
Neath & Port Talbot	3065	9.9	815	4.4	3880	7.8
Newport	3668	9.1	1010	3.7	4678	6.9
Pembrokeshire	3388	12.9	941	5.1	4329	9.6
Powys	1478	4.9	548	2.2	2026	3.7
Rhondda, Cynon, Taff	5541	11.3	1375	3.6	6916	7.9
Swansea	5525	11.4	1397	2.8	6922	7.1
Torfaen	1955	7.6	529	2.9	2484	5.7
The Vale of Glamorgan	2413	7.4	736	2.9	3149	5.4
Wrexham	2147	6.6	627	2.5	2774	4.8
WALES	65638	9.5	17986	3.3	83624	6.7

Source: NOMIS

just 72.6 per cent of the British average and the lowest of any UA in Britain with recorded earnings. A possible explanation for the widening earnings gap in areas such as Blaenau Gwent is that the jobs which are being created are increasingly becoming part-time and temporary. These figures may also be slightly misleading since they refer to the place of work rather than the area of residence so that it is possible for an area to appear relatively poor when a high proportion of its residents work in another authority. This situation is more likely to occur in south Wales where, as seen in Table A, the UAs tend to be smaller in terms of geographical size and more concentrated in terms of population density.

Table D also provides an indication of earnings inequality within the UAs, by reporting the so-called '90/10 differential'. This is defined as the amount that the top 10 per cent of the earnings distribution earn more than divided

TABLE D

Average gross weekly earnings, £'s, and the 90/10 differential, Wales and Unitary Authorities. All industries and services, full-time employees on adult rates, April 1996

	All employees	90/10 differential
Blaenau Gwent	255.1	3.08
Bridgend	–	–
Caerphilly	296.2	2.93
Cardiff	332.9	3.13
Carmarthenshire	303.7	3.34
Ceredigion	–	–
Conwy	–	–
Denbighshire	–	–
Flintshire	334.1	3.24
Gwynedd	275.5	2.78
Isle of Anglesey	–	–
Merthyr Tydfil	–	–
Monmouthshire	–	–
Neath & Port Talbot	338.9	3.68
Newport	331.2	3.19
Pembrokeshire	–	–
Powys	275.8	3.06
Rhondda, Cynon, Taff	306.7	3.06
Swansea	298.6	3.16
Torfaen	323.0	2.54
The Vale of Glamorgan	326.5	3.27
Wrexham	330.9	3.62
WALES	313.1	3.23

Note: – denotes not available as sample requirements were not met.
Source: *New Earnings Survey,* 1996

by the amount that those in the bottom decile earn less than. Earnings inequality is seen to be highest in Neath and Port Talbot, where the top 10 per cent of workers earned in excess of £562.4 a week. This UA was closely followed by Wrexham, where the highest-paid workers earned 3.62 times more than those in the lowest part of the earnings distribution. The most 'equal' UA in terms of earnings is found to be Torfaen, which is the product of the fact that all employees bar those in the bottom decile earned in excess of £188.7 a week. Compare this with neighbouring UA of Blaenau Gwent, where the corresponding amount was just £130 a week. The only other UAs where the 90/10 differential was less than 3 were Caerphilly and Gwynedd.

NOTES

1. Financial assistance from the ESRC is gratefully acknowledged. I would like to thank David Blackaby and Dennis Thomas for helpful comments. The usual disclaimer applies.
2. For details about the continuity between the surveys, see Volume 9.
3. A discussion of trends in GDP in the former counties up to 1993 may be found in Volume 9.
4. These tables are based on the most recent employment estimates, therefore, the December 1995 figures may be different from those published in Volume 9's profile.

REFERENCES

Card, D. and Krueger, A. (1995). *Myth and Measurement: The New Economics of The Minimum Wage*, Princeton, Princeton University Press.

Drinkwater, S. (1997). 'The Welsh economy: a statistical profile', *Contemporary Wales* 9, 171–90.

Dunford, M. (1996). 'Disparities in employment, productivity and output in the EU: the roles of labour market governance and welfare regime', *Regional Studies* 30, 339–57.

Observer (1996). 'Highs and lows in Britain's patchwork quilt of house prices', 24 November 1996.

Western Mail (1997). 'Businesses split over European currency', 12 February 1997.

Yoshimoto, M. (1996). 'On the changing international competitiveness of Japanese manufacturing since 1985', *Oxford Review of Economic Policy*, 12, 61–73.

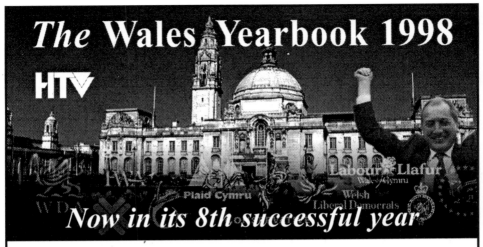